NIETZSCHE:
IMAGERY AND
THOUGHT

NIETZSCHE:
IMAGERY AND
THOUGHT

A COLLECTION OF ESSAYS

EDITED BY

Malcolm Pasley

UNIVERSITY OF CALIFORNIA PRESS

Berkeley and Los Angeles, 1978

UNIVERSITY OF CALIFORNIA PRESS
Berkeley and Los Angeles, California

ISBN: 0–520–03577–1
Library of Congress Catalog Card Number: 77–085748

© 1978 Methuen & Co Ltd

Printed in Great Britain

CONTENTS

PREFACE

Against image and parable

By means of image and parable one can persuade, but can prove
nothing. That is why the world of science and learning is
so wary of image and parable; whatever persuades and makes
things *credible* is here precisely what is *not* wanted; the
aim is rather to provoke the coldest mistrust, initially
by the very mode of expression and the
bare walls: for mistrust is the touchstone for the gold of certainty.

This passage (section 145 of *The Wanderer and his Shadow*) belongs to the
middle period of Nietzsche's career, to the would-be scientific phase
of his philosophizing when he was trying to devote himself to critical
analysis and the establishing of verifiable fact. This not only involved
discarding all metaphysical assumptions, of the kind so readily made
by poets, it also involved the curbing of his own poetic mode of expression at the same time. For 'art', as he now asserted, 'covers life
with a veil of impure thought' (1, 548). However, just how difficult he
found it in practice to abstain from the persuasive tricks of poetry –
above all from the cunning art of metaphor – can be gauged from this
very passage which warns against 'image and parable'.

He starts off bravely enough with the unadorned discourse appropriate to his thesis, but he simply cannot keep it up. '*Coldest* mistrust'
might seem a dead enough image, and as such just permissible for
Nietzsche in his new role as a 'scientific' thinker, but in the context of
the whole book in which the passage appears (*Human, All-Too-Human*)
'coldness' turns out to be a very live image, indeed an image which
controls his arguments. And then, having evoked the 'bare walls'

within which the pursuit of knowledge is conducted – and these sound at least partly metaphorical – he moves over squarely into metaphor, declaring mistrust the '*touchstone*' by which the '*gold*' of certainty is tested. In arguing against images, he falls back on them: he seems to be either refuting his own argument or changing sides.

The above example may serve to indicate the underlying theme which links the following essays: namely, the tension between the two sides of Nietzsche's activity, between the moral heroism of his truth-seeking and his passionate advocacy of cultural change through the power of poetry and myth. He was torn between the urge to weave a glittering and inspiring web out of reality and the equally strong compulsion to lay bare its most painful truths; the image-maker and the image-breaker worked vigorously at cross-purposes, while a superior third Nietzsche made their antagonism a main object of his reflections. The essays in this book approach from a variety of angles that tension between art and knowledge which his work both explores and embodies.

It is not the aim to insist on his shortcomings as a conceptual thinker, on the impatience and incoherence which often mark his handling of traditional philosophical issues, nor is it the purpose to dwell critically on what he attempted in a purely poetic vein. Attention is focused rather on the inseparably hybrid nature of his poetico-philosophical enterprise itself, and on that equally hybrid 'middle mode of discourse' (as J. P. Stern puts it) in which it is typically conducted. Without trying to paper over or explain away the basic antagonism in Nietzsche's work, the book offers a framework for its understanding so that we may better recognize where it took a fruitful and where a self-defeating form.

Not least among the questions raised in these pages is how far he allowed his imagery to dictate his argument even when he supposed that his argument was in control of his imagery; how far his theories and doctrines were formed or swayed – more decisively than he knew and to more damaging effect than he could foresee – by the picture-patterns and the mythical models on which he drew.

It is perhaps especially appropriate to Nietzsche that his work should be made the subject of a group of linked, but independent, investigations. Each contributor speaks, of course, for himself alone, and no attempt has been made to mask or edit out conflicts of interpretation. As far as the judgment of Nietzsche's work is concerned, it is for the reader to say whether some consistency emerges in the balance struck – whether explicitly or no – between approval and rejection.

Quotations from Nietzsche's texts are given in English translation, words or phrases in the original being added where it seems necessary. References are normally to the handiest and most easily accessible German edition, the three-volume edition by Karl Schlechta (Munich, Carl Hanser, 1956; 2nd edition 1960, with the same pagination); they are given by volume and page number, thus: I,548. Where the text quoted is not in Schlechta, the reference is to the *Kritische Gesamtausgabe* by Giorgio Colli and Mazzino Montinari (Berlin, de Gruyter, 1967ff), thus: CM vii 44 (vii being here the volume number). Since the Colli-Montinari edition is not yet complete, some quotations from texts not in Schlechta have had to be located by reference to other editions: these are indicated in each case. Nietzsche's letters are identified by date and recipient only.

In those cases where it has fallen on the editor to determine the English form of Nietzsche's texts, I wish to record my indebtedness to the many translators whose work has been gratefully consulted or used, in particular: Christopher Middleton (*Selected Letters of Friedrich Nietzsche*, Chicago and London, University of Chicago Press, 1969), R. J. Hollingdale (*Thus Spoke Zarathustra*, Harmondsworth, Penguin, 1961; *Twilight of the Idols/The Anti-Christ*, Harmondsworth, Penguin, 1968; *Beyond Good and Evil*, Harmondsworth, Penguin, 1973) and Walter Kaufmann (especially his *The Gay Science*, New York, Random House, 1974) The Oscar Levy translation of the so-called *Wille zur Macht* has been used as a matter of convenience in the case of Mary Warnock's essay: this translation is not suspect in itself, but it should be emphasized that the German text available to the translator had been falsely and tendentiously arranged.

Finally, mention should be made of the debt which all Nietzsche scholars owe to the work of Colli and Montinari, who have already largely given us – and will soon give us completely – the authentic Nietzsche texts in authentic order, on which alone our interpretation and judgment of him can be properly founded.

Malcolm Pasley

ACKNOWLEDGEMENTS

Acknowledgment is due to the English Goethe Society for permission to reprint here, in edited form, F. D. Luke's essay 'Nietzsche and the Imagery of Height'. This appeared originally, under the same title, in: *Publications of the English Goethe Society*, New Series, vol. XXVIII (Leeds, 1959), 83–108.

NIETZSCHE:
ART AND INTELLECTUAL INQUIRY

Peter Pütz

(translated from the German by Roger Hausheer)

In his poem on Nietzsche, Stefan George declares in a tone of re-proachful lament: 'He should have sung,/Not spoken, this new soul!' ['sie hätte singen/Nicht reden sollen diese neue Seele!'].[1] These words go to the heart of the fundamental problem in Nietzsche's life, thought and writing: the antagonism of image and concept, of the creative act which proclaims truth and the analysis which seeks it, of art and intellectual inquiry. But George does not merely define Nietzsche's basic predicament, he believes that he can show a way out, by proposing in retrospect that the predicament be turned into a straight alternative: rather than singing in the language of rational discourse and discoursing in the language of song, he should have sung *instead* of speaking, that is, been a pure poet like George himself. George's advice issues from the reservation which he felt about Nietzsche: instead of presenting images and exemplary models, and renouncing the destructive activity of the intellect, 'you created deities only to destroy them'.

George's criticism of Nietzsche's hesitation between art and intellec-tual inquiry seems to find support from Nietzsche himself, for it is a nearly literal echo of his own words in the late preface (1886) to his *The Birth of Tragedy* (1872). In this 'essay in self-criticism' Nietzsche deplores the fact that he had not been bold enough, in his early book, to attempt a new type of discourse, that he had imprisoned himself in Kantian and Schopenhauerian categories instead of presenting his

new insights and evaluations in the language of poetry. It is in this
context that we find the words which George adopted and slightly
modified: 'He should have *sung*, this "new soul" – and not spoken!'
['Sie hätte *singen* sollen, diese "neue Seele" – und nicht reden!'] (I, 12).
But this almost literal correspondence between Nietzsche and George
holds only for a single aspect of the matter we are considering, namely
the admission of the destructive interlocking of creation and analysis.
Otherwise agreement between the two breaks down. Nietzsche's
utterance applies to his early book, but not to the writings which aim
at enlightenment from *Human, All-Too-Human* to *The Genealogy of Morals*.
George, on the other hand, directs his criticism indiscriminately at the
whole of Nietzsche. What is still more decisive, though it arises from
this difference, is the contrast between the consequences of the two
attitudes. George wants to banish the discrepancy between poetry and
reflection by simply eliminating the destructive element. He overleaps
the abyss and becomes a poet. Nietzsche, by contrast, recognizes this
antagonism, and though he sometimes thinks that he might have
overcome it in *The Birth of Tragedy*, he remains transfixed on the brink
of the abyss. His intellectual honesty will not allow him to avert his
gaze from it, still less to leap across it. Even after the process of self-
criticism, song will not raise him clear of rational discourse, and a
world where beauty and truth are identical remains permanently
inaccessible.

Here we are not dealing with the much-discussed type of poet-
philosopher like Schiller. In a divided state of fruitful tension, such
writers produce works of poetry, and surround them with a flotilla of
preparatory and explanatory tracts on questions of aesthetic principle.
Poetry and thought stand in a clear-cut relationship to one another,
each enjoying a carefully defined sphere of competence. With Nietzsche, on the other hand, this relationship is vastly more complex. At
one moment poetic creation and reflective analysis interpenetrate to
the point where they become indistinguishable, at another they are as
incompatible as fire and water. True, in thematic development,
choice of phrase, syntax and imagery, the poems do tend to over-
intellectualize and stand permanently open to the charge of rhetorical
posturing. And on the obverse side of the coin, the theoretical reflective writings are undeniably poised on the border line which
divides concept from image, and discursive analysis from the fabrication of myth. Yet while poetry and reflection do converge in this way,
they do not achieve a final synthesis. Indeed, their antagonism

threatens them with mutual destruction. The reasons for this are as follows. On the one hand, Nietzsche goes in search of truths which can only be conveyed by myth and by that child of myth, the work of art; on the other, the truth which is reserved to myth and art is dragged before the modern tribunal of the intellect and condemned as falsehood. Nietzsche longs for nothing other than the truth of art, yet is compelled to see in it nothing but lies. It is in this sense, then, that he *would like* to 'sing' but is *forced* to 'speak'. Our task will consist in describing and exploring this fundamental antagonism in Nietzsche's work. In so doing, we will discover that the two rivals, art and knowledge, are not self-justifying activities, but draw their legitimation from a principle underlying them both. This principle in turn will prove not to be immune to inner contradiction, and will thus be seen to split into the dichotomy of poetic creation and analytical thought.

Tensions show up in countless contradictory assertions of the value and worthlessness of knowledge, and, closely bound up with this, of the worthlessness and value of art. Here we will cite only a few of the more representative ones: we hear 'that there is no honey sweeter than that of knowledge' (I, 624); frequently Nietzsche praises the 'urge for knowledge', the 'passion for knowledge', which shrink from no sacrifice and can bear to gaze into the darkest abyss (cf. I, 1223). Thought even acquires a religious aura in phrases where it is consecrated as 'order of truth-seekers' (I, 1148), or the 'holy eucharist of knowledge' (I, 1198). As God demands his all from the believer, so too does absolute knowledge from the thinker: 'we all prefer the decline of humanity to the dwindling of knowledge!' (I, 1223f). Opposed to knowledge is art, a disreputable deceiver and cheat: 'in religion, art and morality we do not touch upon "the essence of the world in itself"' (I, 452). *Pari passu* with the cooling of Nietzsche's attitude to Wagner from *Human, All-Too-Human* onwards, artists are seen increasingly as 'play-actors', as 'glorifiers of the religious and philosophical errors of humanity' (I, 577). As charlatans and liars they are at all times 'henchmen of some morality, philosophy, or religion' (II, 843). They resemble the thoughtless disciples who look only to their own needs and fall asleep instead of participating in the martyrdom of knowledge: '*On Gethsemane.* – The most painful thing the thinker can say to the artist is: What, could ye not watch with me one hour?' (I, 754).

The clear primacy of knowledge over art is rebutted in equally numerous assertions to the contrary. Not only do these give poets priority over thinkers but they see in art the only panacea against knowledge. In *The Birth of Tragedy*, Nietzsche is already engaged in a bitter struggle against 'theoretical man' who, since Socrates, has pursued his disastrous triumphal march, subjecting all things to scientific laws. Nietzsche's sole hope of salvation from the tyranny of concept and number lies in the 'spirit of music'. As early as 1872 he writes: 'Art is more powerful than knowledge, for *art* desires life, and knowledge achieves as its ultimate goal only – destruction' (III, 271). And as late as the 1880s we have the following from the 'Nachlass': 'We have *art* in order that we *may not perish from truth*' (III, 832).

Such contradictory views are voiced not only in the sphere of aesthetics, and in questions as to the respective value of art and knowledge, but in questions of morality, religion and psychology. They also occur in discussions of the most important artists and philosophers. Authorities are repudiated and reinstated only to be rejected again, and so on. So it is with Socrates, Epicurus, Schopenhauer, Wagner – to mention but a few. All these win and lose Nietzsche's esteem several times over, either in one and the same breath or in the course of time. Scarcely any of these great figures can pass muster before this fickle and contradictory judge. Among the very few unshakable authorities are Goethe and, apart from his teaching and historical influence, the person of Christ, with whose passion Nietzsche, as a martyr for the sake of knowledge, still identified in his period of mental collapse, when he signed his letters to Peter Gast and Georg Brandes as 'The Crucified' (III, 1350). The contradictions and ambiguities of Nietzsche's judgments in matters of philosophy, art and science are a source of constant irritation to his interpreters. Connecting threads slip from the critic's hands before he can tie them together. All attempts at systematization and at placing the entire *opus* on sound philosophical foundations have hitherto failed. No single unifying principle has been found. The more competent interpreters have thus recognized the internal contradictions in Nietzsche's work and have not tried to harmonize them. Among these are Ernst Bertram, Karl Löwith, Karl Jaspers, Max Horkheimer, Theodor W. Adorno and Martin Heidegger.[2] Yet others have sought to eliminate these contradictions by one-sided emphasis on isolated aspects of the work. Examples of this are afforded by Alfred Baeumler,[3] who made of the 'will to power' a dominant principle, and by Georg Lukács,[4] who denied the element of enlightenment in Nietzsche and branded him as a proto-fascist murderer of reason. As such he is still taboo in our own day in the Eastern European countries which are under the sway of dialectical materialism.

Apart from the above-mentioned interpretations, yet other possibilities of eliminating, or at least explaining, the contradictions in Nietzsche's works may be considered. Biographical investigations (P. J. Möbius,[5] Erich F. Podach,[6] among others) point to pathological traits in Nietzsche's make-up which become more blatant in the late works and herald his mental collapse, or even anticipate it in the form of logical confusion, so that even before 1889 there was no possibility of any coherent philosophical picture's emerging. But quite apart from the fact that such an approach tells us little about the work and still less about its influence, it misconstrues contradiction from the very outset as a flaw in philosophical thought. It reacts to any departure from the well-trodden paths of rational discourse with suggestions for a medical cure. It frustrates Nietzsche's attempt to shatter rigid normality as the yardstick by which to determine what is true (healthy) and untrue (sick) – although it is precisely from Nietzsche that we could have learnt how sickness can sharpen our cognitive faculties.

Apart from pathological explanations, there is an historical and philological approach to the problem of Nietzsche's contradictoriness. This approach sets out to subsume his divergent opinions under various phases, thus ordering them in a steady line of development. And many contradictions are indeed explicable if one divides up the work into successive stages. In each of these stages we find convergent judgments relating to specific clusters of problems. Very roughly, three phases may be distinguished. The first comprised *The Birth of Tragedy* (1872) and the *Untimely Meditations* (1873-6), and it shows their author as a successor to Schopenhauer and Wagner. His cultural criticism is directed above all against 'theoretical man', against the scientific positivism of the nineteenth century, and against the spirit of the *Gründerzeit*, the period of Germany's economic and industrial expansion, in which he finds genius and organizing power lacking, despite, or perhaps because of, the uplifting national unity which Germany had just achieved. Socrates, the father of both 'theoretical man' and Christianity, undertook with the aid of logic and dialectics to dissolve the life-giving contradictions of ancient myth, and to use morality to mark off good from evil. The culmination, in the nineteenth century, of the resulting optimistic belief that everything can be rationally calculated and amicably ordered is for Nietzsche a pious piece of self-deception on the part of weak natures. They no longer dare to look into the abyss and become cheerful from sheer terror. It is therefore precisely in optimism, democracy and logic that he sees signs of declining vitality and physical exhaustion. A pessimistic vision of life, on the other hand, coupled with affirmation of horror and madness, is an unmistakable sign of strength. Rooted in the spirit of pessimism, Greek tragedy is both an instrument and a product of proud natures who are even prepared to let *nothingness be*. All such tragedy sends us on our way with the metaphysical consolation 'that life, despite all its constantly changing appearances, is in its very depths indestructably powerful and joyous' (I, 47). Here it is already clear how logical inconsistency for the young Nietzsche is not a sign of individual sickness. On the contrary, he elevates it to a principle of existence and defends it against the demands of science for unity and system. At this stage in his development, he appeals to art for assist-ance in his battle against the myth-destroying rationalism of Socrates. For art, above all other things, with its non-scientific images and con-structions, is most likely to revive the myths we have lost. Art (above all the music tragedies of Wagner) triumphs over science.

The second phase in Nietzsche's development can be dated from *Human, All-Too-Human* up to the end of *The Joyful Science* (1882). With *Human, All-Too-Human*, a new conception of science takes shape and with it a new estimate of the relations between art and knowledge. At the beginning of the first section we already hear the following: 'All that we need and that can be had at the present level of scientific development, is a *chemistry* of moral, religious, aesthetic representa-tions and sensations . . .' (I, 447). Chemistry in place of myth, a breaking down into elements in place of the construction of an organic whole, analysis in place of synthesis – all these bear witness to new stirrings of a scientific bent. The 'esteeming of unpretentious truths' (I, 448) takes us out of the realm of the timeless essences preserved by myth, and leads to a decisive insight into the historicity of men, their tools of knowledge and their systems of truth: 'but everything has become what it is; there are *no eternal facts*: just as there are no absolute truths' (*Ibid.*). In place of art and myth (*The Birth of Tragedy*) we are given chemistry and history. Ecstatic celebration of the great interconnected whole is replaced by sober preoccupation with detail, distinctions and exact nuance. In this phase, Nietzsche is the radical sceptic, psycholo-gist and analyst. The sole yardstick of knowledge at any price is that frequently invoked 'intellectual honesty' which is deaf to all wishful thinking. The scientist ranks before the artist, and the dubious activity of the latter is revealed most clearly to the seeker after truth in the case of Wagner. Art has the sole function of helping in 'the transition to a truly liberating philosophical science' (I, 468). The significance of Wagner's music is no longer seen in its capacity to breathe new life into myth, but in its value as material for Nietzsche's analytical forays into the psychology of art.

The beginning of the third phase is announced at the end of *The Joyful Science* (1882). If *Human, All-Too-Human* commenced with an expression of faith in chemistry, in this work the joyful scientist scorns number and calculation, seeing and grasping, as 'coarseness' and 'idiocy' (II, 249). He sums up as follows: 'Consequently a scientific interpretation of the world, as you conceive it, could still be one of the *most stupid*, that is to say, the most empty of meaning, of all possible interpretations of the world' (*Ibid.*). Then from *Zarathustra* on, not only are all demands for a scientific or historical interpretation of the world superseded, but even the heroism of truth at any price is drowned out by the laughter of buffoons, by the mocking wisdom of those who have seen through the little tricks of science, by the rhythmic stamping of the dancer. Now, instead of 'unpretentious truths', the great philosophical and visionary themes hold the field: 'the will to power', 'eternal recurrence', the 'great man', 'breeding', and so forth. After the 'yes' of Zarathustra, the transvaluation of values begins, Nietzsche's great essay in metaphysics. Art is rehabilitated and given a positive function as the opponent of devitalizing knowledge: 'Art and nothing but art! Art is the great enabler of life, the great temptress to life, the great stimulant of life' (III, 692).

The three phases of Nietzsche's development appear again in *Zarathustra* in allegorical disguise: 'Three metamorphoses of the spirit I name to you: how the spirit becomes a camel, and the camel a lion, and the lion at last a child' (II, 293). The camel as beast of burden is the carrier and conserver of the precious cultural tradition (Antiquity, Schopenhauer, Wagner). This fits the first phase of Nietzsche's development during the Basle period when he was a professor of classical philology. But then the 'burden-bearing spirit' takes upon himself the 'heaviest weight' of all (*Ibid.*), namely the cultural heritage, and bears it away into the desert. There he becomes a ravening lion, destroying every 'thou shalt' and every value, including even the burden he patiently carried: 'To create new values – not even the lion can do that yet: but to create freedom for new creation – that the might of the lion can do' (II, 294). The middle period (from *Human, All-Too-Human* to *The Joyful Science*) throws up no new images or exemplary types, the lion is neither a bearer nor a creator of truths but a hunter-down of lies. Analysis and destruction are the sole weapons of the second phase, but through their radical power of negation they prepare the ground for new possibilities. These are taken up by the child in the third metamorphosis. The child heralds a new kind of simplicity, since it is neither to bear the burden of the past nor to destroy it but to remain free to create the things of the future: 'The child is innocence and forgetfulness, a fresh beginning, a game, a self-bowling hoop, a first movement, a holy affirmation' (*Ibid.*). With this we have arrived at the third phase of Nietzsche's work, where intellectual honesty is replaced by love of lies and devitalizing knowledge by art as the 'stimulant of life'.

Any historical and literary interpretation of Nietzsche's works must take account of this three-phase division. It will look for and find reasons for the changes that occurred: the break in personal relations with Wagner, new acquaintances and influences (e.g. Paul Rée, English moral psychology, etc.), the course taken by his illness and the connected shift in his evaluation of intellect and ecstasy. Perhaps it will even discover the root of indecision and fickleness in the fundamentally problematic relationship between art and knowledge. Yet despite all these things, the schematic division fails by a long way to do full justice to Nietzsche's widely divergent judgments. For scepticism towards the artist is still evident in *Beyond Good and Evil* (1886), a work which, according to the above schema, should belong to the third phase. In like manner, in *The Genealogy of Morals* (1887) we encounter, contrary to all expectations, that passionate commitment to truth which we have not been accustomed to since *The Joyful Science*. Nietzsche enjoins us 'to sacrifice all human wishes to the truth, to every untruth, even the truth which is plain, harsh, hideous, repellent, un-christian, immoral . . .' (II, 772).

Apart from the intrinsic difficulties which stand in the way of such a neat division, there are still further objections to resolving the contradictions by the three-phase model. If the texts themselves reveal the simultaneous presence of divergent judgments, so their historical reception only serves to intensify this impression. Thomas Mann, Robert Musil and Gottfried Benn, for example, did not only absorb Nietzsche's writings through the filter of this triadic scheme. Rather they found a fundamental cleavage which in their view ran through the entire work. The extraordinarily high value Nietzsche puts on art on the one hand, and his radical scepticism about art – and above all artists – on the other, is something of which they were equally aware without assigning each of these attitudes to different phases of development. Contradictory stances are not seen as historically remote from one another, but as direct rivals. One insight is not more or less true than another merely for coming earlier or later. Only if we take the contradictions together can we do justice to Nietzsche's own awareness of the problem. We fail if we seek to iron them out by consigning them to different phases of development.

We are still saddled with the problem of Nietzsche's divergent judgments, and have made no progress. True, we have become acquainted with a number of false turnings and dead-ends. Neither a pathological study nor a neat division into phases can resolve our problem. Yet there is a third possibility of reconciling Nietzsche's fundamentally different views, and that is to see thinking in antinomies as being itself Nietzsche's methodological principle. This holds not only for the relationship between art and knowledge but also for many other problem-areas. For this reason we propose here to extend the investigation somewhat and examine the antagonism between art and knowledge in the light of contradiction as a fundamental principle. A whole list of antithetical concepts and images in Nietzsche's language seem to indicate a deep-seated antinomianism of thought and imagination. In *The Birth of Tragedy*, the bright Apollonian element in art and nature is already opposed by dark Dionysian forces. Where the Apollonian principle limits and simplifies, the Dionysian principle overflows boundaries and strives after all-encompassing unity. These two principles are matched by a plethora of dualities and antagonisms: to Apollo, the God of light, corresponds appearance but also illusion; Dionysus on the other hand stands for a loss of grip on appearances, a kind of shuddering horror; the Apollonian principle of individuation and plurality is opposed by the dissolution of individuals and a mystical experience of unity. Similar polarities modelled on the mythical schema of Apollonian/Dionysian are dream and ecstasy, 'appearance' and 'will' in Schopenhauer's sense of these terms, optimism and pessimism, serenity and joyful horror. In the field of aesthetics there is at once conflict and correspondence between plastic art (Apollo) and music (Dionysus), rhythm and melody, cither and flute, Homer and Archilochus, epic and lyric, dramatic dialogue and chorus – examples could be multiplied almost indefinitely. For the images of the Apollonian and Dionysian are not confined to the artistic sphere alone, but stretch out beyond it as elemental 'artistic states of nature' ['Kunstzustände der Natur' (I, 25)].

Karl Löwith, who sees in Nietzsche's philosophy rather a 'tentative experimentation than a completed body of knowledge',[7] deals with another fundamental antagonism. For him, the antinomy of decision and necessity stands in the foreground. Even as a schoolboy, Nietzsche had chosen and treated with intellectual passion the essay-topic of 'Free Will and Fate'. Later, the same problem arises in connection with the enthusiastically embraced notion of 'eternal recurrence' which forms the core of his philosophy. In it a basic contradiction is apparent. On the one hand, man has an urge to self-overcoming and self-aggrandizement ('will to power'), yet on the other, nature, with its law of the conservation of energy, admits only of the aimless repetition of the eternally identical. But how can the will to power rise above itself if the cycle of eternal recurrence obtains? How are we to conceive of Nietzsche's hoped-for 'new man' whose advent he announces, if 'eternal recurrence' only allows of a perpetuation of man as he is and has been?

The antagonism of Apollonian and Dionysian, of will to power and eternal recurrence, and of art and knowledge, seems indeed to confirm those who see in contradiction Nietzsche's ultimate, irreducible first principle. Yet for all that, there are plenty of assertions in Nietzsche which reject contradiction as an instrument for establishing truth. To quote a few of the especially significant ones: 'Antithesis is the strait gate through which error most likes to slip on its way to truth' (I, 563), or, 'There are no antitheses: only from those of logic do we derive the concept of antithesis – and thence mistakenly apply it to things' (III, 541). In the light of such objections, it is no longer permissible to take antithetical structures of thought as forming the basic principle of Nietzsche's philosophy. For here even the principle of *contradiction* is *contradicted*. Antithesis has thus forfeited its validity as the necessary or even sole instrument of knowledge. Nietzsche has seen through it as a mere mechanism pertaining to consciousness. It has no ontological status but is a mere instrument of logic.

Divergences and contradictions accumulate and seem to outdo one another to the point where all meaning dissolves. Even our initial question concerning the relationship between art and knowledge is threatened. But if we refuse to resign ourselves to chaos, yet cannot discover any antithetical principle capable of imposing system on it, we must look beyond contradiction itself. We must look for any approach which, while not perhaps reconciling the contradictions themselves, may nevertheless perhaps be able to oppose the principle of contradiction. An outward sign and first clue is afforded by what Schlechta calls the 'remarkable monotony of the total statement' (III, 1435). For all its contradictoriness, Nietzsche's work is permeated by a kind of unity of intellectual style. This results in part from the relatedness of the basic themes which are presented in ever-new variations. The same or similar phenomena constantly recur in the same or slightly modified form, but no progress is made in the discovery of systematic and logically verifiable knowledge. Despite all the shifts and breaks, the drive for strict continuity may be seen in the late work in Nietzsche's ever-more-frequent and copious quotations from his earlier writings. *Ecce Homo* and the preface to *The Genealogy of Morals* reveal his concern that his works should be interpreted as a unity. He repeatedly speaks of the 'common root', the 'basic will for knowledge', of 'becoming One'. He hopes that all his endeavours as philosopher, poet, and also as scholar, may 'come together as one'. The contradictoriness of individual judgments finds its adversary in that 'monotony' which is an expression of the search for unity. Antithetic reasoning, therefore, can no longer be conceived as the sole basic principle of his work: 'If anything indicates our *humanization*, true and real *progress*, it is to be found in our no longer needing excessive contrasts, indeed, in our dispensing with them altogether . . .' (III, 810). Nietzsche associates the elimination of antitheses with an historical process which either ought to have achieved its goal or will do so in the future. In either case, his expectations are shored up by a utopian idea, for as a simple matter of fact his thought constantly deals in contradictions. Thus the urge to eliminate them contrasts with their continued sway. True, the notion of a totality which would embrace these contradictions is no more than a *desideratum*, but as such it does oppose the massive onslaught of contradictions. *Actual* fragmentation and *longed-for* unity are separate but complementary strands in Nietzsche's thought.

After the problems arising out of conflict and antagonism, we must turn in what follows to those relating to totality and unity. We already find in the cultural criticism of Nietzsche's early writings, particularly *The Birth of Tragedy* and the *Untimely Meditations*, a protest against fragmentation into individual concepts and scientific disciplines, against division of labour and the lack of spiritual unity in Germany, a lack which contrasts sharply with the recent foundation of a new national German Empire. The interconnected totality of all phenomena, including contradictory and destructive ones, which Nietzsche misses in the present, he thinks he finds realized in Greek myth, before Socrates began to destroy it with reason and morality. Only in his earlier works does the *concept* of myth constitute an explicit theme; later he no longer talks *about* it, but sketches out, to the best of his ability, a body of myth which will justify both art and knowledge. The later Nietzsche transfers his basic mythological and aesthetic categories, the Apollonian and the Dionysian, from the realms of tragedy and music to his total vision of human life. Or to put it the other way round, in *The Birth of Tragedy* he already projects his later vision into the Greek myths, which as an archaic symbol of unity and totality prefigure Nietzsche's thought in all his writings thereafter.

The specific linguistic and epistemological concerns of the modern era, which can only express itself in isolated frozen particulars and contrasts, not only forbid any definition of myth but call into question the attempt to talk about it at all, since by its very nature myth resists abstraction and division into opposites. Moreover, unless forms of speech are used which are in turn mythical, myth can only be expressed in permanently provisional and partial statements. Two such individual statements of Nietzsche's that may be taken as representative are as follows: 'In their mythology the Greeks transmuted the whole of nature into Greeks',[8] and 'Myth sought to understand all changes by analogy with human action and human volition'.[9] If we disregard the different *content* of these two sentences and concentrate on the *form* they take as judgments, we will see in both cases, as in many others, the ubiquitous use of words like 'whole', 'entire', 'all', 'every', 'always', etc. All these terms reveal a tendency to seek totality. Since myth breaks down definitions and overcomes the barriers set between rationality and irrationality, between good and evil, beauty and ugliness, it can itself only be defined in terms of the constant elimination of definitions. On the one hand this occurs through the use of the above-mentioned epithets of totality, on the other, through a progressive negation of individualizing particulars. Hence Nietzsche is permanently in a position where he can only say what myth is *not*. If he wants to tell us what it *is*, he must take the leap into seemingly empty generality which allows of no analytical division and hence no definition. With sarcastic undertones he quotes the words of Anaxagoras: 'in the beginning everything was of a piece ['beisammen']: then came human reason and created order' (1, 74). So long as 'everything is of a piece', scarce a word is necessary for the whole edifice to fall apart. Thus the provisional and sole concept adequate to myth and its unruly and contradictory nature is – totality. But this term is used not in a Hegelian sense to express *reconciliation* of opposites but rather their *toleration*. Nietzsche conceives of myth as a form of totality to be striven after by progressive negation of distinctions, a totality which must be left open. This conception, we may note in passing, is rooted not in the thought of antiquity but in early romanticism, and hence stands at the beginning of the modern age. Nietzsche is fully aware that myth is irreconcilable with modern awareness, but his certainty of this is intimately bound up with his conviction of the necessity for a mythical renewal; 'Without myth every culture loses its healthy and creative natural powers: only a horizon ringed about with myths can confer unity on an entire cultural movement' (1, 125). The more remote and strange myth is to the modern age, the more urgent is its need of myth and yet the more hopeless is the attempt to reconcile the two. Here lies the basic, tormenting contradiction at once of Nietzsche's thought and of the modern age itself. Like no one else, Nietzsche suffered from this wound. But he not only suffered from it, with biting sharpness of perception he made the wound deeper and more painful, so that his contemporaries and followers would be forced to cry out, or at least be shaken out of their mental torpor and their complacent acceptance of scientific habits of thought.

In his early writings Nietzsche glorifies ancient myth as the lost guarantor of the universal interconnection of all things, though he does not cast off the myth-destroying spell of modern awareness. In his later writings, similarly, he does not abandon the search for an all-embracing whole amid all the antagonisms. But what exactly lies hidden behind this all-encompassing totality which is supposed to embrace and settle all questions of truth and falsehood, art and knowledge, a something which can no longer be expressed in the language of myth alone? The answer seems simple, at least as far as terminology goes, for there is one constantly invoked word in Nietzsche's writings which forces itself on our attention, and that is 'life'. 'Life' is the foundation and interconnection of things, and embraces and determines all there is. The secondary literature on Nietzsche is very ill at ease with the vagueness of this concept, if indeed it should be called a concept at all; terms like 'metaphor' or 'figure' seem preferable. And even the oft-repeated assertion, especially in the 'Nachlass' of the 1880s, that the formula for 'life' is the 'will to power', has no abiding validity since it is contradicted, as we have seen, by the idea of 'eternal recurrence' (cf. Löwith). For how can the 'will to power' raise man above the limits set down for him in a universe ruled by iron fate? From our inability to answer this question it is plain that every specific interpretation of the sought-for whole, of 'life', restricts the totality of this principle and opens the way to contradiction. Restriction of the whole entails the loss of its universality.

What we said earlier about myth holds also for 'life'. Nietzsche can conceive of 'life' only as a totality to be striven after and kept open by progressive negation of particular distinctions. This totality is the only concept adequate to life and its unruly contradictoriness, not in Hegel's sense of *reconciliation* but of *toleration* of contrasts. The totality of 'life', which in The Birth of Tragedy Nietzsche still projects on to the Greek myths, comprises a radical openness and affirmation of self-destructive antagonisms, including the notion of nothingness as a complement of totality. It is not the recognition and acceptance of *nothingness* that Nietzsche stigmatizes as *nihilism*, but its covering up and disguising by Christianity and morality.

But this notion of totality as a conceptual basis for Nietzsche's ideas about ancient myth and for his later scheme of a myth of 'life' does not culminate in quasi-religious worship and the invocation of chthonic mythical powers. On the contrary, it is bound up with modern aspirations to exact knowledge, and still more with an awareness of the problems of epistemology. This is revealed in the very inadequacy of language: 'every word is a prejudice' (I, 903), or, 'Words are only symbols for the relations of things to each other and to ourselves, and at no point do they touch upon the absolute truth' (III, 390). Words are not merely inadequate, they are false because they are the instruments of distortion. On the one hand we are dependent upon them, on the other they not only fail to serve us but actually get in the way. When we talk of something in conceptual language we do not grasp it in its totality but only in isolated aspects, and are led to rest content in this partial view. In this way we suppress the multi-faceted ambiguity of the object of knowledge and with it the sought-after wholeness: 'So far as the word "knowledge" has any sense at all, the world is knowable; but it can be variously *interpreted*, there is not one single meaning hidden behind it, it has countless meanings. – "Perspectivism" ' (III, 903). Here Nietzsche states the notion which most tellingly characterizes his method of thought. The constantly renewed attempts to grasp the totality of 'life' come to grief and are repelled by relative partial judgments which are at loggerheads with one another. Through the constant shifts of position by which his entire work is marked, Nietzsche seeks the desired totality in ever-renewed nuances which are mutually contradictory and point to new perspectives. Such a perspectivist way of seeing things both relativizes individual judgments and yet at the same time preserves them from onesidedness. It keeps our eyes open to that totality which is the realm of open possibilities. The permanent isolation of one perspective as a universally valid way of seeing things would establish an ideal and hence a principle inimical to 'life'.

In the light of such changing perspectives, contradictions and opposites acquire a new function. Since the manifold facets of the whole can never be stated exhaustively, let alone simultaneously, the perspectivist approach first stakes out the extremes; and in this way there arises that appearance of plain contradiction. In reality, however, the opposites have the function of poles which mark off those extreme points of the whole between which a multiplicity of other perspectives are possible. And antithesis, encompassing as it does the greatest conceivable sweep, is the best suited to embrace these multifarious possibilities. Such poles do not therefore constitute absolute opposites but rather correlated extremes which stand in relation to a totality, even if it is one that cannot ultimately be encompassed. Thus contradictions not only have a solvent and relativizing function, but they also acquire a role as the necessary means of modern perspectivism, which has become an indispensable tool of knowledge and expression. Whether the sought-after totality is called 'myth', as by the early Nietzsche, or 'life' as in the later works, its content remains his own attempt at myth; and his method of seeking knowledge is perspectivism. The *goal* of knowledge is the *myth* of the prophet, and the *path* to knowledge is the *perspectivism* of the sceptic.

Both these concerns remain for ever separated, and yet they are related to one another. The will to mythical renewal alone is bound to get bogged down in a bottomless speculation, unable to meet the requirements of exactness laid down by modern science. On the other hand, commitment to shifting perspectives would lose sight of that all-embracing interconnectedness and reduce the search for the whole to a string of detached fragments, individual disciplines and specific truths. The deeper and ultimately insoluble contradiction of

Nietzsche's work lies in the fact that contradictoriness and totality as opposites must stand to one another in a simultaneous relationship of hostile opposition and mutual co-operation. This antagonistic role determines the relations between art and knowledge, both of which are rooted in the quasi-mythical totality of 'life' but yet at the same time are exposed to all the perspectivist, particularizing views of modern scepticism.

Even art is not immune to this inner dissension, although in *The Birth of Tragedy* it is still unambiguously in favour of the lost world of myth that must be regained. Indeed, in the shape of Wagner's music tragedies it is glorified as the sole guarantor of the rebirth of myth. Since in the later Nietzsche 'life' assumes the inheritance of Greek myth, art might be given a clear and unimpeachable position relative to 'life' as the champion of mythical totality against the perspectivism of knowledge. We will see, however, how art, like 'life', has to relinquish its unambiguous and impregnable posture *vis-à-vis* other equally divided functions of 'life'. At this point we may look for the sake of comparison at Hegel's aesthetics. There art is integrated into the 'system of Spirit'. 'For us the concept of beauty and of art is a presupposition given by the system of philosophy.'[10] Here natural beauty is largely excluded, for the spirit alone is truth, and beauty must partake of it if it is to acquire real value. Art is still touched by sensuous and unreflected elements, and as such does not rank in the higher echelons of the system of spirit. It is forced to recognize higher stages in religion and, above all, philosophy. Only philosophy is capable of attaining to the absolute idea in which all traces of nature are transcended and purified. Art, on the other hand, remains permanently dependent upon lower forms which are less true. Works of art, therefore, do not bear their value within themselves, for this accrues to them only when they are made objects of philosophical understanding: 'Art invites us to reflective thought, not for the purposes of producing more art but for understanding systematically ['wissenschaftlich'] what art is.'[11] Thus, in the system of philosophy, art takes a subordinate but, for that very reason, assignable and legitimate place. In its function of reconciling spirit and nature it even acquires a purpose.

In Schopenhauer's philosophical system, too, art occupies a fixed and important place, albeit in a quite different set of relations from Hegel's. Man can liberate himself from the fetters of desire in the degree that his self-awareness frees him from the drive of his will. The searcher after knowledge must cease wishing to be an individual subject, renounce the promptings of the will, and in contemplation purified of desire become a mirror of the object. In this he succeeds in varying degrees on various levels of awareness. In the naive state pure will largely prevails: in religion man projects the fulfilment of his wishes into a higher kingdom conceived in various ways; in science and philosophy he already operates with the principle of sufficient reason, but for the time being he only uses it to grasp individual phenomena. Only in art does man rise above particular appearances and contemplate underlying ideas, that is, the respective essences of particular stages of objectivization. Thus architecture grasps the idea of things inorganic, landscape gardening that of botanical species, drama the idea of human action and history, etc., until we reach music which, as the highest of the arts, is in direct possession of the idea of the will. In Schopenhauer's system, therefore, art towers above all else, and music is even supposed to achieve the shedding of individuality.

Nietzsche is just as concerned as his predecessors to create a coherent aesthetic. At least he is convinced of the necessity of such a task, as emerges from letters to Erwin Rohde[12] and Peter Gast.[13] At the same time he insists on the liberation of art from all bonds. It shall be neither the handmaid of philosophy as in Hegel, nor a vehicle on the road to Nirvana as with Schopenhauer. It must be indifferent to all moral, religious and political aspirations. 'Art as a feeling of superiority and a 'mountain' set against the lowlands of politics, Bismarck, Socialism, and Christianity etc., etc.'[14] Where Hegel and Schopenhauer investigate the place and role of aesthetics on the ladder of knowledge, and determine the relations of art to other manifestations of the human spirit, Nietzsche must forgo all this. He is thus unable to rest content with a phenomenology of art since he lacks a system within which to integrate it and assign its functions. Consequently his questions concerning the ontological status of aesthetics constantly draw a blank, are retracted, reformulated, variously answered, and so on. He aims at a detachment of art from all ideals, concepts and presuppositions which makes it impossible for him to assign it a fixed place. Were his ambitions more modest, less absolute and radical, and were he to consider art in connection with other cultural phenomena, an aesthetic might be more easily possible. But, as it is, the conferring of an independent status upon aesthetics dooms to failure all attempts at a systematic solution. In contrast with Hegel and Schopenhauer, Nietzsche, by bestowing the highest possible value on art, namely independence, finds himself in the peculiar position of exposing it to every conceivable attack, since neither priest, philosopher, nor politician can see it serving his purposes. Even if Nietzsche does deny to art all goals external to itself, he nevertheless seeks desperately for a conceptual theory of aesthetics. This means that he cannot conceive of art as wholly isolated from other concerns. But in so doing he does not relinquish the principle of aesthetic autonomy, for he does not inquire into the *ends* of art but into its *origins*. It is not the functions and purpose, but the springs of art that interest him. In taking this path he pursues a two-fold aim: he must *justify* art without *binding* it to non-aesthetic ends.

In his Preface to *The Birth of Tragedy*, written at a later date, Nietzsche emphasizes that in his early works he already interpreted existence in the light of ancient myth as 'beyond good and evil'. Religion, morality, philosophical reasoning, all must be disarmed as evaluative principles lest they should diminish the living whole. Yet, as we have seen, Nietzsche's entire work shows that at the latest from Socrates onwards, a disinterested acceptance of life as a whole has not been possible. The indispensable totality of 'life' is opposed by the changing and contradictory perspectives of modern knowledge. And if art is to have its origins in the totality of 'life', then at the same time it inherits 'life's' antagonistic nature. 'Life' as the source of all there is, including art, imposes on the latter the stamp of its own dividedness. The most striking expression of this is the Apollonian/Dionysian dichotomy which marks ancient myth and art in the early work, is later extended to cover 'life' itself, and finally, as the principle of 'life', also draws art into its sphere of influence. In the 'Nachlass' of the 1880s, from which we here quote an extended passage, these two elements in art and 'life' appear as the two poles of the mythical whole. In this confrontation the contrasts and consonances between these two elements become apparent:

The word '*Dionysian*' expresses: an urge for unity, a reaching out beyond persons, routine, society, reality, beyond the abyss of transience: the passionately painful welling-over into darker, richer, more indeterminate states; an ecstatic affirmation of the total character of life, as identity in change, immutable power and immutable joy through constant change; the great pantheistic common joy and common compassion which welcomes and hallows even the most terrible and questionable characteristics of life; the eternal willing of procreation, fertility, and recurrence; the sense at once of the necessity for creation and destruction.

The word '*Apollonian*' expresses: the urge to achieve total self-sufficiency [Für-sich-sein], the typical 'individual', and for everything that simplifies, emphasizes, and renders strong, clear, unmistakable, typical: freedom under law.

The future development of art is just as much bound to the antagonism between these two forces at work in nature and art ['Natur-Kunstgewalten'] as is the future development of humanity to the antagonism between the sexes (III, 791).

Both these forces then ['Natur-Kunstgewalten'] pursue unity, but in each case of a radically different character. The *Dionysian* element strives after universality which will embrace all extremes and blot out all boundaries. This sense of unity is emphasized by the language of the above quotation, which embraces opposites: pain-ecstasy, change-identity, common joy-compassion, creation-destruction. The fixing of extremes and their overcoming affords an indirect description of Dionysian unity as totality. The *Apollonian* element strives for unity too, but not for the all-embracing totality of the Dionysian. It achieves unity rather by simplification and emphasis of certain strands drawn from the plenitude of the whole. Ambiguity is eliminated by an act of self-limitation, and subordination to a law entails simplicity and individuality. The Apollonian fixes unambiguous detail and captures a part of reality. The Dionysian strives after the unity of the *whole* and the Apollonian aspires to the clarity attainable from a particular *perspective*.

Despite their antagonism, the two elements are necessarily related, for left to itself the Dionysian principle represents a chaotic and permanent pursuit of excess. It thus requires the simplifying, ordering, and crystallizing function of the Apollonian principle. If, however, the latter were to isolate itself, it would become fossilized and barren. Hence its dependence on the rich, the whole, the overflowing principle. The totality of the world is constantly breaking down the one-sided, partial perspective, and restoring the claims of the Dionysian principle. This in its turn can only manifest itself in ever-renewed Apollonian forms of partial expression. In this duality of the Dionysian and the Apollonian principles as a mythical conception of 'life' we can see a reflection of the tension between totality and changing perspectives. Both these principles are equally necessary, and only the threat posed by a preponderance of the abstract and over-conceptualized view of life of the nineteenth century led Nietzsche to give temporary priority to the Dionysian principle. But in their conflict and interaction with one another they enjoy in principle equal status. Nietzsche's over-emphasis of the Dionysian element, which he feels to be threatened, reveals the desire to work towards a renaissance of myth beyond scientific consciousness, but without disregarding the demands of intellect. The quest for mythical renewal is, moreover, the deeper reason for Nietzsche's consistent polemics against every moralistic interpretation of the world, and against Christianity in particular. Unlike other critics of religion in the nineteenth century, he does not even attempt to rebut its articles of faith by rational argument. Instead he simply rejects them instinctively 'We deny God as God. . . . If the existence of this God of the Christians were *demonstrated* to us, we would find it even harder to believe in him' (II, 1212). The reproach against Christianity is directed less against the truth-claims of its fundamental tenets than against the historical fact that they could not preserve their binding power; by the nineteenth century at the latest they had lost their mythical efficacy in life and thought. Christianity had once upon a time completed the moral and rational work of 'theoretical man' (Socrates), and encompassed once and for all the downfall of Greek myth. In so doing it had sinned against 'life' but was nevertheless justified so long as it could gain credence for its interpretation of existence. So long, that is, as it was itself myth. Only in its death-pangs did it become untrue, and then because it lost all credibility. From that moment it must be dealt the death-blow to make way for a new myth. This will lean heavily on the myths of antiquity with their affirmation of the *whole* of 'life', of luminously buoyant but also of darkly tragic existence; of the Apollonian *and* the Dionysian elements.

The images used to express the Apollonian and the Dionysian principles belong not only to the aesthetic sphere (music, tragedy, epic, etc.) but also to nature and ordinary human existence. In so far as they designate the totality of 'life', art is no longer completely isolated. It is drawn by the antagonistic dualism of the two 'Kunstzustände der Natur' (I, 25) into a broader context which transcends the narrow sphere of aesthetics. And this has a decisive effect on the evaluation of art. Beauty and ugliness are not independent phenomena peculiar only to the world of art; nor yet are they an expression of rationally fixed goals or of moral and social ends. Rather the 'beautiful and the ugly are seen to be *determined*; namely with respect to our most basic *values of survival*' (III, 576). Beauty thus takes its place among the life-enhancing categories. All living things, according to Nietzsche, press for an increase in vitality and summon up all the means at their disposal to secure survival and self-fulfilment. At the zenith of his power, man too braces all his energies, but without strain, lightly and serenely, even when he is suspended over the abyss. At such moments he is beautiful and capable of producing beauty, the great work of art, which bears the same attributes as himself. By way of analogy Nietzsche points to animals that in the mating season acquire greater strength and become correspondingly more colourful and beautiful. Just as heightened energies are manifest in the enhanced beauty of the living creature, so too is human art an expression of the heightened will to live. The artist acquires power over the world by arranging things as his existence demands. The original significance of melody and rhythm consisted in compelling other beings, above all the gods, to be mindful of the needs of mortal existence: 'they were ensnared by poetry as by a magic noose' (II, 93).

Art answers to the instinct in man to transmute unbearable reality into beautiful illusion, and to become, like the Greeks, 'superficial – *out of profundity*' (II, 1061). Here art is obedient to the will to power which is the servant of 'life'.

If, in obedience to 'life's' imperatives of survival art creates a world beyond truth and falsehood, it cannot pay heed to the demands of reality and logic. For terms like 'true' and 'real' must first justify themselves before the bar of 'life'. The transformation of the world into bearable illusion, which 'life' requires and directs, is the more justifiable as both truth and knowledge are also rooted in the will to power. As such they do not describe the world of things in a strictly objective fashion, but like art interpret and reinterpret it in obedience to the demands of 'life'. The inadequacy of our cognitive equipment and its dependence upon the life-enhancing principle empower art to create its own world. The demand for aesthetic transformation of reality thus rests upon two presuppositions: first, the endeavour to trace art back to its origins, to 'life', and second, the epistemological insight that all truth reposes upon the changing conditions determined by the instinct for survival. *Totality* on the one hand and sceptical *perspectivism* on the other are the constitutive elements of Nietzsche's philosophy of art.

Perhaps at this point one might raise objections to what looks like that very functionalization of art which was supposed to be avoided. For has not the derivation of art from 'life' created a new purpose, a new goal? Have not ends alien to art been smuggled through the back-door into the edifice of aesthetics? And is not art conceived of here as but an instrument for 'coming to terms with life'? Here again we must attempt to forestall a misunderstanding of what is meant by 'life'. It cannot be confined to a biological and social instinct for well-being which seeks to steer clear of everything repellent. 'Life' as a quasi-mythical notion also embraces what is sick, ugly and evil. Hence art does not merely take refuge in the idyllic but in its moments of great-est strength seizes hold of horror and tragedy. Thus Greek tragedy, for example, teaches 'that life, despite ever-changing appearances, is in its depths indestructibly powerful and joyous' (I, 47). Since 'life' as the open totality of all phenomena, including those in opposition to one another, remains indeterminate, it cannot yield that calculable meaning which would prescribe the goals of art. What 'life' demands in specific cases cannot be established, since even sickness and things hostile to life can still fulfil a function in the total process. The por-trayal of horror itself supposes a plenitude of 'life' without which the artist could never achieve mastery over the absurdity of existence. The creator of Greek tragedy is thus distinguished by the 'pessimism of *strength*' (I, 9), whereas weak artistic natures take pleasure in the pretty and the unproblematic, the elegant and the harmless. And neither does artistic depiction of the hateful and terrible pursue any educative goal. It is not the purpose of tragedy on the stage to instruct men how to lead more fortunate lives from the example of the misfortunes of the tragic hero. Art seeks to stand firm in the face of inevitable horror but does not attempt to elicit from it any positive moral or religious meaning. In the service of 'life', the tragic artist recognizes what is hostile to it as an undeniable element in it. His affirmation of the horrible in no wise diminishes horror. Its very intensity is rather a measure of the force with which the tragedian experiences the abyss and is able to bear it. By giving free play to the totality of 'life', he pre-serves it from the one-sided interpretations of morality, science, Christianity and politics. In considerations such as these art acquires for Nietzsche its most monumental significance; for him it becomes 'the highest task and truly metaphysical activity of this life' (I, 20). The capacity to fulfil this task he grants (initially) to Richard Wagner.

But perspectivism would have no validity were it to find no objections to this 'metaphysical' evaluation of art. And surprisingly enough it falls to Richard Wagner, the supposed reviver of mythical art, to serve as the representative of its opposite, that is, of modernity and inner disharmony. There may well be external biographical reasons for this in the break-up of the friendship between the two men. But deeper reasons are to be found in the inherent contradictoriness of the concept of 'life' as the source and criterion of art. We have seen how 'life' is split between the rival Dionysian and Apollonian principles, and how the sought-for totality is revealed to the knowing subject not as a unity but from a variety of ambiguous perspectives. We have seen, too, how this duality is communicated to all 'life's' products, including art. Yet life does not split up into these two principles alone, for from another angle it is subject to a further dichotomy. It is realized in the opposing forms of health and decadence. These are not merely descriptive but also normative categories, which have taken the place of logical and moral value-judgments: 'The *sickly* are the greatest enemy to man: *not* the wicked, *not* the "beasts of prey" ' (II, 863).

Now 'sickness' in this sense, like 'life', is not a biological concept drawn from the natural sciences. In its broadest physical and moral sense sickness connotes fragmentation of the totality of things. Its symptoms are over-emphasis on the theoretical, the priority of analytical reason over instinct, and the predominance of knowledge over art. Nietzsche detects its further expression in the excessively high value put on learning, in democracy, equal rights for women, the religion of compassion and Wagner's *Parsifal*, and so on. All these symptoms display a preference for the theoretical and the ideal. They stand for a singling out and delimitation of separate strands which always entail exclusion and distortion of what remains. Every aesthetic ideal – and atheism, too, which denies itself the lie of God's existence – is grounded in an impoverishment of 'life' and seeks to attain mastery over existence by exaggeration of a single segment. Where the *décadent*, in the light of his own ideal, denigrates instinct, passion, wickedness and bestiality, the adherent of full and vigorous 'life' gives them free rein in their interplay with one another. He does not lose himself in supine obedience to any one of them. Health consists in being able at all times to sustain any powerful stimulus without blindly succumbing to it at its very onset. The chaste man who suppresses his instincts is not healthy; health is reserved for the man who gladly accepts and enjoys them, without becoming their slave in the way that the ascetic is enslaved by his ideal. The strong do not squander their powers in this one-sided fashion but balance them all in a creative tension.

Health and *décadence* are two antagonistic manifestations and criteria of 'life'; and since art is rooted in 'life', the same principles apply to it too. In forming aesthetic judgments also we ask of the artist or the work of art whether they accommodate a great and multifarious variety combined with playful ease, or give one-sided prominence to some things at the cost of others. The strong in spirit are slow and do not respond to every stimulus; they despise effect and exhibitionism. What Nietzsche calls the 'great style' as a sign of health he discovers in Gottfried Keller, Stifter, Lichtenberg, Jung-Stilling, and always in Goethe. By contrast, the overwrought style, with its richness and refinements which are disproportionate to the flimsy content, is a sign of diminished vitality. Wagner, who was praised in *The Birth of Tragedy* and even in the *Untimely Meditations* as the saviour of myth and beauty, is now presented from a changed perspective as the *décadent par excellence*. For Nietzsche he is the type of the play-actor, the virtuoso of nuance and effect, overburdened with detail yet without any unifying creative power, brimming with knowledge but devoid of instinct. A typical example of aesthetic judgment based on the contrast between health and decadence is Nietzsche's characterization of the Old and the New Testaments.

> All my respect for the Old Testament! In it I find great men, a heroic landscape and one of the rarest things on earth, the incomparable simplicity [Naivität] of *stout hearts*; still more, I find a people [Volk]. In the New, by contrast, I find nothing but petty sectarianism, an insipid rococo of the soul, mere flourishes, whims and crotchets, the unbreathable air of the conventicle . . . (II, 884f).

This judgment on the two parts of the Bible squares perfectly with the criteria of health and sickness. The evaluative terms are on the one hand 'great', 'heroic', 'simplicity', 'stout heart' – expressions of a noteworthy generality and sweep. On the other, there is the petty, narrow world of the New Testament: 'whim', 'crotchet', 'flourishes'. In the one case he finds the immediate and the all-embracing; in the other, the particular, the peculiar, the patchy. The Old Testament still embodies totality ('a people'), the New reveals the fragmented and the remote ('sects', 'conventicles'). For Nietzsche, Richard Wagner is an heir of the New Testament, above all in his *Parsifal*. Here modern critical awareness prevails over art which should draw its inspiration from the depths. Instead of health Nietzsche sees only sickness, in place of totality only singular perspectives. 'Impoverished life' is opposed by 'great healthiness'. And as art springs from 'life' so it inherits antagonism in the opposition between decadent style and 'great' style. The epithet 'great', which is a remarkably indeterminate word, occurs with striking frequency in Nietzsche's writings. It is associated with every possible type of emotion, action and event: 'great longing', 'great disgust', 'great danger', 'great chase', 'great healthiness', 'great noonday', etc. The first effect of this ever-recurrent epithet is one of intensification, whereby the notion to which it is attached is given greater emphasis. But with this greater emphasis comes an enlargement of meaning. The 'great chase', for example, means more than the 'chase' in its customary sense. The chase is governed by rules, the needs of life, utilitarian considerations (it is customary to hunt only particular animals, and so forth); but the 'great chase' transcends all barriers and spares neither man and his values nor the gods. And least of all does Nietzsche's 'great chase' stop at his own thought and writing, for truths already established are hunted down and killed.

The semantic enlargement secured by the word 'great' has nothing to do with abstract logic. Yet while 'great' resists any formal conceptual definition, it is not pallid and empty but dense with sensuous qualities. Its meaning is partly conceptual and partly metaphorical, partaking of abstraction and intuition. The tension between sensuousness and intellect, image and concept, which we find in 'greatness' makes it possible to establish connections between the most disparate, indeed opposite, phenomena. A prerequisite for 'greatness' in man as laid down by Nietzsche is that 'the multiplicity of elements and the tension of opposites should grow' (II, 595). Wickedness and cunning belong to 'greatness', but so too do innocence and the serene peace of the strong and vital; intellect, sensuality and health, but also their refinement through their opposite, *décadence*. The precondition of 'greatness' lies in the multifariousness of desires and their control. This has nothing to do with the ascetic's repression of a part of his desires to favour others in the name of some ideal. The curbing of emotions is meant to guarantee the maintenance of a sphere of freedom, and safeguard the full range of human possibilities, so that no one part acquires power over the whole and thus destroys it. Curtailment of desires in the 'great' man does not entail the breathless exertions of asceticism. It ensures rather that his forces are kept in easy balance. What holds for the 'greatness' of man in general also applies to the artist and his work. His work is 'great' when it is at once simple and contains the greatest possible range of perspectives; when it has given rise to conflicting interpretations and remains a permanent source of contrasting influences. Goethe, the man and his art, represents the essence of such 'greatness'. He ties himself to neither dogma nor doctrine, and is full of inner contradictions almost in the manner of a god. And for Nietzsche he achieves the higher freedom of the 'great' in his willingness to let things be, even those most opposed to one another.

Goethe, as the embodiment of living totality, remains for Nietzsche an unapproachable ideal. Richard Wagner, on the other hand, is a contemporary against whom he does battle and whose modernity he at the same time sympathetically shares. In contrast with the ideal of 'great' healthiness is the actual impoverishment of life which Nietzsche diagnoses in his own age and in himself. His writings are filled with scorn and anger at every form of decadence, and his outbursts against Wagner are so excessive that they can only be explained as expressions of agonized self-destruction. His criticisms of lack of proportion, of exaggeration of the particular at the expense of the whole, of play-acting, are indeed directed against supposedly pathological monstrosities in Wagner's music. Yet every single objection could be applied word for word to Nietzsche's own thought and work. His work, too, is anything but the expression of a unity and plenitude of overflowing life. In his writings, also, isolated features are thrown up in too high relief and disproportionately emphasized; witticisms and sleights of hand are used with virtuosity to gloss over the sought-for but decidedly absent organization of the whole. If Nietzsche calls Wagner the 'greatest *miniaturist* in music' (II, 918), then *he* is the 'greatest miniaturist' in words and ideas. He, too, like Wagner is a romantic threatened by his own multifarious nature, but with an insatiable craving for classical unity.

Yet even Nietzsche's consistent condemnation of degeneracy does not provide the starting-point for a (negative) value-system. For as always with Nietzsche, contradiction is not far away. In the preface to *The Case of Wagner* he says: 'I am as much a child of this age as Wagner, I mean a *décadent*: the difference is that I grasped the fact and resisted it. The philosopher in me resisted it' (II, 903). This revealing quotation is informative in many ways: we know from what has already been said that decadence arises out of the predominance of the theoretical and the burden of modern knowledge. Wagner as artist is too self-aware, possesses too much knowledge, to succeed in the production of 'great' art. This now gives rise to the apparent paradox that one's entanglement in modern consciousness can only be made plain, and perhaps even overcome, by one's being made conscious of it. It is not the artist languishing in the chains of knowledge who may free himself but – at any rate in dreams – the self-conscious seeker after knowledge who is aware of their existence: 'The philosopher in me resisted it.' The artist suffers from a surfeit of philosophical awareness and yet the philosopher is his only physician. He alone at least recognizes the sickness even if he cannot cure it. Only full awareness of his own sickness allows Nietzsche to sketch a picture of its opposite, 'great' healthiness. Only when the latter has been destroyed does it become something desirable that must be restored. In a certain sense, therefore, 'great' healthiness requires sickness before it can be recognized as a corrective.

Thus, not only 'greatness' but decadence too, like all else, has its origin in the totality of 'life'. Like the apparently irreconcilable opposites of wholeness and perspectivism, so health and sickness too are correlates in that they work together in complicity. Hence decadence is at once a consequence and an agent of particularizing knowledge where 'great' healthiness corresponds to the aesthetic and mythical construct of the all-embracing whole. Health and decadence constitute the same kind of antagonistic duality as do totality of 'life' and perspectivist particularization, the Apollonian and the Dionysian, art and knowledge. We have seen that both health and decadence as well as art and knowledge are rooted in 'life' and bear the stamp of its antagonisms. Art, which is wedded to beautiful illusion, is not alone in resting upon non-rational judgments of value, for so too do knowledge and truth. They are responses to a vital urge which must believe things true, not because they are 'objectively' true, but because their posited truth subserves some set of human needs or wishes. The epistemological dichotomy of things-in-themselves and mere appearances here becomes obsolete, for both truth and falsehood arise at the bidding of the will. 'We have projected *our own* conditions for survival as the *predicates of Being* itself' (III, 556). This not only limits and makes more difficult of attainment the ideal of exact, 'objective' knowledge, as was hitherto the case, it shows it to be mistaken in its very conception.

Nietzsche's destruction of the prevalent theory of scientific knowledge depends on demonstrating that science – whether in the guise
of epistemological realism or idealism – can only rest upon objects
which have been filtered through the senses and the understanding;
and that the relevant vital interests which affect this process are never
taken into account. Thus, to him the philosophical dichotomies of
Plato and Kant are vulnerable not because they are unable to with-
stand logical scrutiny, but because they have been prized out of an all-
embracing totality and have become as such a symptom of decadence.
Philosophical systems are criticized not because they break the rules
of rational argument, but because they are a function of impoverished
'life'. The cry for knowledge at any price, regardless of the claims of
lies and myths, is a sign of sickness and only serves to exacerbate this
condition. So long as knowledge accepts that the 'predicates of being'
derive from our vital needs, it does not come into conflict with art,
for both are active in the service of health-giving 'life'. But whenever
the search for truth strays from its moorings to take soundings on its
own account, that is, when it becomes 'objective', it comes into conflict with life-preserving art.

Precise concepts and exact inferences, or for that matter sceptical
questions, are held to be a source of peril. To protect himself against
ruinous scepticism, Nietzsche thus banishes his desire to know everything, and in his wisdom sets firm limits to knowledge. These serve
to ensure that critical analysis of emotions and ideas shall not destroy
the healthy simplicity of existence nor the freedom from scruple
indispensable to the artist. But if theoretical reflection still succeeds in
asserting itself, it soon comes up against limits which no man has set.
The resultant despair at this transforms itself then into an imperious
need for art. Beauty acts as a panacea for the suffering which arises out
of the defeat of the will to knowledge. 'Our religion, morality and
philosophy are forms of *décadence* in humanity. – The *counter-movement*:
art' (III, 717). On this view art takes clear precedence over knowledge
in the scheme of vital activities.

The quotation that follows also appears at first to give clear confirmation of the primacy of art. Yet we shall see how in one and the
same quotation the ideas presented can turn full circle, so that we see
the truth the other way round. Here again we see how fruitless must
be the attempt to schematize the contradictions in Nietzsche's work.
'Compared with the artist the appearance of *scientific* man is indeed a
sign of a certain constriction and levelling of life (– but also of *intensi-*

fication, severity, hardness, will-power)' (III, 774). Here Nietzsche gives absolutely no indication as to whether one side of this dichotomy is subservient to, or dependent upon, the other; nor does he even tell us whether they are related at all. The laconic 'but also' does not indicate a clear opposition, for the contra-distinction expressed by the word 'but' is at once cancelled by the juxtaposing effect of the word 'also'. Of course, both art and knowledge are related to a third factor, 'life', which science is supposed on the one hand to abase, on the other to enhance. And art, too, has a similarly ambiguous function. From the point of view of the totality of 'life', it might appear wise to inject the sickness of knowledge into 'life' itself, thus as it were conferring greater immunity upon its 'great' healthiness. But the will to truth at any price does not permit the integration of knowledge into a system which would draw its poisonous fangs. The powerful emotional requirement of 'intellectual honesty', so repeatedly invoked, is a match for the urge to make the world bearable through beautiful illusion, and it develops an independence which denies itself all wishful deception.

Seen from this angle, 'Scientific man is a further development of artistic man' (I, 582). The upward revaluation of knowledge proceeds apace; the effort alone which it requires of us deserves our sacrifice. 'Reason' and 'experience' are gods 'which are within *ourselves*' (I, 1037). If, from the point of view of health, concepts and logical inference were a dangerous source of sickness, here Nietzsche esteems it the most important achievement of modern intellectualism that men 'learn to *draw correct inferences*' (I, 613). When knowledge is spoken of in this radically unattached sense, Nietzsche has in mind the path to it and not the goal, the search for knowledge and not its crystallization in dogmatic forms. Seen from this standpoint of uncompromising intellectual experiment, art recedes into the shadows. It no longer by any means enjoys the dominant place accorded to it from other points of view, but even on occasions sinks into complete insignificance, as may be seen particularly from *Human, All-Too-Human*. If the three-phase division mentioned earlier might just still be able to explain this, it breaks down utterly when we turn to *Zarathustra*. According to the genetic schema, the primacy of aesthetics should be evident here. Yet not only do we encounter a casual slighting of art, as in *Human, All-Too-Human*, but hear the gravest charges levelled against it. The oldest and most serious charge of all we hear on Zarathustra's lips: poets are guilty of lying.

The chapter 'On Poets' in the second part of *Zarathustra* opens with a declared commitment to the body and its impermanence, to historical and empirical existence in the here and now. The rejection of everything unearthly and eternal is clothed in a parody of the '*Chorus mysticus*' at the end of Goethe's *Faust* II: 'Everything transient/Is but a parable.' ['Alles Vergängliche/Ist nur ein Gleichnis.'] In Nietzsche we have by way of typical contrast: 'and everything "intransient" – that too is a mere parable' (II, 382) ['und alles das "Unvergängliche" – das ist auch nur ein Gleichnis']. In an earlier chapter, 'On the Fortunate Isles', Zarathustra has said exactly the same almost word for word, adding: 'And the poets lie too much' (II, 345). Already at this point he bestows his praise on process and impermanence, warning all creative spirits not to discredit but to justify the temporal. If intransience is a mere parable, that is, a symbolic fiction whose claims to reality and eternal value are empty, and if such fictions are the stuff peculiar to poets, then it is a part of their trade to create a hazy world of unearthly permanence. When, in the chapter 'On Poets', Zarathustra once again makes a mock of intransience, he suppresses the earlier rider that the poets lie too much. This is a charge which is already voiced by Solon and Plato, and in the Middle Ages.[15]

When Zarathustra's attentive disciple points out the omission, the missing utterance takes on great but problematic significance. Zarathustra, who refuses to carry about with him as a burden the opinions he has expressed in the past along with his reasons for doing so (he compares them to a flock of escaping birds), now repeats the missing sentence, but this time in the form of a question: 'But what did Zarathustra once tell you? That the poets lie too much?' – and then he adds: 'Yet Zarathustra too is a poet' (II, 382). And a little later he extends his charge still further when he says: '*we* lie too much' (II, 383). Mendacity resides in the vain, shallow and arrogant claim to have 'special secret access to knowledge' (*Ibid.*), although the personages and deities of poets, and our own too, originate in the realms of dream. This is the reason why Zarathustra makes a rhyme on 'Dichter-Gleichnis' ['poets' imagery'] and 'Dichter-Erschleichnis' ['poets' trickery'] (*Ibid.*). When he despairs of poets yet calls himself a poet too, his criticism is directed in part against himself. Hence he has grown weary not just of mythic deities and gods, but of the 'superman', whom he had proclaimed in their stead. Now this mythic construction, too, appears to him the mere product of 'Dichter-Erschleichnis', born of the wish for healing and salvation at least in this world. He is now filled with deep sadness and scepticism, scepticism not just of poets, but also of himself. For this he is scolded by his disciple who would see his master strong and free of doubt. He is aroused by enthusiasm for the sought-after 'great' healthiness, but, unlike Zarathustra, does not succumb to the evil spell of modern awareness. Zarathustra's eyes rest upon the poets, his own self, and 'us', showing him only shallowness and self-admiration; only when he turns his gaze inwards does he see beyond past and present away into the future, where the poets stand before him 'transfigured' (II, 385).

Zarathustra's speech is characterized by a progressive extension of the reproach of lying. The stages are these: the poets lie; as a poet Zarathustra also lies; we lie. Hence art is by no means exceptional, but only a heightened form of modern human existence. Lying consists in losing oneself to isolated segments of life and raising them up as deities, values and ideals, which are then worshipped and mistaken for the whole. Instead of making use in their lives of the possibilities opened to them by the whole of history, men in the modern age have invented 'intransience' and been stupefied by it. They have set up deities knowing full well whose minds have fathered them. They will only be able to acquit themselves from the charge of lying if, like Zarathustra, they turn their gaze inwards and become 'penitents of the spirit' ['Büsser des Geistes'] (*Ibid.*), whose advent Zarathustra sees in the poets of the future. 'Penitents of the spirit' – we are told no more than this – as used by Nietzsche, is a thoroughly ambiguous figure of speech. It signifies on the one hand the penitent who, in the name of the spirit, does penance for the vanity of lying illusion, and by applying critical intellect exposes modern artists in all their ambiguity. To the Greeks it was still permitted to invent the Olympians as a counterweight to the absurdity of existence. But what in antiquity was once a sign of greatness is here unmasked as a cunning lie. The reason for this is that the thinkers of modern times have come to see that the myths of antiquity were historically determined. They have also seen through modern attempts at mythical renewal as a mere ministering to our instinct for survival. But the phrase 'penitents of the spirit' does not only signify that such penitents will be active *for* the spirit, but that they will assume its burden like a cross and do groaning penance for the fact that it is holy to them. They atone for the sins of art against knowledge, but they also do penance for the knowledge that they may *wish* to preserve the hopeful myths of art but cannot be *permitted* to do so.

In not rejecting the self-conscious awareness of the modern age, and in expressing it in the antagonistic principles of totality and perspective, the Dionysian and the Apollonian, health and sickness, art and knowledge, Nietzsche avoids betraying knowledge but frustrates the beneficial revival of myth, even if only in the shape of art. By continuing in the face of his own self-criticism to 'speak' and not 'sing' – or we could even say, not 'dance' – he meets the unavoidable demands of the modern analytical mind without relinquishing his longing for mythical totality. It was not given to him to enter the Promised Land, nor even – like Moses – to see it from afar. He can but dream of it, and even then only in concepts in which, as Anaxagoras has it, nothing is any longer 'of a piece'.

NOTES

1 The poem appears as the fourth of the 'Zeitgedichte' in Stefan George's collection *Der siebente Ring* (Berlin, 1907).

2 Cf. Ernst Bertram, *Nietzsche, Versuch einer Mythologie* (Berlin, 1918); Karl Löwith, *Nietzsches Philosophie der ewigen Wiederkunft des Gleichen* (Stuttgart, 1935); Karl Jaspers *Nietzsche, Einführung in das Verständnis seines Philosophierens* (Berlin-Leipzig, 1936); Max Horkheimer and Theodor W. Adorno, *Dialektik der Aufklärung* (New York, 1944); Martin Heidegger, *Nietzsche*, 2 vols (Pfullingen, 1961).

3 Cf. Alfred Baeumler, *Nietzsche, der Philosoph und Politiker* (Leipzig, 1931).

4 Georg Lukács, *Die Zerstörung der Vernunft* (Neuwied-Berlin, 1962).

5 P. J. Möbius, *Über das Pathologische bei Nietzsche* (Wiesbaden, 1902).

6 Erich F. Podach, *Friedrich Nietzsches Werke des Zusammenbruchs* (Heidelberg, 1961).

7 Karl Löwith, *op. cit.*, p. 14.

8 Nietzsche, *Gesammelte Werke, Musarionausgabe*, vol. IV, p. 253.

9 Nietzsche, *Musarionausgabe*, vol. IV, p. 271f.

10 Hegel, *Ästhetik*, 2 vols, ed. Friedrich Bassenge (Berlin and Weimar, 1965), vol. I, p. 35.

11 Hegel, *op. cit.*, p. 22.

12 Nietzsche's letter of 7 October 1869 to Erwin Rohde.

13 Nietzsche's letters of 19 November 1886 and 19 April 1887 to Peter Gast.

14 Nietzsche's letter of 19 November 1886 to Peter Gast.

15 Cf. Maria Bindschedler, *Nietzsche und die poetische Lüge* (Basel, 1954).

2

NIETZSCHE'S CONCEPTION OF TRUTH

Mary Warnock

My aim in this essay is to state as clearly as I can Nietzsche's theory of truth, and, in doing so, to point to some connections between Nietzsche and other philosophers, both earlier and later. I am not interested in the question of influence, of who had read what, who admired whom. The connections I want to trace are connections of meaning, similarities of thought; they are more logical than causal or historical. For Nietzsche has to some extent suffered, in England, from being thought a highly outlandish and non-serious thinker, and to point to some such connections may help us to understand his thought. Again, I want to avoid historical discussion of the development of Nietzsche's thought itself, though this may seem an even more dubious aim. For it is difficult to write about Nietzsche without becoming at least partly biographical. Nevertheless it seems to me that this way of approaching him tends to obscure the philosophical interest of his work. It is seldom that other philosophers, with the possible exception of Wittgenstein, are treated firstly as men with biographies and only secondly as philosophers. On the whole, for good or ill, their philosophical works are taken as given, as if they had descended like tablets from heaven, timelessly there to be criticized, analysed and appraised. It is in this unhistorical spirit that I want to discuss Nietzsche's theory of truth. But it must be admitted at the outset that to speak of his *theory of truth* is probably misleading. For, as will become evident, he is not consistent; and this inconsistency springs not so much from the

gradual development of a view in which the earlier stages are contradicted or overtaken by the later, but from a tension in his attitude
towards truth. And his attitudes find expression in his theory. Moreover, as we shall see, there is an ambiguity in the very subject-matter
under discussion. We shall not find a way to reconcile these tensions
and ambiguities; but it is by considering their nature that I hope to be
able to clarify Nietzsche's own thought, and incidentally to bring out
what he has in common with certain other, very different, philosophers.

I

After these preliminaries, then, let us go back briefly to the eighteenth
century, and consider Hume's views about our knowledge of the
external world. Hume regarded the consciousness as first and foremost the recipient of impressions which came into it through the
senses. He distinguished, among the contents of consciousness, between impressions and ideas, which were derived from impressions in
the way that a copy is derived from an original. Ideas are what we think
with, the materials of reflection and reason; but there can be no idea
which is not derived directly or indirectly from an impression. Now,
if one takes the word 'impression' seriously, as Hume did, it is clear
that my impressions must be different from yours (impressed, that is
to say through the agency of *my* sense-organs on *my* consciousness,
while yours are impressed on *your* consciousness and are part of *your*
experience). It is also clear that both for me and for you, on this
theory, the existence of *objects* of awareness, things we can know, cannot be separated from our being there to experience them as objects
for us. What has to be explained for Hume, as for his predecessors in
the empirical tradition, is *how* we know, and *what* we can be said to
know. The very idea of knowledge is, for them, dependent on that of
consciousness, and after consciousness comes the idea of objects of
consciousness. There are no objects without consciousness of which
they are the objects. So *things* are dependent upon someone's knowing
or experiencing them. And what we actually experience is, Hume
thinks, a series of impressions. And yet, as he was perfectly well aware,
we do not, in fact, think of the world in this way. We think of it as
external to ourselves, as common to all the different people who experience it, as permanent and independent of any observer. So how is
this fact to be accounted for? How do we come to have a conception
of a world so utterly different from the fleeting, shifting, mind-

dependent world which ought to be all that we know, if the theory is correct?

Hume's answer to this question is contained in a famous section of his *Treatise* entitled 'Of Scepticism with regard to the Senses'. 'The subject of the inquiry', he says, 'is concerning the causes which induce us to believe in the existence of body.' He argues that besides reason, which deals in the relations between ideas, and sense, which receives original impressions, we have a third faculty, imagination, and it is by means of this faculty that we construct for ourselves the stable and separate external world with which in fact we are familiar. The imagination keeps a kind of storehouse of ideas and can produce them when required. If, for example, I see a cat sitting on the hearthrug in front of the fire, what is happening is that I am receiving certain cat-impressions which cease when I turn away, leave the room or even blink. But the imagination produces ideas or images derived from this cat-impression and others like it, and with these fills up the gaps in my actual experience. And since the gaps are filled by images which are so very like the original impressions, we come to believe that there were no gaps, or rather that the gaps were unimportant, because the object, the cat, was there all the time waiting for us to look at him again. Imagination can produce ideas, or images, which are *actually like* the impressions we receive. It does not normally produce ideas to fill up gaps just at random. There is real coherence and real similarity among our impressions themselves, and thus between our impressions and their derived ideas. The cat now is like the cat five minutes ago, and if it has changed, it has done so in a manner we are accustomed to; perhaps it has stretched, or turned to warm the other side. So, relying upon this genuine regularity in appearances, the imagination makes us feel as if the cat sat there all the time. We think that the idea we have of it while we were not looking at it *is* the thing itself.

So imagination, for Hume, assumes a crucial role in the construction of our world. When we speak of permanent and independent objects we are really speaking, Hume says, of a fiction. But it is a fiction which we cannot help believing. 'An easy transition or passage of the imagination along the ideas of these different and interrupted perceptions is almost the same disposition of mind with that in which we consider one constant and uninterrupted perception. 'Tis therefore very natural for us to mistake one for the other.' We are subject to a psychological necessity, the force of a very strong habit; and he speaks elsewhere of the 'smooth transition and propensity' of the imagination in this habitual working. But he is not happy with his solution. 'I cannot conceive', he says, 'how such trivial qualities of the fancy, conducted by such false suppositions, can ever lead to any solid and rational system.' But he can think of no other. He is perhaps unnecessarily alarmed by the derogatory connotation of the word 'imagination', and still more of what he takes to be the synonymous 'fancy'. It seems to him somehow contemptible that our whole notion of the world should rest on something so volatile, frivolous and positively misleading as imagination, which, after all, is supposed to deal not in truth but in fiction. And yet we are bound to put our trust in it. Hume has in fact got into exactly such an ambiguous position as it is the purpose of this essay to explore. He has, he thinks, exposed to our view the shaky and disreputable foundations upon which our knowledge of the world rests; and at the same time he is bound to admit that we cannot do without these foundations.

> Thus, tho' we clearly perceive the dependence and interruptions of our perceptions, we stop short in our career, and never upon that account reject the notion of an independent and continu'd existence. That opinion has taken such a deep root in our imagination that 'tis impossible ever to eradicate it, nor will any strain'd metaphysical conviction of the dependence of our perceptions be sufficient for that purpose.

And in the end he advocates carelessness and inattention as alone affording any remedy for the fatal ambiguity of his conclusion.

Hume, then, has argued that in all our knowledge of the external world, we ourselves contribute a crucial part, namely the belief that there really are objects separate from ourselves and capable of being known. He also argues, in a different passage, that when it comes to scientific knowledge, to general knowledge, that is, which applies to the past and future as well as to the present, we contribute, by imagination and habit, an equally unjustifiable belief. For we simply come to expect that objects will behave in the future as they have behaved in the past. We contribute these beliefs, but in a sense we *ought not to*. Bare perception, impressions on their own without addition from the imagination, would lead us neither to general nor indeed to particular statements of fact. Even if we say something as unadventurous as that the cat has been in the chair all the afternoon, we base this on our own additions to the evidence of the senses. We cannot prove the continuous existence of the cat by appeal either to senses or to reason.

We are left with the uneasy feeling that what we assert is dependent on the nature and quality of our own imaginative powers.

Now Kant was deeply impressed by the sceptical arguments of Hume, and by the hopelessness of the position into which they led him. It was indeed largely to find a way out of Hume's apparent dead-end that his Copernican Revolution was invented. He agreed with Hume that we cannot be aware of anything except what appears to us, and that therefore all our knowledge is knowledge about what *appears*, to you, to me, to each individual. But he did not, in consequence hold that knowledge is all of it 'subjective', or confined to the individual. On the contrary, he maintained that there is, and we all know that there is, such a thing as *absolute* knowledge of what appears. We do know for certain that the truths of physics, for example, apply to what is before us in the world, and will continue to be applicable tomorrow, just as they were yesterday. There *must*, therefore, be a way out of Hume's difficulty. Kant's solution was in terms of the categories or pure concepts of the understanding, which we all, as rational human beings, apply alike to our experience, and which it can be shown that we *must* so apply. Logic can enable us to draw up a list of all the concepts of the understanding, concepts of unity, cause, substance and so on, to which our experience conforms, because we make it do so. This is his revised account of our contribution to our world-picture. We could not experience anything, nor could we understand or describe our experience unless it were subject to the laws of these categories. Kant, like Hume, has a role which he assigns to the imagination in our knowledge of the world. If it were not for this faculty, he maintains, there would be no possibility of giving any content to the pure concepts of the understanding. We would have pure logic, and we would have, therefore, laws, but we would not have laws which apply to actual experience. Imagination is the link between sensation and thought, between our having certain chaotic sensations and our organizing these into *things* which have unity or plurality, which have causal relations with other things, and which are permanent spatial and temporal objects. But with these details we are not here concerned. The essential difference between Kant and Hume is that for Kant our contribution to the world we know, though it certainly exists, is not just a matter of habit, it exists necessarily in one and only one possible form. He believes that he can prove that there could be no *other* possible categories except those which we in fact apply. They are not just the most general features which we find experience to have. We do not, that is to say, frame the categorial rules by contemplating our experience in particular and then generalizing. On the contrary, the nature of reason itself is supposed to give us the clue to what the categories are, and we know independently of experience, *a priori*, that these categorial rules must hold. So the foundation upon which our knowledge rests is no longer so whimsical and trivial a thing as the force of habit, or the power of a fancy that we may happen to possess. It is bound to be common to everyone (even though each person's experience is his own) just as reason and logic are common, and it could not be other than it is. Even the contribution of imagination by which we *apply* the categorial laws to experience is common to everyone. For Kant distinguishes between the empirical and the *a priori* functions of imagination. The latter is the same for everyone, and so we can be sure that the categorial laws will not only be conceptually the same for all alike, but that they will apply always, to everyone's experience alike.

It is this categorial necessity and universality which entitle us to claim, as we do, that there are some things (such as that every event has a cause) which are *absolutely* true and will always be true as long as experience exists. We can claim knowledge, in that we know that such laws will always apply to our experience. But, although there are such truths, nevertheless the subject-matter of them, and of all our knowledge, is the world of *appearances*. Behind the appearances are the things-in-themselves, of which we experience the appearance. And of things-in-themselves, apart from how they appear, we can know nothing whatever.

Now Nietzsche's theory of truth can be seen first and foremost as a denial of what Kant asserted on the two major issues sketched above. First, he did not believe that the categories which we apply to the world are the only possible categories. Our contribution to, indeed our construction of, our world is a fact; but we could construct it a different way. And second, he did not believe that we apply our categories to the mere appearances of things, because he did not believe that it made sense to draw a distinction between what exists and what appears. There is only one world, not two. I hope in the following pages to suggest in rather more detail how the rejection of Kant's doctrines on these two issues led Nietzsche into a sceptical *impasse* no less puzzling than Hume's. His recognition of the dilemma sounds, it is true, more heroic, perhaps more tragic than Hume's. But intellectually speaking, they were in the same tight corner.

It may perhaps be worth saying a little more about the relation between Kant and Nietzsche before going on, in the next section, to a more detailed examination of Nietzsche's views on truth. Kant himself had interpreted Hume in the following way: Hume had, he thought, demonstrated that since all our knowledge is about our own experience, there can be no real knowledge of the world as an objective, rule-governed, predictable object. Not only can we not make accurate or justifiable predictions about the future, since the future is necessarily *beyond* our experience, but we cannot even justify our belief in the existence of coherent independent objects of knowledge at all. Objective knowledge is impossible; it is a mere fiction. But, Kant said, we actually *have* such knowledge. Both in the sphere of mathematics and that of physics we know how things will be; we can, and know that we can, predict, beyond the range of experience. In order to account for this fact, as he took it to be, he invented the Copernican Revolution.

To know, Kant held, is to understand the laws which govern both the present and the future behaviour of objects. Now, an object is something observed from a particular point of view. To demand to know objects as they *are* absolutely, in themselves, rather than to know objects seen from a certain point of view, or as they appear, would be like demanding that we should see without eyes, or describe without language. An object *is* an object-as-it-appears. Knowledge of objects, then, must be *our* knowledge of objects *for us*. So the point of the Copernican Revolution is that we should realize that our knowledge does not conform to objects as they are; but rather that objects as they appear conform to our knowledge and our reason, which is all we could possibly have. 'Knowledge' and 'object' both imply the fitting of a scheme or pattern on to experience. An object must have some form, that is some definite *way* of appearing. This, on Kant's view, applies to the spatial and physical form in which we actually see things, and also to the conceptual form in which we classify them and conceive of their past and future behaviour, their objectivity, independence and causal interconnections. The mathematical regularities of things, which constitute our mathematical knowledge, derive from the ways in which we necessarily *see* them; their conceptual regularities, constituting scientific knowledge, derive from our ways of *categorizing* them.

Nietzsche denies all of this, because he denies the original notion of *objects of consciousness*. Indeed the idea of mind or consciousness, as a

separate inner entity, enclosed within the body, the mark of distinction between humans (and perhaps animals) and other beings, is,
according to Nietzsche, a myth. There is no such thing as the mind
looking out on a world, from behind the eyes. Instead, there is a whole
number of different things in the world each of which struggles to
survive, to do better than its neighbours, in its own way. People un-
dertake this struggle through their own peculiar contacts with the
rest of the world. If you are not committed to the idea of *consciousness*,
to the preconceived idea of the mind separate from its observed
objects, then you should not be committed either to a Humean view
of impressions on the consciousness, or to a Kantian distinction between objects-as-they-appear-to-the-mind and objects-as-they-really-
are. By abolishing consciousness, Nietzsche hoped to have abolished
in one stroke both Hume's predicament and Kant's solution to it. But
it is doubtful whether he can be said to have succeeded.

In order to understand Nietzsche's denial of consciousness upon
which his opposition to Kant ultimately rests, we must anticipate, to
a certain extent, some ideas which I will explore in more detail in
section II. The centre of his argument is that we can have no possible
category by which to draw a distinction between what appears to us
and what really is. For the very notion of an 'appearance', whether, in
Hume's terms, an impression on the consciousness, or in Kant's, the
form of all our experience, essentially depends on a distinction between 'inner' and 'outer'. But this is the very distinction which it is
impossible for us to make. We cannot even attempt a critique of our
own mind. There would be nothing *else* to criticize it with, no possible
standpoint from which we could view it. Nietzsche does not deny
that we use the distinction between inner and outer, between mind
and object of mind; nor does he deny that we are unthinkingly committed to using it, because it is embedded in our language. But he does
deny that we can *justify* such a distinction on any rational grounds. If
we cannot, then the question of the difference between what enters
our consciousness and what is outside it, between what appears to us
and what really is, simply disappears. There is no need to puzzle our
philosophical heads, as philosophers since the pre-Socratics always
have, with the question of the relation between the real and the
the apparent, nor with the relation between the outer and the inner.
The question simply does not make sense. And once this question has
been eliminated, then Kant's whole theory has gone with it. For the
essence of the Copernican Revolution was to identify and demon-

strate the categories, which were *a priori* and the products of the mind
and inner sense, and were that by which the appearances of things
were organized. But we cannot distinguish the appearances of things
from things, and we cannot say what is 'in the thing' and what is
contributed to its form by us. 'Is it within the range of probabilities
for an instrument to criticise its own fitness?' Nietzsche asks (*WP*
§ 410).* And the answer is that it is not. He says: 'We have no categories
which allow us to separate a "world as thing-in-itself" from a world of
appearance. All our *categories of reason* have a sensual origin; they are
deductions from the empirical world.[. . .] If there is nothing material,
then there can be nothing immaterial. The concept no longer *means*
anything' (*WP* § 488). Again, in *Twilight of the Idols* he says (II, 963): 'We
have abolished the real world: what world is left? The apparent
world perhaps? But no! *With the real world we have also abolished the apparent
world!*' There are, then, no *a priori* concepts, and so there is nothing
which we can be said to *know* in the way in which Kant thought we
knew that the laws of Newtonian physics would apply to the physical
world. What happens, then, to the notion of truth? Nietzsche says this:

> The most strongly credited *a priori* 'truths' are, to my mind, mere
> *assumptions pending further investigation*; for instance, the law of causation
> is a belief so thoroughly acquired by practice and so completely
> assimilated, that to disbelieve in it would mean the ruin of our kind.
> But is it therefore true? What an extraordinary conclusion! As if
> truth were proved by the mere fact that man survives! (*WP* § 497).

It is now time to examine the implications of this in more detail.

II

The consequence of denying that we can distinguish between what
the mind contributes to the world and what is *in* the world, independently, is the denial that we can find any such things as *brute facts*.

* I.e. paragraph 410 of *The Will to Power*, in Oscar Levy's English version (re-issued
in 1964 as a Russell reprint).
 Editor's note: In the case of this essay, passages from Nietzsche's posthumously
published late writings are located simply by reference to the paragraph numbers
of Levy's English version of the compilation entitled *Der Wille zur Macht*. This is
because chronology is not here at issue, and the numbered paragraphs make for
ease of reference. But this is a matter of convenience only: it should not be taken
as support for the false notion that this compilation, *Der Wille zur Macht/The Will to
Power*, is a work which Nietzsche himself composed.
 Unbracketed dots do not indicate omissions. They are part of Nietzsche's text
and a regular feature of his style.

We can never strip off the interpretation and describe how things would be without it. Hume thought that we could. He believed that, if it were not for the seductive and perhaps inevitable contribution of the human imagination, we know that our experience would be a series of discrete impressions, resembling one another, it is true, and coming in an observable order, but following each other like pictures on a screen. Kant, it may be said, realized that we could never know what experience would be like without our own contribution to it. It is a *condition* of experience that we do employ the categories of the under-standing. He clearly saw that we cannot begin to *describe* our experience without already employing the categories in the description, those categories of unity, substance and so on which constitute the form of all the experience that we have. But, in Nietzsche's view, this realiza-tion was vitiated by his belief that we could nevertheless *say* what categories we were using, and show that we could use no others, and by the belief that what is so categorized is the world of mere appear-ances behind which lay the ineffable world of things in themselves. It is as if Nietzsche thought that Kant was too cowardly to follow his argument wherever it led. For if we contribute *anything* to the world, then we contribute the idea of a 'thing'; and 'the psychological origin of the belief in *things* forbids us to speak of "things-in-themselves" ' (*WP* § 473).

What was this psychological origin? According to Nietzsche it was a kind of false and naïve introspection which led people first of all into the belief that there is a world of beings, *of things which appear*. There seemed to be three basic 'facts' revealed to introspection, namely: that we are causal agents; that we can find out how we come to bring things about; and that all our feelings and thoughts derive from the *ego*, the 'I thinking' revealed by the Cartesian *cogito*. 'I think', if nothing else, seemed to be an indisputable brute fact; and by 'think' Descartes meant 'will' and 'perceive' and 'feel'.

> Man projected his three 'inner facts', what he believed in most firmly of all, will, spirit, ego, outside himself – he derived the con-cept 'being' only from the concept 'ego', he posited 'things' as possessing being according to his own image, according to his con-cept of ego as cause. No wonder he later discovered in things only *what he had put into them*! The thing itself, to repeat, the concept 'thing' is merely a reflection of the belief in the ego as cause' (II, 973).

Thus the idea of things and of causal connections is something we impose on the world. But, having said that, does Nietzsche think that we ought to try to eliminate these concepts? Here we may perhaps begin to see the similarity between his dilemma and Hume's. Hume told us that the notion of a 'thing' existing independently, and endowed with causal powers, was a figment of the fancy. But he admitted that 'nature has not left it to our choice' whether to believe in things or not. We do, but we cannot *justify* it. Is Nietzsche then perhaps saying the same thing? He, more than Hume, is aware how totally dominated we are by the language that we use to describe the world. There has been no philosopher, apart from Wittgenstein, so clearly aware that philosophical problems are somehow embedded in grammar. In *The Wanderer and his Shadow*, Nietzsche wrote (I, 878f): 'Through words and concepts we are still continually seduced into thinking of things as being simpler than they are, as separated from one another, as indivisible, each existing in and for itself. There is a philosophical mythology concealed in *language*.' Again, some years later, he wrote: 'Language is built upon the most *naïve* prejudices'; but:

> *we cease from thinking if we do not wish to think under the control of language*; the most we can do is to attain to an attitude of doubt concerning the question whether the boundary here really is a boundary. *Rational thought is a process of interpreting according to a scheme which we cannot reject* (*WP* § 522).

We are caught in the net of language and grammar. The blind belief in substances, in things, independently acting and being acted upon, in qualities, in essences; all these are the products of the grammar which we use, and cannot wholly escape. The most that can be hoped from the philosopher is that he should understand that the thrall in which he is held by grammar *might* be broken, or that he might be in a different thrall. It is a contingent matter that he is bound as he is. He cannot see *what* might be different, perhaps, but he need not acquiesce in the *a priori* inevitability of thinking the way he does. 'Where our ignorance really begins, at that point from which we can see no further, we set a word; for instance the word "I", the word "do", the word "suffer" – these concepts may be the horizon lines of our knowledge, but they are not "truths" ' (*WP* § 482). It follows, of course, that such words as 'soul', 'will', 'I', are not names of *things*. There are many words, as Nietzsche well understood, which appear name-like, but which do not function as names. These particular words are established and used when a certain complex of relationships has become manifest. There is not, for example, a *will* lying behind the complex connections entailed by striving to control this or that bit of the environment; nor is there an 'I' which thinks, as a separate entity from the relations which persons have to the world in general. Nietzsche denies that one can suppose any inner *thing* apart from its expression in relationships.

> To require of strength that it should *not* express itself as strength . . . is just as absurd as to require of weakness that it should express itself as strength.[. . .] Popular morality separates strength from expressions of strength, as if there were a neutral substratum behind the strong man.[. . .] But there is no such substratum; there is no 'being' behind doing, working, becoming; the 'doer' is merely invented to accompany the doing – the doing is everything (*The Genealogy of Morals*, II, 789).

One is here irresistibly reminded of the kinds of things which Wittgenstein says in the *Philosophical Investigations* about inner entities, and inner processes. Indeed, the central passage of the *Investigations* (§ 303ff) is so strikingly like Nietzsche's thought that it must be treated as positively casting light on it. Wittgenstein writes as follows:

> 'But you will surely admit that there is a difference between pain-behaviour accompanied by pain and pain-behaviour without any pain?' Admit it? What greater difference could there be? 'And yet you again and again reach the conclusion that the inner sensation itself is a *nothing*.' Not at all. It is not a *something*, but not a *nothing* either! The conclusion was only that a nothing would serve just as well as a something about which nothing could be said. We have only rejected the *grammar* which tries to force itself on us here. The paradox disappears only if we make a radical break with the idea that language always functions in one way, to convey thoughts, which may be about houses, pains, good and evil, or anything else you please.

And again (§ 307):

> 'Are you not really a behaviourist in disguise? Aren't you at bottom really saying that everything except human behaviour is a fiction?' If I do speak of a fiction, then it is of a *grammatical* fiction. How does the philosophical problem about mental processes and states and about behaviourism arise? The first step is the one that altogether

escapes notice. We talk of processes and states and leave their nature undecided. (The decisive movement in the conjuring trick has been made, and it was the very one that we thought quite innocent.)

And then follows the famous statement about the aim in philosophy: 'To show the fly the way out of the fly-bottle'.

The theory, whether Nietzsche's or Wittgenstein's, that we are trapped by grammar, has bearing on the concept of truth. For the notion of truth is, and always has been, hard to distinguish from the notion of 'correspondence with the facts'. Nietzsche is saying that we interpret as a fact what we are trapped by grammar into so interpreting. But we can never get at the facts freed wholly from our own interpretation of them, so there is no such thing as the truth; no true statement which corresponds to the separately existing, hard facts. Philosophers have all been guilty of what he calls the 'Stoicism of the intellect', 'That *wish* to remain stationary in front of the actual, the *factum brutum*, . . . that renunciation of all interpretation whatsoever' (II, 890). But such a renunciation is impossible. All one can do is to show that interpretations might be different, that there could be another way of organizing experience and describing it. What a philosopher must at all costs try to avoid is the kind of *deference* which Kant manifestly felt to that naïve and fetishistic past which is encapsulated in language and in logic, a deference based on the belief that language, equipped with the grammar of subject and object, unity and plurality, verb and noun, active and passive, is rational, and is a *picture* of how things are. ' "Reason" in language! Oh what a deceitful old woman! I fear we are not getting rid of God because we still believe in grammar' (II, 960).

Erich Heller, in an illuminating article on Wittgenstein (*Encounter*, 1959) remarked that in the *Tractatus* Wittgenstein still suggested that language could picture a discoverable reality, and that its function was to do this, although the area of reality which could be so pictured had been narrowed and limited to almost vanishing point. All round the describable, lay acres of the ineffable, that about which one must be silent. By the time he came to write the *Investigations*, Heller suggests, like Nietzsche he had given up the idea that language *could* so picture reality, even a limited and circumscribed part of it. This account of the difference between the early and the late Wittgenstein may be unduly simple, but it is not wholly misleading. Broadly, his interest is constant; namely, it is interest in the relation between language and the world. And in the *Investigations* he was concerned to try to demonstrate the complex way in which we are trapped in our fly-bottle linguistic prison.

The similarity between him and Nietzsche is indeed striking. But what they made of this common thought that we are caught in the net of language was equally strikingly different. Both, it is true, held that the task of the philosopher is to expose the trap into which he and all other language-users have fallen. But Wittgenstein held that therefore the philosopher's work must be very largely descriptive. In the *Investigations* he says:

> We must do away with all *explanation,* and description alone must take its place. And this description gets its light, that is to say its purpose, from the philosophical problems. These are, of course, not empirical problems; they are solved rather by looking into the workings of our language, and that in such a way as to make us recognise those workings: *in despite of* an urge to misunderstand them . . . Philosophy is a battle against the bewitchment of our intelligence by means of language (§ 109).

Again, after quoting from the *Tractatus*, he says:

> One thinks that one is tracing the outline of the thing's nature over and over again, and one is merely tracing round the frame through which we look at it. A picture held us captive. And we could not get outside it, for it lay in our language and language seemed to repeat it to us inexorably (§ 114).
>
> Philosophy simply puts everything before us, and neither explains nor deduces anything. Since everything lies open to view there is nothing to explain (§ 126).

Finally, on the connection between grammar and reality, he says:

> Grammar does not tell us how language must be constructed in order to fulfil its purpose. It only describes and in no way explains the use of signs. . . . If someone says 'If our language had not this grammar, it could not express these facts' it should be asked what *'could'* means here (§ 496).

The philosopher, then, must be struck by the most ordinary and familiar assumptions which lie embedded in the way we talk about things in the world. But, having been so struck, he must simply point out what features of grammar have come to his notice, and what assumptions they will tend to carry, for according to Wittgenstein these are precisely the assumptions which breed philosophical puzzles For Nietzsche, too, there is no doubt that it is the philosopher's role to be struck by what remains unnoticed for other people. Language is something all-too-familiar to us, and therefore it takes a philosopher to be struck by it. But having raised the question whether language was an adequate expression of reality, and found that it was not, that it was rather a kind of enshrining of a primitive metaphysic of truth, Nietzsche was inclined to draw the conclusion that there could be no such thing as truth. We cannot by any possible means get at the truth, since that would mean getting at the bare uninterpreted facts, or objects with real being. But we know there are no such things despite our temptation to follow language into a belief in them. Therefore the word 'true' becomes meaningless, and we must learn to do without it.

Saying that there was no such thing as correspondence with the facts at first led Nietzsche into saying 'therefore there is no such thing as truth' and hence 'everything is false'. This was the extreme 'pessimism of the intellect' into which he naturally fell as he rejected first the possibility of metaphysics, and then the 'Kantian trick' by which reality was, as it were, let in again by the back-door. For Kant had salvaged the thing-in-itself, what there really is, by insisting that it must lie behind the appearances which we know. And on Nietzsche's view this was no better than a dodge. For Kant had both argued that we can assert truths only about appearances (since these truths are the rules which we ourselves apply and cannot conceive to be otherwise) *and* had said that behind these appearances there was a realm of reality, about which we could say nothing. But Nietzsche held that Kant could therefore safely believe whatever he wanted about this 'reality'. In particular he could go on believing in God, Freedom and Immortality; and this was a trick. So, calling all this into question, Nietzsche thought that he must assert that there is no such thing as truth. That one can see no way to deny something does not entail that its assertion 'fits the facts'. There *can* be no facts for it to fit. 'The inability to contradict anything is a proof of impotence but not of "truth" ' (*WP* § 515).

But the question must next be raised, what is one to do with this total scepticism? If it has been shown that to speak of truth is a deception, how can one go on doing it? For manifestly even Nietzsche *does* so. The question arises, he says, 'whether one *can* abide consciously

in untruth? or if one must do that, whether death be not preferable?'
Here we have, in heightened and tragic tones, the same dilemma as
afflicted Hume. For if Hume had indeed shown that we have no solid
basis for our claim to know that the external world exists, and is
predictable by science, how then, he asked, can we bear to go on be-
having as if it did exist, and as if we could rely on its behaviour? Is it
not somehow absurd to be so totally dependent on mere 'fancy'?
Hume found, as we have seen, that the only solution to this dilemma
was to stop thinking about it. Carelessness and inattention would
alone afford a remedy. He was capable of acknowledging that he
practised philosophy only part-time. When he was not a philosopher,
he could play a game of backgammon and remain unworried. But
such a solution was inconceivable for Nietzsche, who said of himself
'I have at all times thought with my whole body and my whole life'.
He was bound to try to find an intellectually and emotionally respectable solution to the problem posed by the fact that while one
needs and uses the notion of the true and the false, yet there is no
possibility of reaching a means of distinguishing the one from the
other. This impossibility is what leads him either to say 'everything is
false' or, more circumspectly, but no less damagingly, that the notion
of truth and falsity is *meaningless*. So, in this form, the question is
how can we bear to go on employing meaningless concepts. It is to
Nietzsche's solution of this problem that we must now turn our
attention.

III

For Nietzsche, the question appeared in this form: if there is no such
thing as absolute truth (or if we have no way of distinguishing true
and false) why do we value truth? His scepticism about truth is in fact
a special case of his scepticism about values in general. Why do we
continue to prefer what we call truth to falsehood; why are we un-
willing to deceive or be deceived? '*What* is it in us that really wants
"the truth"?[. . .] Granted we want the truth: *why not rather* untruth?
And uncertainty? Ignorance, even? – The problem of the value of
truth stepped forth before us' (*Beyond Good and Evil* 1; II, 567).

Since Nietzsche did have some form of answer to these questions, it
follows that in some sense he had an account of truth which was not
wholly negative. And yet he never lost the sense that, in a way, he
ought not to value truth at all.

For we have no organ whatever for *knowledge*, for 'truth': we 'know' (or believe or fancy) precisely as much as may be *useful* in the interest of the human herd, the species: and even that which is here termed 'usefulness' is only a belief, a fancy, and perhaps precisely that most fatal piece of stupidity through which we shall some day perish (*The Joyful Science* 354; II, 222).

In this last passage the broadly speaking pragmatist nature of Nietzsche's positive doctrine of truth begins to emerge into sight. But, though a kind of pragmatism was in fact acceptable to him, he did not really solve the dilemma which must face all pragmatists. If the true is the useful, then it is certainly easy to see why it is valued. But in saying that the true is the useful what are you in fact understanding by the word 'true'? What is true seems now to depend on what people *hold* to be true, because they find that it works. If something else worked better then *it* would become true. Whether something is true must, on such a view, depend on whether it is believed. But the trouble is that the word 'truth' does not in fact mean 'what is believed', and, obstinately, it refuses to mean this. It goes on, whether we like it or not, meaning 'what fits the facts'. Now Nietzsche had told us that there are no facts. So there should be no truth. Yet we persist in valuing truth, and seeking it. This is the very tension to which I referred at the beginning.

It could be said, and has indeed been said often, that Nietzsche was confused here by using the word 'true' in two different senses. He used it to mean 'fitting the facts'; and in this sense he asserted that there was no such thing as truth. But he also used it in a 'transvalued' sense, according to which the true was the useful. In this sense, he asserted that truth not only exists but is valuable and must be pursued. The same confusion arises, it is suggested, over the whole area of the transvaluation of values, of which the redefinition of 'truth' forms a part. Sometimes he seems to be saying 'There is nothing good' (old sense, meaning 'commanded' or absolutely good). Sometimes, on the other hand, he says 'I will tell you what to value instead of the old values . . . i.e. I will tell you what is *really* good'. And in this case, 'good' is being used in a *new* sense. But perhaps this way of presenting the conflict is a bit misleading; at any rate it is certain that it is not a conflict of mere terminology. It is rather that Nietzsche genuinely did not know how to answer the question whether or not there is anything good (or true). It is, it seems, the fate of all thoroughgoing sceptics.

Once again, there is an analogy with Hume. For he, too, genuinely seemed not to know whether he was telling us that we ought not to believe in the continuous and independent existence of objects, on the grounds that this was merely 'fancy', or whether, accepting that we do believe in them, he was explaining to us what causes induce us to have such a belief. Was he, in fact seeking to *undermine* our belief, to show it to be irrational and therefore fit to be abandoned, or was he simply *analysing* it? Was Nietzsche undermining or analysing our preference for the true?

There is, then, a familiar tension in Nietzsche. But in addition to this, there is, I suspect, an actual shift in his view of truth, a shift, this time, not so much of attitude as of subject-matter. For the sceptical views which we have considered so far have had reference to the possibility of saying anything absolutely true about the state of affairs which is before one. The argument against 'brute-facts' is designed to show that, even in the simplest situation, where I seem to be reporting on a matter of fact available to the senses, there is, all the same, an element of interpretation which leads me to describe the situation in one way rather than another, to see it as one thing rather than another thing; and so my interpretation could always be countered by another interpretation. Nothing is *mere* reporting.

This kind of scepticism may be regarded as largely anti-Cartesian, as intended to demonstrate the futility of the philosopher's 'search for certainty', which leads him into the realm of 'basic' or undeniable facts. Such was the mainspring not only of Cartesianism, but also of the empiricist tradition. According to Nietzsche the certainty they sought could never, in principle, be achieved, since neither introspection nor the most cautious possible recording of the 'facts' of the external world could release one from the net of interpretation, or of the grammatical necessity for framing one's description according to certain presuppositions. As Hume had seen, we contribute all too much ourselves to the simplest situation. In *Beyond Good and Evil* 16 (ii, 579) Nietzsche wrote:

> There are still harmless self-observers who believe that 'immediate certainties' exist, for example 'I think'[. . .]: as though knowledge here got hold of its object pure and naked, as 'thing in itself', and no falsification occurred either on the side of the subject or on that of the object. But I shall reiterate a hundred times that 'immediate certainty', like 'absolute knowledge' and 'thing in itself' contains a

contradictio in adjecto: we really ought to get free from the seduction of words! Let the people believe that knowledge is total knowledge, but the philosopher must say to himself: when I analyse the event expressed in the sentence 'I think' I aquire a series of rash assertions which are difficult, perhaps impossible, to prove, – for example that it is *I* which thinks, that it has to be a something at all which thinks, that thinking is an activity and operation on the part of an entity thought of as a cause, that an 'I' exists, finally that what is designated as thinking has been determined – that I *know* what thinking is (ii, 579).

But alongside this theory concerning basic truths, Nietzsche also developed a theory of *science*, the concern of which was not so much statements of how things are here and now, in detail, but general theories and scientific laws. Most of what he says of a positive kind about truth relates to this kind of theoretical statement, not to simple propositions at all. And in the end it seems that the most he could do was to lay the two parts of his theory of truth alongside one another. He could never really bring them together, nor could he make one part follow from the other. In this sense, just as he had two different attitudes towards truth, so he also had two different subjects to discuss, about one of which his views were wholly sceptical, about the other, to some extent at least, constructive. Nor need this greatly surprise us. For Nietzsche was not a systematic philosopher (and *systems* of philosophy were the subject of some of his most violent attacks). His remarks about truth were scattered, and even random. We should not therefore lament a lack of coherence among them. It is enough to try to understand what he said.

So it seems to me that Nietzsche was able to give an answer to the question why we value truth, the question which he said 'stepped forth' before us, in terms of a concept of truth as the goal of scientific method, that is, as *theory*. And in doing so, he tended to lose sight of the nature of truth as it may occur in particular statements of fact – that today is Wednesday, or that the carpet is green. What we are seeking on this 'scientific' view of truth, is a complex of hypotheses, by the adopting of which as true and therefore as the basis for prediction, we can master, control and change the world to fit it for our own survival. This is, broadly speaking, the pragmatist aspect of Nietzsche's theory, and it is worth remarking how close he comes to the pragmatists, and especially to Peirce, in his willingness to concentrate, at least sometimes, on the notion of truth as the *goal of science*. A. J. Ayer, writing about Peirce, says that if we are thinking of the truth of simple propositions concerned with the present, it is obviously absurd to suggest that their truth consists in their being accepted by a consensus of future scientists or anything of the kind, since many propositions which we wish now to assert as true will cease to be candidates for truth or falsity in the future. They will, as it were, have lapsed altogether (for example no science, however complete, could chronicle and assess such propositions as 'this pudding is hot') and Ayer says that Peirce does not offer any reply to this kind of objection, because he does not think it worth taking seriously.

> He was not interested in obtaining an adequate formal definition of truth. He thought that such a concept would be idle, that it would do no work for us. . . . We must remember here . . . that the position which Peirce takes is that of a man engaged in a process of enquiry. It is of no help to such a man to be told with classical propriety that a proposition is true if it states what is so. He wants to know what is so, or rather he wants to know how best to find out what is so; which means, in concrete terms, how to select his hypotheses and how to test them. It is not surprising, therefore, that Peirce's theory of truth should devolve into a theory of scientific method (*The Origins of Pragmatism*, pp. 39f).

These words could with equal propriety be applied to Nietzsche, as far as concerns one important aspect of his writings. Thus we have two phenomena to consider: on the one hand there is, in Nietzsche, a vacillating attitude to the possibility of truth, to the very meaningfulness of the concept; and on the other hand there is a switch in interest between two different *kinds* of question, of which now one and now the other occupied his attention.

Let us now look in a bit more detail at his discussion of truth as the goal of science. Nietzsche believed that the only possible general explanation of the nature of things was to be found in the notion of the will to power. He demanded an explanation of *everything*, which would not markedly separate human behaviour from other phenomena. For he believed, as we have seen, that everything is, as it were, made of the same stuff. Long before he had come upon the idea of the will to power, he wrote: 'When we speak of *humanity* our basic idea is that this is what *separates* and distinguishes man from nature. In reality, however, there is no such separation: "natural" properties and those specifically called "human" are inseparably entwined' (III, 291). The general consequence of Darwinism, that one must think of man as a part of his whole environment, not as a god-like and alien visitant in a foreign world, was totally absorbed into Nietzsche's thought. 'Consciousness' is a myth, ultimately derived from grammar. It is not a *thing* which marks off human relations to the world from all others; nor can it be taken to justify a distinction between appearance and reality. 'The universe exists.' That is about all one can say.

Now in the universe as a whole, if you seek to understand changes, actions, reactions, or any kind of activity or behaviour, the hypothesis of the will to power is the most explanatory, because the widest in scope. Nietzsche believed that he had discovered the will to power empirically, not through any exercise of reason *a priori*. If he could not claim it as an empirical concept, then of course he would be open to a charge of inconsistency; for he would both be denying the possibility of *a priori* truths to explain the world, and at the same time asserting such a truth. But he insisted that 'experience' had taught him of the will to power. He could therefore assert it itself as a hypothesis, though a hypothesis so far unchallenged. Nietzsche assumes that the processes of evolution themselves, the survival of one kind of vegetation or of animal in a particular area at the expense of other vegetation or animals can be explained in terms of the will to power, once the notion of 'will' has been divorced from its mythological association with consciousness, felt striving, internal cause or freedom. One cannot, that is to say, separate the notion of causality from that of will. But far from this leading to the positing of a *special kind* of causation which operates only among conscious beings, it should lead in the other direction, to the positing of a will wherever, in our search for scientific knowledge, we come upon causal sequences. 'We *must*', he writes, 'make the attempt to posit hypothetically the causality of the will as the only form of causality' (II, 601). This is a sort of anthropomorphism in reverse.

Once this most general hypothesis is accepted, then, in so far as his interest turns to epistemology, to questions of knowledge or truth, the question for Nietzsche can be put in this form: How is the will to truth related to the will to power? For since, as we have seen, the whole notion of truth is necessarily to some extent a deception, the need arises for a critique of the will to truth. In *The Genealogy of Morals* Nietzsche wrote:

Turn to the most ancient and the most modern philosophers: they all fail to recognise to what extent the Will to Truth itself requires a justification. Here is a gap in every philosophy – what is it caused by? Because up to the present the ascetic ideal *dominated* all philosophy, because Truth was fixed as Being, as God, as the supreme court of appeal. Because truth was not *allowed* to be a problem.[. . .] From the minute that the God of the ascetic ideal is repudiated, *there exists a new problem*, the problem of the *value* of truth. – The Will to Truth needs a critique [. . .] the value of truth is tentatively to be *called in question* (II, 891).

The ascetic ideal depended on a belief in the possibility of attaining absolute truth (perhaps guaranteed, as in Descartes' system, by God). Once this has gone, then the question of truth can be raised. And the *justification* for the pursuit of truth rather than falsehood or deception turns out to be achieved by subsuming the will to truth under the will to power, as a part of it.

The so-called *thirst for knowledge* may be traced to the *lust of appropriation* and of *conquest*: in obedience to this lust the senses, memory, and the instincts, etc., were developed. The quickest possible reduction of the phenomena, economy, the accumulation of spoil from the world of knowledge . . . (*WP* § 423).

We must, then, consider truth only in the context of the scientific advance of man, attempting all the time, as he becomes more and more highly evolved, to master and control more and more of the universe. 'Pure' science, the pursuit of truth for its own sake, is not possible, if 'truth' actually *means* that which leads to practical mastery over the environment. We must stop thinking of truth as something to which we can lay claim when we, as perceptive subjects, come across statements which fit the facts, that which we look out upon and perceive. Nietzsche writes,

It is not a question of 'subject and object', but of a particular species of animal which can prosper only by means of a certain *exactness*, or better still *regularity* in recording its perceptions (in order that experience may be capitalised). . . . Knowledge works as an *instrument* of power[. . .]. In order that a particular species may maintain and increase its power, its conception of reality must contain enough that is calculable and constant to allow of its formulating a scheme of conduct[. . .]. A species gets a grasp of a given amount of reality, *in order to master it, in order to enlist that amount in its service* (*WP* § 480).

It is perhaps in this placing of truth in the context, or under the banner, of power that Nietzsche is most prone to swing between the old 'fitting the facts' sense of the word 'true' and his new, pragmatic sense. (But any pragmatist, or indeed any defender of a coherence theory of truth, must find the same difficulty.) He argues that *what* it is that we find effective may change from time to time. 'To the extent to which knowledge has any sense at all, the world is knowable: but it may be interpreted *differently*, it has not one sense behind it, but hundreds of senses' (*WP* § 481). Therefore it follows that 'truth' may change. This is a sense of 'true', however, which it is very difficult to adopt. Our language rebels against it because of the 'old' (some may say the 'real') meaning of 'true', according to which 'true' means 'as the facts are' and according to which, also, there is an implied contrast between a statement of fact and a hypothesis. So Nietzsche can also write,

> Truth is [. . .] more fatal than error or ignorance, because it paralyses the forces which lead to enlightenment and knowledge [. . .] It is more gratifying to think 'I possess the truth', than to see only darkness in all directions . . . (*WP* § 452).

> *How* is truth *proved*? By means of the feeling of increased power, – by means of utility, – by means of indispensability, – *in short, by means of its advantages* (that is to say, hypotheses concerning what truth should be like in order that it may be embraced by us). But this involves *prejudice*: it is a sign that *truth* does not enter the question at all . . . [. . .] What was needed was always belief – and *not* truth . . . Belief is created by means which are quite *opposed* to the method of investigation: *it even depends upon the exclusion of the latter* (*WP* § 455).

Now, in these passages alone all the ambiguities to which I referred are manifest. Interpreted in one way, Nietzsche is saying that those who have sought for truth have always, in fact, sought for some dogma in which they could rest, and save themselves the painful exertion of investigating any further. But what would they, if they were honest, have been investigating *for*? Surely only in order to discover the truth in a different sense, namely in the sense of that which seems, for the time being, to increase their power. This is the real meaning of truth, but one must of course, in this sense, never claim to have reached it. At best it is an unattainable ideal. Nothing that we *actually* grasp can be more than a hypothesis. If 'true', however, *means* 'the best hypothesis we have' then of course we cannot say 'nothing is true'; we must say 'such and such is true for the time being'. But at this point we come, once again, up against the deep recalcitrance of language. We come up against the impossibility of sincerely saying 'I know but I may be wrong' or 'It is right, but perhaps it won't be tomorrow'. Similarly, if one is referring to general laws or regularity statements, one must *either* say they are hypotheses, or assert them as true. But if one does the latter, one cannot also say in the same breath that they may be shown to be false. We cannot make the claim involved in the use of the word 'true' or 'know' with one hand, and withdraw it with the other.

So, once again, we seem to have come to a point where what Nietzsche is offering is not so much a theory of truth as a theory of science. He is answering the question how do we discover more about the world, and why do we want to. But even within this theory, in which there is no place for any discussion of the truth of simple single propositions, but only of explanatory hypotheses, he is sometimes sceptical, sometimes not; he sometimes thinks that we can, sometimes that we cannot achieve the truth. But at least, consistently, he recognizes that there is a motivating will to truth. This is the motive of science, but as it is a manifestation of the will to power, it is in fact a universal motive for the whole of the human species; it is that form of the will to power which characterizes the human species. So science is defined as 'The transformation of Nature into concepts for the purpose of governing Nature' (*WP* § 610). But of course Nietzsche insists that we recognize the status of these concepts: 'Parmenides said: "One can form no concept of the non-existent"; – we are at the other extreme, and say, "That of which a concept can be formed, is certainly fictional" '(*WP* § 539). The process of science thus becomes an endless pushing forward of boundaries, by the only possible means, namely the questioning of established hypotheses, and the critique of presuppositions.

The will to truth is a process of *establishing things*; it is a process of *making* things true and lasting, a total elimination of that *false* character [i.e. which the world has], a transvaluation of it into *being*. Thus, 'truth' is not something which is present and which has to be found and discovered; it is something *which has to be created* and which *gives* its name *to a process*, or, better still, to the Will to overpower, which in itself has no purpose: to introduce truth is a *processus in infinitum*, an *active determining* – it is not a process of becoming conscious of something, which in itself is fixed and determined. It is merely a word for 'The Will to Power' (*WP* § 552).

Nietzsche recognizes that some scientific 'fictions' have become so useful that they are positively necessary to life. For instance, the law of causation has become so totally built into human thought that 'to disbelieve in it would mean the ruin of our kind' (*WP* § 497). In another note (*WP* § 550) he says that he agrees with Hume that belief in causality is nothing but habit, though it is not the habit of the individual so much as of humanity as a whole. But despite the strength of such a habit, because the will to truth is the will to power, which has no external goal or purpose, the process of questioning and undermining hypotheses will in fact continue whatever its consequences, and it is the philosopher's task to encourage and to justify the questioning. For the philosopher it is who says that a belief may be a necessary condition of life and *yet* be false (*WP* § 483). Darwin had held that any species is dominated by, indeed in some sense formed by, its environment. Nietzsche thought that this was a great exaggeration of the influence of the environment and of external circumstances upon the species. The essential factor in the development of the species is the power which it has to create an environment which it can manage and exploit. But the will to power is not *for the sake of* the development of the species. It *is* the life itself of that, and every other, species. It follows that the most valuable, though not necessarily the least destructive, members of a species are those individuals who can, as it were, pit their own strength against the environment; and, translated into human terms, this means those who can question things held to be totally unquestionable by their fellows, even if this questioning leads to ruin. As Kaufmann puts it: 'When Nietzsche describes the will to truth as "a principle which is hostile to life and destructive" he is entirely consistent with his emphatic and fundamental assertion that man wants power more than life' (II, 602). So it must be wrong to think of truth as defined in terms of its usefulness to life, because if truth (that is power) and life conflict, then it will be the desire for truth which wins; but this is not incompatible with the acceptance *as* true of whatever is conducive to life and the convenience of life. The fact is that a genuinely great and free spirit will not accept such 'truths' for long. In *Beyond Good and Evil*, Nietzsche wrote:

'The strength of a spirit might be measured according to how much of the "truth" it would be able to stand, more clearly, to what degree it *needed* to have it watered down, shrouded, sweetened, blunted and falsified' (II, 602).

The true scientist and philosopher, then, is perpetually creating new truths which are explanations of the real world. But of course the ambiguity in Nietzsche's view still remains. For on the one hand his notion of a search for truth may seem necessarily empty, content-less. The only characteristic of the truth-searcher is that he should *not* be content with what he has got, and that he should realize the *inventiveness* of his own role. The idea that he should *reach* the truth is absurd, since the search, as we have seen, is a process *in infinitum*. On the other hand, since error and falsehood are condemned, truth is *ipso facto* to be admired. The ideal is before us. What we can never reach is the complete or total explanation; but truth is this total explanation. It is what gets it right, what says how the world is. So the old sense of 'fitting the facts' has by no means been expunged. We must settle perhaps for saying that seeking the truth by seeking to falsify less than complete explanations is seeking for what we can never get. At least we can never know whether we have got it or not. It seems to me that, with regard to this part of his theory, though Nietzsche was less of a scientist and far less of a logician than Karl Popper, nevertheless the resemblance between his views and Popper's is so striking that a quotation from Popper's essay 'The Aim of Science', may throw light on Nietzsche's position. Popper writes as follows:

> If it is the aim of science to explain, then it will also be its aim to explain what so far has been accepted as an *explicans*; for example, a law of nature. Thus the task of science constantly renews itself. We may go on for ever proceeding to explanations of a higher and higher level of universality . . . unless indeed we were to arrive at an ultimate explanation.

He then raises the question whether we must suppose that there *are* ultimate explanations. And, just like Nietzsche, he connects the view that there are with the Cartesian kind of belief in essences, perhaps connected with a belief that God made the essences as they are. If we can discover what they are, according to Cartesianism, we can go no further. But, on the other hand, Popper does not wish to accept what most critics of Cartesianism have offered instead, namely instru-mentalism. Such critics have interpreted scientific theories as *nothing but* instruments for prediction, devices, that is, which will enable us to manage the world. Like Nietzsche, Popper cannot accept the thought that a theory is invented *with this end in view*. His preferred view, the 'third view' is this:

> Although I do not think that we can ever describe, by our universal laws, an *ultimate* essence of the world, I do not doubt that we may seek to probe deeper and deeper into . . . the properties of the world, that are more and more essential or of greater depth. I believe that this word 'deeper' defies any attempt at exhaustive logical analysis, but that it is nevertheless a guide to our intuitions.

This might well be taken as a statement of Nietzsche's belief; it might express the extent, in his words, to which he 'remains pious'. The consequence seems to be that, just as some philosophers have suggested that we must always analyse the word 'good' in terms of 'better', so we must analyse the word 'true' in terms of 'more true', 'less false' or 'possessing more depth of insight'.

Nietzsche would hold that the real scientist, the man who could achieve this greater depth of insight, and for whom the will to truth was more important than life itself, was necessarily a man superior to the general run of men. It is perhaps worth noticing that here the two parts of Nietzsche's theory of truth may be seen to come together. For not only will truth, in the sense of scientific explanation, be the goal of the superior, the superman, but also, in the sense in which truth is the property of single, simple propositions which 'fit the facts', rather than theories, it is only the superman who will be critical of the grammar in which such propositions are expressed, and will see through the mythology of the bare simple subject/object facts. He will be able to see for what it is the stranglehold that the metaphysics embedded in language has upon us. Obviously one cannot predict what substitute for such metaphysics he will make. One cannot both say that one is enmeshed in a particular grammar and at the same time and in the same language say how it would be if one were freed. Otherwise one would not be wholly enmeshed. But it is not inconceivable that *some one* might be able to take such a step. So, in both parts of the theory, Nietzsche is envisaging a wholly creative kind of being, quite free from the kinds of presuppositions that we can guard against and uncover piecemeal, but from which we cannot entirely free ourselves. Such a being could as he put it 'live without truth', that is without the comforting security of belief in the rightness of his theories, or the bareness of the facts which are reflected in his simple propositions. But in another sense he will be the only possible master of the truth. Wittgenstein once said that he felt as though he were writing for people who would think in a quite different way and breathe a different air from present-day men. So Nietzsche's theory of truth, whichever aspect of it we consider, strongly suggests a quite different mode of thought, unattainable by us, both about language and about explanations of the world.

IV

It is time now to attempt some kind of brief summary. We can best see the force of Nietzsche's theory of truth by regarding it first and foremost as an example of a thoroughly sceptical theory. Hume's scepticism about the existence of the external world (and to a lesser extent his scepticism about the possibility of general scientific statements with regard to the future – his notorious 'problem of induction') led him to adopt a position of ambiguity which, as I argued, throws some light on Nietzsche's own ambiguities. Hume was reduced to the position where he saw that we contribute, through our own imagination, to the picture which we have of the world, and that this picture is one which we use and rely upon for the ordinary conduct of life. But since there is this 'fanciful' contribution of our own, we can never claim that our picture is correct, however useful or familiar it may be. The imagination is subject to no checks either of reason or experience, and therefore in the end must be regarded as a trivial and misleading faculty. Although Hume attempted to offer an analysis of what our knowledge of the world amounts to, again and again he was led away from dispassionate analysis into an expression of the feeling that we ought not to have to rely upon so volatile and flighty a faculty as the 'fancy', and therefore that in some sense we ought not to profess the view of the world as solid and orderly which we do in fact profess. And he could see no way out of this difficulty except as often as possible to forget about it.

Kant, starting from the hopelessness of Hume's position, argued that we do indeed, by understanding and imagination, contribute to the scientific view of the world; but this must necessarily be a view of the world *as it appears*. The world itself which appears cannot be discussed because, necessarily, it is beyond the view of an observer, who must see things from some point of view or other. What this point of

view is is described in terms of the categories he employs in his perception and his scientific statements. If there is an observer at all, then
the object of his observation must be the appearance *to him* of the world.
But about this appearance we need not be sceptical, because we can
state exactly what are the contributions which we bring to it. There are
therefore absolute truths which are known *a priori* and which apply
to the world as we see it.

Nietzsche, as we saw, rejected Kant's belief in appearances, rather
than things, as the object of our knowledge. He rejected it on the very
radical ground that it was nonsensical. No such distinction between
'thing' and 'appearance of thing' can be made. For the dichotomy
which justifies such a distinction, namely the dichotomy 'consciousness' and 'material world', is itself a myth. His belief that the subject-
matter of science is the world itself and not any mere appearance is
part of his general monolithic view of the world – there is no 'inner'
as opposed to 'outer', no 'mind' as opposed to 'body'. And in rejecting
this part of Kant's beliefs he also rejected the Kantian argument that
we can discover for certain *what* categories it is necessary for the understanding to apply to the appearances of the world. There can be no
deduction of the categories which, once discovered, lay down for ever
the form in which we will acquire all future knowledge. He has
therefore put himself back into the unstructured world of Hume: what
we claim to know is partly created by ourselves and we cannot
lay down any rules for creation, nor justify the validity of the construct we have made. All we can say is that we employ *some* categories,
make *some* assumptions. But we might see things differently, and perhaps some day we may. What we know for certain is that every 'fact'
is partly constructed into such by ourselves. So, if truth is the property
of a statement exactly to fit the undoctored, unconstructed brute
facts, there can be no such thing as truth, for there are no such facts.

But alongside this wholly negative theory there is, in Nietzsche,
another theory concerned with the progress of scientific knowledge
in general rather than with the concept of truth as a property of
particular statements. And in this theory, Nietzsche comes very close
to saying that for the scientist, the true description of the world is
that hypothesis which is most useful and which covers the most
ground in its explanation. However, even in that part of the theory
which, like the pragmatism of Peirce, is concerned with the general
not the particular, Nietzsche vacillates between the view that the enlightened scientist will learn to give up the notion of truth altogether

when he realizes that what have been accepted as truths will in their turn be falsified, and saying, on the other hand, that truth is the ideal towards which the scientist works, albeit without hope of total success. So I have argued both that Nietzsche is concerned with truth in two different aspects, which are never very clearly brought together (though the treatment of each aspect has some features in common with the other), and that within the second of these, he does not always treat 'the will to truth' wholly consistently.

Perhaps, finally, it is necessary to add one further complication. Although we have seen that, for Nietzsche, the search for truth was never to be the search for *certainty*, only the search for freedom from a particular kind of entanglement, whether linguistic or more generally conceptual, yet there is, paradoxically, a quite different element in Nietzsche's thought. For he himself simply *asserted* what he took to be a truth about the nature of things, namely that there will be recurrence, that what is happening now will happen again in all its details. And of this, it seems, he was simply *certain*. How could he consistently claim to know that this was true? or was it itself merely an hypothesis which would one day be shown to be false? The consideration of this question throws some light, I think, on the necessarily paradoxical nature of any sceptical theory of truth. For in order to assert something, as I have said, one must assert it as true; and this means not 'true for the time being' or 'true for me' but simply 'true'. Now there may be some things which one *must* assert, because one sees them immediately to be true, or because one feels them inescapably in one's bones. About such things, one must either keep silent or assert them as positively true, no matter what *theory* of truth one may hold. I would maintain of the doctrine of recurrence, that Nietzsche felt it as a passion, and therefore asserted it: that he could not, and did not wish to, apply his own critical apparatus to this assertion. At one level, of course, if one says 'everything will recur' and is careful to add 'but not yet, and at no predictable time', this is a statement which could never be falsified; and therefore it could be said everlastingly to remain as an hypothesis. The only drawback is that it might also seem to lose any possible interest it might have had. It might be true, it might not, but it makes no possible difference.

However, I would maintain that it was not at this level that Nietzsche asserts the proposition of recurrence. It was rather the expression of a way of perceiving life, the expression of a belief that things carry with them a certain kind of eternity. A particular moment

cannot be dead and finished when it is over. Its whole significance while
it is experienced is *that it will recur*, or, in other words, that it is eternal,
as it were stored up to be had again. It would take us too far from the
present theme to speculate about the nature of this kind of perception, the grasping of a *meaning* in experience beyond its mere superficial
characteristics. But it seems plausible to mark it off, roughly, as imaginative rather than 'merely' cognitive, and to see connections between
it and the ordinary interpreting of the world of perception which
Nietzsche, like Hume and Kant, was sure that we were bound to indulge in every time we perceive anything at all, and which Hume and
Kant ascribed in part to imagination. But this kind of imagination
could be called creative. For Nietzsche, the belief in recurrence meant
acceptance of the world; a willingness that just as it is, it should *be*
everlastingly. And it is not perhaps fanciful to connect this acceptance
itself with the will to power. In *The Joyful Science*, it is the man of power
who is the man fully to accept the whole of his own nature, and that
of the universe. And in *Ecce Homo* Nietzsche writes: 'My formula for
the greatness of a human being is *amor fati*: that one wishes to have
nothing otherwise [. . .] Not merely to bear what is necessary, still less
to conceal it [. . .] but to *love* it' (II, 1098).

Such assertions, it seems to me, cannot be used as an argument
against Nietzsche's theory of truth; nor should the theory be used in
turn to undermine the assertions. All words are interpretations; all
categories of descriptions and laws of prediction are contributed by us
to our world, and may be examined, criticized and changed. But in the
case of recurrence, here is an interpretation which wells up from a
way of understanding the world which is essentially creative, emotion-
laden and imaginative. It expresses not what we *have to think,* but what
we *ought to feel.* So Nietzsche seems to imply. It is a statement exempt
from the criticism of the intellect, only because such criticism could
not be made to latch onto it at any point. There is yet one more inconsistency here; there is a tension between thought and feeling,
reason and sentiment. It is arguable that without some such tension
the irritant which gives rise to works of genius would be lacking. But
however that may be, in the case of Nietzsche it seems clear that one
should merely observe the inconsistency, and not try to interpret it
out of existence.

3

NIETZSCHE AND THE IDEA OF METAPHOR

J. P. Stern

... were it not that I have bad dreams.
(*Hamlet* II, 2)

How are we to read Nietzsche? How are we to understand the characteristic style of his philosophizing and the mode of language in which it is cast? Two important circumstances of his biography offer a possible start. The first is the fact that his creative life is confined to the astonishingly short period of about sixteen years, from 1872 (when, at the age of twenty-eight, he published *The Birth of Tragedy from the Spirit of Music*) to January 1889, when he wrote the last pathetic letters and postcards to his friends, and was taken from his Turin lodgings by the ever-faithful Franz Overbeck, to spend the remaining twelve years of his life, mindless, confined, in the hideous care of his sister. He tended to see his writings, now as a single venture in the apparently absolute freedom of uncommitted philosophical speculation, now again as purposeful critical thinking about the state of Western mankind in an age of decadence, as reflection consistently committed to a number of concrete moral and existential concerns (though these are not the terms he himself would have used). And this is the two-fold way we must approach his work. We can see that his philosophizing begins by taking issue with, and remains grounded in, the contemporary cultural situation of the Second German Reich founded in 1871, and that his care for the contemporary world and his critique of it are not so very different from the concern and critique of writers like Karl Marx, Thomas Carlyle and Matthew Arnold[1] (and again these are comparisons he would have scorned); but we can also see that he tried to rid himself of the burden of criticism and strove for a greater freedom.

The second circumstance that needs recalling is simply his immense, all-consuming passion for *writing*, and the fact that we cannot imagine what his 'thought' would look like without its very particular, highly purposeful wordings (as we can imagine the thought of Descartes, or Kant). From the days of his solitary boyhood onwards, even when, writing to his sister or mother or aunt, he has no more to communicate than his observations on the progress of the seasons or the content of a school lesson, this love of writing dominates his hours and days. And from his adolescent years at Schulpforta to the end of his conscious life, writing remains inextricably connected with that endless series of migraines, stomach cramps and colics and states of near-blindness from which no single week was wholly free[2] – a grace and a deliverance nevertheless. Writing had for him strong compensatory erotic overtones (which it is the foolish prejudice of French structuralists to identify with sexuality), but so has all creativeness. What distinguishes his books, apart from their intellectual energy, is his passion for shapeliness, balance and clarity *over brief stretches of prose*. Nietzsche loathed the idea of democracy in all its forms, yet his utmost concern with intelligibility is present in almost every sentence he wrote: to find him accused of 'obscurantist' and 'elitist' tendencies by Marxist detractors whose own prose is rendered inaccessible by wilful mannerisms and obscurities to all but the smallest circle of initiates, is one of the many ironies that make up the posthumous fate of his writings.

Value-judgments adhere to Nietzsche's every thought. It is the characteristic style of his philosophizing to infuse every one of his insights – whether they be philosophical or psychological, moral or historical or even physiological – with his personal value-judgments, to pose questions as searching as he can make them, to offer no more than provisional, hypothetical or perspectivist answers, to impose further questions on these, and to pour suspicion on all static resolutions. Because so much of the man is in the thinking, the destructive treatment to which he often subjects his own earlier arguments is self-destructive, too. But then, he was hardly ever intent on his own or his readers' peace of mind, nor did he succeed in creating a 'system of opinions', let alone an ideology, although in that fragmentary collection of notes and excerpts to which at the end of his conscious life he gave several titles, among them 'The Will to Power', he planned

to do just that. It is characteristic of him, as it is of few other philosophers, that he distrusted 'the will to system'[3] as a sign of defective intellectual integrity, and yet his work is rich in continuities and abiding
concerns. The three I shall single out here seem at first sight to have
little in common, but I hope to show that they are in fact closely
related:

1 How seriously are we to take the life of men in the world?
2 What is the function of the aesthetic in life?
3 How is the modern fragmentation of knowledge – the division of
   areas of knowledge which to Nietzsche are always areas of experience – to be overcome?

From the ever-renewed attempts at exploring these questions Nietzsche brings back a number of insights which are more penetrating
and which throw a more brilliant light on various aspects of our
experience than more systematic and 'scientific' thinkers have done.
His work is open, in every sense unconcluded. The points at which he
stopped writing, and we stop thinking out what he wrote, are apt to
be arbitrary: the game of philosophical leapfrog on which he was
engaged is endless, 'eternal'.

In 1873 (a year after *The Birth of Tragedy*) Nietzsche dictated to his old
schoolfriend, Carl von Gersdorff, an essay entitled 'On Truth and
Falsehood in an Extra-Moral Sense' (III, 309–22). Although this is only
a short essay of fifteen pages, which Nietzsche hardly corrected and
which was not published until 1903, it is probably the longest single
piece on a traditional 'philosophical' subject he ever wrote. Its subject
is the metaphysics of language. I shall examine it here in some detail,
partly for its own sake and partly also as a sort of seed-box of later
arguments, relating my consideration of it to a number of much later
reflections and *aperçus* in order to show – or at least to offer some evidence for suggesting – that this early essay not only charts the area of
a life-long concern, but also helps us by its own example to understand that manner and style which we recognize as Nietzsche's own
mode of philosophizing.

The purpose of this early essay is to elucidate a linguistic variant of
Kantian criticism. (This is not to say that Nietzsche's re-interpretation
in terms of language owes anything to Kant, whose linguistic views
had been entirely naïve and uncritical.) Kant had maintained that we
are incapable of unmediated knowledge of whatever is outside ourselves – of 'things-in-themselves' – since we know these things only

under the forms of our perception; and Kant's position had traditionally been exaggerated, indeed falsified, to the point where it
amounted to a denial of the possibility of any reliable knowledge and
to the assertion of a radical subjectivism. Similarly, Nietzsche claims
that language, far from giving us a true account of things as they are
in the world, and far from having its grounds in 'true reality', is in
fact no more than a referentially unreliable set of almost entirely
arbitrary signs, made up by us for various very concrete and practical
ends, mainly to do with the safeguarding of life and the preservation
of the species. And whereas we like to think that the value of language
is commensurate with the amount of truth about the world it secures
for us, its real value to us is merely a pragmatic one, to do with whether
or not it works. The function of language is related to what Nietzsche
in the second of the *Untimely Meditations* calls 'the hygiene of life' (I,
282): its principal function is to hide the hostile nature of the universe
from men in order to preserve them from destruction – at least for a
little while. *The lie*, therefore – the lie about what the universe is
really like – is not a contingent aspect of language, but its very essence.
The lie of language in an *'extra-moral sense'* (as the title of the essay puts
it) consists in the vital pretence that language is able to relate the
world of men to some wider, benevolent cosmic scheme by offering
them reliable knowledge of that scheme (whereas the universe can
get on perfectly well without the world of men and is merely waiting
for an opportunity to continue on its desolate journey through man-
less aeons). The *'moral'* sense of lying, on the other hand, is confined to
violating the linguistic, lexical or semantic conventions men have set
up in order to get on with each other as best they may. There is no
knowledge of a world beyond our world – all statements pretending
to such knowledge are false, whereas all statements claiming to be
true accounts of our world are mere tautology: 'If someone hides a
thing behind a bush, looks for it there and indeed finds it, then such
searching and finding is nothing very praiseworthy: but that precisely
is what the searching and finding of "truth" within the realm of reason
amounts to' (III, 316). (One may, incidentally, wonder how men, said
to be incapable of knowing anything about the universe in which
their world is travelling, nevertheless 'know' that it is malevolent,
destructive and desolate. The answer to that question is contained in
Nietzsche's first book, *The Birth of Tragedy*, where a pre-rational, instinctive intuition of primal suffering and fear is postulated as the
grounding[4] of humanity.

How then (Nietzsche asks), if we are incapable of positive contact with the real world, can we sustain life? How is it that the world works? The world works on an illusion, an *as if* principle. We act in the world as if we were in touch with a benevolent reality, as if we were capable of comprehending its cosmic purpose, as if there were a divinity whose decrees we fulfil and who gives meaning to our individual lives – as if God were alive.

(This 'as if' mode enters Nietzsche's style, or rather the many styles he acknowledged as his own, at the most intimate and instinctive level of his writing, sometimes to its detriment. For while it is true that all he wrote is distinguished by a splendid liveliness and adaptability to the purpose in hand, a curious mannerism escapes his conscious control. It is his very frequent and often redundant use of the particle *'als'*, meaning 'as', 'in the role or function of . . .'. There is no need to resort to the tedium of 'stylo-statistical' word counts in order to note whole paragraphs, especially in the early writings, where his use of this particle is impossible to justify on grammatical or stylistic grounds. This linguistic tic is not meaningless. What it signifies, to excess, is an instinctive, monotonous re-enacting of a fundamental movement of Nietzsche's thought: a movement in which a never-ending interchange in the function of words – metaphorical intimations of divers spheres of experience – is allowed to become the dominant feature of his language – the metaphorically inexact intimation of our being in the world.)

While we establish and try to stabilize this *as if* relationship through language, the functions of language nevertheless remain *ad hoc* and its uses largely arbitrary. Between words and things there is neither a direct relationship (things are in no sense the causes of words), and yet the two are not completely unrelated, for words are said to be the distant and distorted echoes of sense-perceptions. These rudimentary elements are poeticized and given coherence according to rules which are entirely 'created' or invented by man. Thus the relationship that obtains between words and 'the real world' is a metaphorical or aesthetic one. Man as the idealist philosophers saw him – that is, man as the unstable and arbitrary perceiving subject of an objective world – is re-interpreted in Nietzsche's scheme as man the creator of language. The relationship which obtains between subject and object – between human language and the real things in the world from which language is excluded – is not a causal relationship, for between two such heterogeneous things as subject and object no direct relationship can

exist ['denn zwischen zwei absolut verschiedenen Sphären, wie
zwischen Subjekt und Objekt gibt es keine Kausalität, keine Richtig-
keit, keinen Ausdruck . . .']. It is not mimetic or expressive, but what
Nietzsche calls an 'aesthetic attitude':

> I mean an intimatory transference, a sort of halting, stammering
> translation into an entirely foreign language: for which purpose we
> need a freely poeticising, a freely inventive middle sphere and middle
> faculty (III, 317).

(We shall see that the designation of these words – 'a middle sphere
and middle faculty' – is more self-revealing than Nietzsche is likely
to have intended.) This 'poeticizing translation into an entirely
foreign language' Nietzsche now likens to the production of Chladny's
figures, which are obtained by playing the bow of a violin against a
board of very thin plywood covered with fine sand; the regular geo-
metrical patterns into which the grains of sand arrange themselves
thus reflect or reproduce the vibrations of the music. These figures
are as it were metaphorical representations of the music – metaphors
of a metaphor – but on the other hand it would be absurd to claim that
you can tell from these patterns what it is that men mean by the word
'tone', let alone that from these patterns they can tell anything about
the nature of music.

This picturesque yet accurate image aptly illustrates Nietzsche's
historical situation. We note his predilection for an analogy drawn
from the realm of the natural sciences – it is, as always, a not very
sophisticated bit of science – such as was fashionable in the heyday of
the scientific ideology; and we seem to be left with the impression that
in order to explain the mental operation involved in the creation of
language, all we need do is translate the mechanical causality of
Chladny's figures into the sphere of mind. A good many of the psychological insights and reflections in the books of Nietzsche's most
mature period – especially in *Beyond Good and Evil* and its sequel, *The
Genealogy of Morals* – are founded in analogies which involve just such a
psycho-physical causality, so much so that it looks as though Nietzsche were on the point of accepting one of the mechanistic and
materialist psychologies current at the time. Almost the opposite is
the case. By pointing to Chladny's sound patterns, and to the fact that,
whatever else they do, they do *not* explain what music is, Nietzsche is
in fact showing how inadequate the analogy – the argument from
metaphor – really is, and thus pointing to the break between the

psychic and the physical, between mechanical purpose and human meaning.[5]

The system sketched out in the essay 'On Truth and Falsehood in an Extra-Moral Sense' is a system not without meaning, but meaningful only in itself. The way Nietzsche chooses to describe this system (and it may be recalled that he started life as a classical philologist) is by saying that words do not designate things and are not little labels stuck on to things, but are *metaphors* for real things in the world:

> What then is truth? A mobile army of metaphors, metonymies, anthropomorphisms – in short, a sum of human relations which, poetically and rhetorically intensified, became transposed and adorned, and which after long usage by a people seem fixed, canonical and binding on them. Truths are illusions which one has forgotten *are* illusions [. . .].

If, so far, the passage was cast in the form of a fairly neutral *constatation*, now the point has been reached where Nietzsche can no longer let go without using the entire energy of his style to thrust a heavy value-judgment over the whole argument: 'Truths are illusions which one has forgotten *are* illusions, worn-out metaphors which have become powerless to affect the senses, coins which have their obverse effaced and are now no longer of account as coins but merely as metal' (III, 314).

Certainly there is no need to emphasize the powerful imagination at work in this metaphorical account of the nature of metaphors, an imagination that points to and intimates rather than setting out to prove its insights. (In this respect, at all events, Nietzsche seems to agree with Schopenhauer, who had claimed that 'erweisen' rather than 'beweisen' was philosophy's proper task.[6]) What is less obvious is the way this passage, and the essay as a whole, illuminates the nature of Nietzsche's own philosophical project, and should help us to come to a fuller understanding of it.

Let me now draw some of the implications inherent in this metaphysical fiction and in the later arguments that grow out of it.

1. The essay does not offer a radical criticism of the language of universal and metaphysical concepts in the way that, for example,

Wittgenstein's work does. It sanctions generalizations and conceptual statements of every kind – metaphysical or empirical – as a part of that complex system of linguistic conventions by means of which men are enabled to live in the world. Concepts (Nietzsche writes in the concluding section) are not fundamentally different from other aspects of our language. He likens them to dice – 'they are made of hard bone . . . octagonal and negotiable, like dice . . . but even as such they are the residue of metaphors' (III, 315), that is, of sense-impressions translated into particular names.[7] When Nietzsche likens concepts to coin (money), he illuminates their nature in much the same way as the young Marx had illuminated the nature of money (coin) by likening it to concepts and thus identifying the function of coin as that of a mediator between men and the goods they would have, their 'demande':[8] but whereas Marx's ultimate aim is to subject the metaphorical shift to radical criticism, Nietzsche accepts it as part of 'the lie' and thus as the *donnée* of our situation in the world. Yet at the same time we note that, although Nietzsche shows how 'the language of science', too, springs from the common ground of metaphor, none of the important passages in the essay itself is cast in the language of concepts and 'Wissenschaft'. Again, Nietzsche does not criticize the Kantian and Schopenhauerian notion of 'the things in themselves' beyond saying that for us they are convenient because life-sustaining fictions. Without these fictions we would be victims of the paralysing spell which an unmediated expectation of suffering casts over us; to put it in the succinct phrase of one of the fragments for 'The Will to Power', it is the function of language to turn all the transient phenomena of the world – all 'becoming' – by means of a lie into 'being': 'dem Werden den Charakter des Seins *aufzuprägen*' (III, 895).

Yet how can we ever speak of 'fiction', 'myth' and 'lies' without implying some kind of truth? 'Truth', for us, may be no more than the agreement to play a game of dice in a certain way, to count the spots on the die always in the same way, and we may hardly ever cease to be aware that 'for us, [truth] can be no more than . . .': but does the formulation, 'for us', not imply that there must be something other, something more . . .?

2. By identifying it with 'a mobile army of metaphors', Nietzsche proposes to consider language primarily as an aesthetic phenomenon. But the 'system' he creates – or rather intimates – is quite unlike other, more traditional, aesthetic systems, beginning with that of Kant's

teacher, Alexander Gottlieb Baumgarten (the first to use the term
'aesthetics' in our sense) through Schiller to Schopenhauer. Nietzsche's sketches for such a 'system' differ from all these in being tied
to an historical dimension. Its changing nature – that is, its historicity
– is built into this scheme by means of its very formulations:[9] he speaks
of the 'long usage' in the course of which words become 'fixed,
canonical and binding on' a people; metaphors become 'hard' and
'rigid', or again they wear out and 'lose their sensuous power', images
are effaced and cease to be valid . . . In all this there is change, movement, a course of history. It is a process which runs all one way, from
pristine freshness to ossification, decadence, and an apocalyptic
ending; and this is indeed the way Nietzsche saw European history
from the golden age of pre-Socratic Greece to his own day and the
early twentieth century as he prophetically envisaged it. The German
literary tradition, from Hölderlin through Heine to Stefan George,
Karl Kraus and beyond, is full of such apocalyptic visions, in which
moral prophecy combines in strange ways with a destructive, Samson-
ite intent.[10] Nietzsche's catastrophe-mindedness, too, entails a powerfully negative evaluation of each subsequent historical stage, but –
and this is inherent in his value-judgments – it also entails an unequivocal condemnation of everything that is 'fixed, canonical, and
binding', *because it is hostile to 'life'*. Being, we recall, is the lie imposed on
becoming. Words make no sense unless they are arranged in a way
that makes them 'fixed, canonical, and binding', yet once they are so
arranged, they cease to communicate with 'life'. To place this paradox
in a wider Nietzschean context: the regularization of the elements of
language is condemned as an aspect of the institutionalization of all
individual experience.

And here we come to an all-pervasive and, I think, unacceptable
limitation of Nietzsche's thinking: he is fundamentally uninterested
in, and often undiscriminatingly hostile to, what we may call *the
sphere of association*. By this I mean that in all his philosophizing he has
nothing really positive to say about, and much suspicion of, all those
human endeavours – in society, art and religion, in morality, even in
the sciences – whereby single discrete insights and experiences are
transfixed, stabilized and made reliable by means of rules and laws
and institutions, seeing man's search for stability almost always only
as an arrest of experience, an inauthentic pursuit,[11] a fear of solitude,
a failure of independence and courage, a defection from the heroic
acceptance of singularity. It is not merely that in the dialectic which

lies at the core of all human experience he always favours the unique
against repetition, genius against justice, but that he hardly admits
the presence of a genuine dialectic, of an authentic human problem.
Nietzsche has written splendidly on Goethe, and seems to have
understood more finely than others the nature of Goethe's poetic
genius and humanity. Yet for Goethe's love of custom and habit,
for his ability to hallow the everyday and thereby give it lasting
value –

> O, gedenke denn auch, wie aus dem Keim der Bekanntschaft
> Nach und nach in uns holde Gewohnheit entspross.
>
> [Oh, remember then, too, how in us, out of acquaintanceship's
> seed, sweet habit has gradually grown.][12]

– for this mode of being Nietzsche shows no spontaneous understanding at all. Among the reasons why he is so ready to assign to the
aesthetic activity a central role in human existence is his understanding of it as a mode of experience which, more than any other mode,
escapes the sphere of association and lives by the appearance of
uniqueness. Its true celebrant is not Goethe but Rilke:

> Einmal jedes, nur einmal. Einmal und nicht mehr. Und wir auch
> einmal. Nie wieder. . . .
>
> [Once, each thing but once. Once and no more. And we also are once.
> Never again. . . .][13]

Nietzsche's consistent rejections of the sphere of association form
an important limitation of his philosophical thinking. It is the most
disturbing of his limitations, because it is breached by no dialectic of
questions and hypothetical answers, by no speculative experiments.
Moreover, in this attitude he is in no way original, in no way 'the
unique event and exception' in the culture of his country: here he
forms part of a dominant German tradition that goes back to Martin
Luther and perhaps beyond.

3. In speaking of language as a dynamic system of signs with an inherent organization of meanings, Nietzsche goes in some ways beyond
the traditional linguistics of his period – the theory which looks on all
words as static names of things. Though he does not anticipate
Saussure's insight,[14] on which modern linguistics is founded, that the
elements of language cannot be physically described (Chladny's

figures illustrate a causal relationship of sorts), yet he argues throughout on the assumption that these elements receive their particular
meanings only from the determining contexts in which they occur.
But is there anything beyond these contexts? In trying to answer this
question, we come to the characteristic turn of the argument: by
calling it 'an army of *metaphors*', Nietzsche implies a non-metaphorical
order of things to which language does not belong, but to which it is
somehow – 'aesthetically', by way of a 'halting, stammering' translation – related.

That there is a non-metaphorical, 'true', or perhaps numinous order
of things, to which language does not belong, was the central metaphysical (and Schopenhauerian) claim on which *The Birth of Tragedy*
was founded. The anti-Socratic attitude, central to that book, cul-
minated in an attack on all language-dominated cultures. Sixteen
years later, at the end of Nietzsche's meteoric course, in *Twilight of the
Idols* (ii, 1005), he writes in that tone of fatal bravado characteristic of
his last reflections, under the heading 'From a Moral Theory for the
Deaf and Dumb, and Other Philosophers':

> We no longer set a high enough value on ourselves when we com-
> municate what is in our minds. Our real experiences are not at all
> garrulous. They couldn't communicate themselves, even if they
> wished to. That is because they lack the right word. Whatever we
> have words for, we have already outgrown. In all talk there is a
> grain of contempt. Language, it seems, has been invented only for
> the average, for the middling and communicable. Language vul-
> garizes the speaker.

How, then, should he convey his vision of the metaphysics of
language, his conviction that 'man is a rope, tied between animal and
superman' and that 'what may be loved in man is that he is a transition'?[15] There is no direct way of doing it, and yet Nietzsche does not
believe that 'whereof one cannot speak, thereof one must be silent':[16]
his passion for *writing* remains dominant to the end; it seems like the
obverse of his fear of silence and insanity. It is at this point that the
language of indirection and metaphors, and the argument by 'intimation and transference', come into their own.

The existence of a non-metaphorical, perhaps numinous, world
remains merely implied (implied in the word 'metaphor'), and so does
the relationship between it and the phenomenal world (the world
represented by metaphors). But again the implication is not fortuitous.

Nietzsche's assertion of an *'eternal* justification of Being through the Aesthetic'; his later image of an *'eternal* recurrence of all things',[17] as well as that lurid statement, also from *Thus Spake Zarathustra*, that 'God is dead'[18] (a metaphor: for what? for the fact that God was once alive?) are all examples of a metaphysics of which the least confusing thing to say is that it consistently avoids the dangers of dogma and petrifaction at the price of being consistently paradoxical. It reminds us of the central image of Rilke's *Duino Elegies* – the image of the angels who are 'messengers' from nobody, without a message of any particular kind, yet intimating 'aesthetically' an order of some kind. Of that order which Nietzsche may have in mind we know no more than we know of 'the Beautiful', of which the First Elegy proclaims that it is

. . . des Schrecklichen Anfang, den wir noch grade ertragen,
und wir bewundern es so, weil es gelassen verschmäht,
uns zu zerstören.

[. . . the beginning of Terror we are still just able to bear,
and we adore it so because it serenely disdains to destroy us.]

4. How are we to understand that 'aesthetic attitude' from which language arises? If language is an army of metaphors, then the activity of artists – traditionally seen as makers of metaphors – and the aesthetic activity in general assume an entirely central position in the world, at the very heart of things. Art is then neither esoteric and marginal, nor in any way dispensable, but becomes the human activity *par excellence*: it *is* creative existence. In *The Birth of Tragedy* Nietzsche had used that strange sentence I have just mentioned, and repeated it three times: 'Nur als aesthetisches Phänomen ist das Dasein und die Welt ewig gerechtfertigt.'[19] [Only as an aesthetic phenomenon is the world and the being of man eternally justified.] That assertion was in no way explained by its context and remained enigmatic; it is only the essay of the subsequent year which gives it a fuller meaning. The 'justification' the world is said to achieve 'as an aesthetic phenomenon' – i.e. through 'the aesthetic attitude' – is identical with the 'justification', or validation, or meaning imprinted on the world through man the maker of linguistic conventions, that is, of a system of 'metaphors'. This in turn implies that gnosis on which Nietzsche's original idea of tragedy was founded and with which the present essay begins – the existence of a hostile universe of silence before and beyond language,

within which the little human world of language is an oasis of life, of comfort and sustenance, *but not of truth*.

5. However, it is only when man ignores the 'aesthetic' or metaphorical nature of his being in the world by taking it for granted, 'when, [in his function] as an *artistically creative* subject, he forgets himself' (III, 316), that he is able to live at peace with himself and the world. Except for these precarious moments of harmony, achieved and experienced in the act of creation, the antagonism between the world and its aesthetic theodicy remains unreconciled. The artist is one who is and is not aware of the shifting grounds, the metaphorical and 'lying' nature, of his productions. To him there applies that image from chapter 1 of *The Birth of Tragedy* (1, 22f), which again receives a fuller meaning through this later essay: what the artist and 'the aesthetically sensitive man' experiences is

> . . . the whole divine comedy of life, including the inferno . . . not like mere shadows on the wall – for he lives and suffers with these scenes – and yet not without that fleeting sensation of illusion. And perhaps many will, like myself, recall how amid the dangers and terrors of dreams they have occasionally called out to themselves in self-encouragement and not without success: 'It is a dream! I wish to dream on!'

The formulation is among the most accurate and beautiful in Nietzsche's work, yet it is as precarious as the moment it describes. The next step in the argument (e.g. in the second of the *Untimely Meditations*) will be the exaltation of a healthy, creative life at the cost of a 'true' knowledge of the world, followed by Nietzsche's strange paeans to the unconscious, 'the natural' and 'the instinctive' as authentic modes of experience. We cannot blame Nietzsche for the ghastly company in which this enthusiasm for authenticity in its various forms will land him in our time, when he can no longer 'prevent people from doing mischief with me' (II, 1152). Yet we must marvel at the paradox whereby this most intellectual and conscious of modern thinkers invokes values to which he is himself a stranger – a paradox for which we have lost all taste.

6. What are we to make of that strange, idiosyncratic insistence on the 'lying' nature of language? Why does Nietzsche refuse to distinguish clearly between 'fictions' and 'lies'? Does he simply follow Plato in the tenth book of the *Republic*? In the event, Nietzsche's concern is the opposite. Plato ignores the distinction because by branding

fiction as a lie he hopes to safeguard the *polis* from the effects of poetic irresponsibility. (The myths of poets, Plato suggests, are hardly better than the evil lies of demagogues.) Nietzsche, on the other hand, cares little for the *polis*, and *seems* to care hardly more for truth, seeing that he delights in inventing situations in which life is shown to be possible only at the cost of sacrificing the pursuit of truth; situations of this kind do not seem to worry him enough.

'Life', not the *polis* nor even 'the world', is the real object of Nietzsche's concern. And life, he will argue, being the source and origin of rational distinctions, can never be defined and designated by them – and again this is a sophistry that does not worry him enough. Thus life, for Nietzsche, is never a concept but a vision, a metaphor which embraces all kinds of being but – and here we return to the point of our earlier criticism – is devalued when it is seen unheroically, under the aspect of association. Yet it is clear that the difference between myth or fiction or poetry on the one hand and the lie on the other derives its entire meaning from an organized legal or social context; and that only to one who is prepared to take institutionalized life in the world seriously is this difference of any consequence. *Sub specie aeterni*, in terms of an aesthetic justification, it disappears.

And here is the point at which we may look for an answer to the first of our three opening questions. If (as we have seen) 'life' as Nietzsche envisages it can neither provide nor endure the unqualified truth about itself; if, furthermore, the most gifted of men are merely makers of metaphors, merely poets, and 'poets lie too much';[20] and if, finally, all that happens in the world is enacted in unreality, on an 'as if' principle, then assuredly there is no good reason for taking life without its 'aesthetic justification' – life as it is – seriously.

The aesthetic attitude (and here we turn to our second question) is the human attitude *par excellence*. It justifies man's being in the world and gives order and shape to it, but this again is a pursuit which cannot be taken seriously. On the contrary: merriment and laughter ensue whenever we recognize what man's being amounts to – an immense, finely structured cosmic joke. The metaphysics of metaphor is a sample and paradigm of the metaphysics of being: 'Around the hero everything turns into tragedy, around the demi-god everything turns into satyric drama; and around God everything turns into – what? maybe the "world"?' (*Beyond Good and Evil* 150; II, 637). There is hardly a book of Nietzsche's which does not contain a sketch of such an aesthetic re-interpretation, or at least an assurance that this is a vital part of his philosophical undertaking. And yet: to the end this pan-aestheticism remains a mere speculative possibility, a mere intention. For however much Nietzsche aspires to it (and his admiration of the aesthetic attitude has occasionally an unpleasant undertone of self-conscious worldliness about it); however much he approvingly discerns it in certain 'monumental' historical characters (reminding us occasionally of the *kitschig* 'Renaissance men' of Conrad Ferdinand Meyer, his contemporary[21]), Nietzsche cannot forgo his moral-existential concern for long. It is as though he were haunted by a demon of that truth, the impossibility of which he has argued; as though he were compelled to insist not on the fiction but on *the lie* at the root of the metaphors which enable us to come to terms with the world into which we have been thrust; as though he were at the mercy of that 'spirit of gravity' which is also a burden of weightiness ['Geist der Schwere'][22] and which he had so often ridiculed and renounced. For this emphasis on a moral terminology is certainly incompatible with the dream in which a central and all-embracing function is ascribed to the aesthetic, seen as a game, a sport of the gods, a jolly and colourful army of metaphors. And this contradiction receives its final image in the anti-historical and 'extra-moral' Nazarene figure of Jesus in Nietzsche's *Antichrist* – an image and a metaphor, but not a resolution. The contradiction remained unresolved, as far as I can see, to the end of Nietzsche's conscious life. He would indeed justify the whole world aesthetically, 'were it not that I have bad dreams'.

7. Finally, the essay with which I have been concerned, and in particular the idea of metaphor that is central to it, help us to understand and appreciate the nature of Nietzsche's philosophical undertaking, his use of language generally as well as his unsettling mode of thinking.

Numerous critics of Nietzsche have read his work as that of a traditional nineteenth-century German conceptual philosopher or ideologist who, from irresponsibility, demagogy or sheer ineptitude, made things unnecessarily difficult for himself and his readers by indulging in metaphor-mindedness; critics of this sort see it as their task to demythologize Nietzsche's writings and, having freed them from their metaphors, to consider how much – or rather how little – remains valid in terms of a conceptually legitimized scheme or system. Other critics have taken the opposite view: they have seen him as a poet – either as a heroic poet of the German soul (in a tradition that goes from Hölderlin to Rilke, George, and Paul Celan), or as a pre-fascist poet *manqué* with a penchant for art nouveau heraldic beasts and a permanent place in Pseud's Corner. I believe he is none of these things, and that the alternative, poet versus philosopher, is misleading.

Assuming that the way a writer conceives of language and the way he describes it is also indicative of the way he uses it, we can see that what Nietzsche has evolved in those few years he was granted for his philosophical venture is a language and variety of styles which are metaphorical in something like the sense outlined in this early essay of his and the later observations that spring from it. It is a mode of writing somewhere between the individuation and concern with particulars which is the language area of fiction and poetry, and conceptual generalities and abstractions which make up the language area of traditional Kantian and post-Kantian philosophy. As we have already seen, although the last (and weaker) section of the essay is concerned with the way in which 'Wissenschaftlichkeit' – the language of science – is fashioned, and with the way in which it too is related to 'the mobile army of metaphors', yet this language of science is not the language in which most of the essay itself is written. And again, when Nietzsche refers to the image of the silver coin with its effaced inscription, its value reduced to that of the metal alone, he has in mind neither the coin itself (he is not telling a story), nor a generality which would make the precise image of the coin merely an illustration and therefore dispensable. The metaphor of the coin is intended as an intermediary between two modes of thinking and writing, as a pattern which determines neither a narrative line nor a piece of philosophical poetry or 'Begriffsdichtung',[23] but a philosophical argument.

This middle mode of discourse can certainly be *shown* (and to show it has been the purpose of this paper), but I am not clear how it can be defined more precisely. It is not poetry; Nietzsche's poetry seems to me much less distinguished than his prose. Nor is it poetic prose – the poetic prose he wrote is in every sense (in itself and in its influence) a disaster.[24] Nor is it aphorism – Nietzsche's strictly aphoristic utterances are much less interesting[25] than those of other practitioners of the genre, especially La Rochefoucauld and Lichtenberg, whom he admired. Then again there are the passages in which he is concerned with traditional conceptual problems (e.g. in his polemics against Kant), which are impatient, repetitious and mostly perfunctory. What is truly distinguished in his work (and also, incidentally, the true ground of his immensely wide and often overpowering influence) is this middle mode of language – which I suppose we may call 'literary-philosophical' – and to have devised this mode and applied it to an almost endless variety of contemporary issues is his greatest achievement.

The disdain with which Nietzsche treats the sphere of association and the consequent limitations of his view of life in the world have been mentioned, but there is another, positive side to this story. The guiding intention of his philosophical prose is to convey not the general or the average but the unique, to preserve the dynamic, unsteady, the irregular and above all the individualized nature of life. Schopenhauer once described his own philosophical style as the outcome of 'my trick . . . of suddenly and instantly freezing the most living sense-experience or the deepest feeling the hour has brought with the coldest abstract reflection, in order to preserve it in a transfixed state'. Nietzsche intends the opposite. His aim is to let the process of 'Becoming' speak, to challenge 'all those who swear by the gradualness of all development as by a moral law' (I, 368f), to alienate 'life' as little as possible from its uncertain, unstable, catastrophic origins, even at the price of intellectual coherence inself. Language, metaphor and thought are related to 'the real world' as patterns and paradigms of our being in its relationship to 'the real world': there is no such thing as 'Being at rest with itself, identical with itself, unaltering: the only "Being" vouchsafed to us is changing, not identical with itself, it is involved in relationships'.[26]

Being involved in relationships: the ever-renewed attempts to preserve these 'relationships' from petrifaction fill Nietzsche's books and notebooks, this is what he sees as the task of his philosophical *and* literary undertaking. It is not surprising that Nietzsche's hybrid mode of writing is forever in danger of being impatiently dismissed as 'neither one thing nor t'other', for it constitutes a provocation of the genre theories and tacit assumptions on which French and English kinds of discourse are founded. But it has its antecedents (great writers are hardly ever formal innovators), in the early works of Plato, in Pascal, and a host of German writers as well as a few English ones like William Blake; and it has countless successors, among them the (equally irreducible) language of 'family likenesses', 'blurred photographs', and metaphors of games of Wittgenstein's *Philosophical Investigations*.

And here lies the answer to our third opening question: in challenging, through this mode of writing, the absurd dichotomy of 'scientific' *versus* 'imaginative', or again the antitheses between 'concept' and 'metaphor', 'abstract' and 'concrete', Nietzsche is at the same time intent on challenging that division in our areas of knowledge-and-experience, that fragmentation of knowledge which he (together with men like Marx, Carlyle and Matthew Arnold) saw as one of the chief blights of modern Western civilization, as the sign of our decadence.

What Nietzsche teaches us is not to read philosophy as literature, let alone literature as philosophy, but to read both as closely connected forms of life.

NOTES

1 Nietzsche knew nothing of Arnold nor, surprisingly, of Marx; Carlyle (see, *Twilight of the Idols*) was one of his pet hates.

2 See Karl Jaspers, *Nietzsche: Eine Einführung in das Verständnis seines Philosophierens* (Berlin, 1947), pp. 91–101.

3 See *Twilight of the Idols*, 'Maxims and Arrows' no. 26: 'I mistrust all systematizers and avoid them. The will to a system is a lack of integrity.' In 1882 Nietzsche improved a number of Lou Salomé's aphorisms; in one of them she wrote: 'Perhaps the most honest philosopher would not get as far as philosophizing.' Nietzsche's revision: 'Perhaps the most honest philosopher would not permit himself to get as far as a "system".'

4 The reality of 'das Ur-Eine' ('the primal unity') of suffering, as opposed to the appearance of individuation; see *The Birth of Tragedy*, sections 1, 5, etc.

5 'We feel', writes Wittgenstein in the *Tractatus*, 6.52, 'that even when all *possible* scientific questions have been answered, our problems of life have still not been touched at all.' This is not the only point where Nietzsche's and Wittgenstein's thinking come together. The *Tractatus* is another scheme in which a parallel is established between the propositions of language and 'the logical form of reality' (4.12ff); and in the *Tractatus*, too, this relationship is not simply 'representative' but remains indeterminate, though it is not 'aesthetic' in Nietzsche's sense.

6 For Schopenhauer's view that philosophical arguments are established by a process of 'erweisen' ('demonstrating') as opposed to scientific 'beweisen' ('proving'), see *The World as Will and Idea*, Book 1, section 14.

7 Hegel too derives 'Begriff' from 'begreifen' but tries to preserve the dynamic character inherent in the verb (see his *Ästhetik*, Berlin, 1955, pp. 136–7).

8 See Marx's section on money in the *Paris MSS* (*Ökonomisch-philosophische Manuskripte*) of 1844, which includes the famous quotation from *Faust I*: 'Doch alles, was ich frisch geniesse,/Ist das drum weniger mein?' and from *Timon of Athens*: 'What is here?/Gold? Yellow glittering, precious gold?' For a stimulating, if frequently bizarre, discussion of some of the philosophical problems of metaphor, including Nietzsche's 'effaced coin', see Jacques Derrida, 'White Mythology: Metaphor in the Text of Philosophy' in the *Metaphor* number of *New Literary Review*, vol. VI, no. 1 (Autumn 1974), especially pp. 12ff.

9 See also Heinrich von Staden, 'Nietzsche and Marx on Greek Art and Literature: Case Studies', *Daedalus* (Winter, 1976), p. 89.

10 See J. P. Stern, *Re-interpretations* (London, 1964), pp. 221ff.

11 This is not contradicted by his positive interest in the Greek *polis* (in *The Greek State* of 1872), which he sees entirely as a means toward the cultivation of (aesthetic) 'Genius'.

12 From 'The Metamorphosis of Plants' of 1798.

13 From the Ninth Elegy. For the relation between Rilke's 'nur einmal' and Nietzsche's 'eternal recurrence' see Erich Heller, *The Disinherited Mind* (Cambridge, 1952), pp. 128–30.

14 Ferdinand de Saussure, *Course in General Linguistics* [1915] (New York, 1959), especially chapter iii.

15 *Thus Spake Zarathustra*, Book I, sections 3 and 4 of 'Zarathustra's Prologue'.

16 *Tractatus*, last proposition.

17 *Zarathustra*, Book III, section 13, 'The Convalescent', anticipated in *The Joyful Science*, section 341.

18 *Zarathustra*, Book I, section 2 of 'Zarathustra's Prologue', anticipated in *The Joyful Science*, section 125.

19 Sections 5 and 24; only at the end of the second mention in section 5 does the word 'ewig' occur; cf, also § 5 of the 1866 preface.

20 *Zarathustra*, Book II, section 17, 'Of Poets', and Book IV, section 14, 'The Song of Melancholy'; cf. also the first of the *Dithyrambs of Dionysus*, 'Only a fool! Only a poet!'

21 It is a curious coincidence (noted with approval by Heidegger) that one of the most sensational of C. F. Meyer's stories, *Jürg Jenatsch* (1872/4) opens with a highly 'Zarathustrian' description of the Oberengadin, where in August 1881 Nietzsche conceived the thought of 'the eternal recurrence' (see his own account in *Ecce Homo*).

22 The issue remains profoundly ambiguous. In *Zarathustra*, e.g. Book III, section 11 ('Of the Spirit of Gravity'), in *Beyond Good and Evil*, section 193, and a good many other places, all signs of weightiness, heaviness, difficulty are disparaged, ridiculed, and at their most ridiculous (as in Schopenhauer) attributed to the Germans: 'the Germans consider themselves profound when they feel heavy and gloomy . . .' (CM, VIIIi, 311). Yet in other contexts (e.g. *Zarathustra*, Book I, section 1, 'Of the Three Metamorphoses'; *The Joyful Science*, section 341, 'The greatest weight'; 'the depth of one's capacity to suffer is almost what determines the order of rank', 'I want the severest trials ever faced by any man' [both quoted by Thomas Mann in his essay *Nietzsches Philosophie im Lichte unserer Erfahrung*]; 'my task is *to set up the most difficult ideal* of a *philosopher*' [CM, VIIIi, 151]; and especially in the repeated claim that the idea of the eternal recurrence is supremely valuable because it is supremely hard to endure) the evaluation of 'das Schwere' (what is heavy, burdensome, difficult) is entirely positive – more than that: here if anywhere Nietzsche's evaluation is consistent, this if anything in his work is his positive 'table of values'.

23 See H. M. Wolff, *Friedrich Nietzsche: Der Weg zum Nichts* (Berne, 1956).

24 Nietzsche himself, alas, does not heed his own counsel: 'The tact of a good prose writer in the choice of his devices consists in approaching *close* to poetry, *but never* moving *over* into it' (*Unschuld des Werdens*, I [Kröner edn, vol. 78], 'Zur Lehre vom Stil' p. 191).

25 The reason is that they are *consistently* 'unmasking' and disparaging: see e.g. *Beyond Good and Evil*, the 'Maxims and Interjections' (Sprüche und Zwischensprüche').

26 '*An sich klar* ist aber, dass Vorstellen *nichts Ruhendes* ist, nichts Sich selber Gleiches Unwandelbares: das *Sein* also, welches uns einzig verbürgt ist, ist *wechselnd, nicht-mit-sich-identisch*, hat Beziehungen [. . .]. Dies ist die *Grundgewissheit vom Sein*' (CM, vii, 468).

4

NIETZSCHE'S MASKS

W. D. Williams

Everything profound loves a mask; the profoundest things of all even have a hatred of image and parable. Could it not be that *antithesis* is the one proper disguise for the modesty of a god to walk abroad in? A questionable question: it would be strange if one of the mystics had not ventured some such speculation before now. There are happenings of so delicate a kind that one does well to bury them and make them unrecognizable with some expression of coarseness; there are acts of love and extravagant nobility which one is best advised to follow up by taking a stick and belabouring the man who witnessed them, so as to confuse his memory[. . .]. A man who is profound in his modesty meets his vicissitudes and his delicate decisions along paths which few people ever reach and of whose existence even his closest intimates ought never to learn[. . .]. Every profound spirit needs a mask: what is more, around every profound spirit a mask is continually growing, thanks to the constantly false, that is to say *shallow* interpretation of his every word, his every step, of every sign of life that he gives (*Beyond Good and Evil*, section 40; II, 603f).

Nietzsche could hardly warn his reader more clearly than he does here that his writing is never to be taken at its face value, that he is consciously addressing an audience and adopting a particular *persona*, which will continually vary. Indeed, one of the more puzzling and fascinating characteristics of his work is the very wide range of these 'masks' which he adopts and the extraordinary skill with which he will switch from one to another at short notice and even on occasion combine several in one passage. He is thus continually playing a game with the reader, forcing him not only to think about the subject under discussion but also to follow the elusive scent that is being laid and to attempt to discover the 'real' Nietzsche underneath the mask.

In the passage quoted above there is much talk of modesty ('Scham'), and it is almost as though we were being told that self-masking, even self-distortion, were a matter of decency and *bonton*. And here he talks of expressing one's deepest feelings through articulating the opposite. This is an extreme position. Usually the masking is more subtle, and frequently Nietzsche deliberately allows it to slip, so as to use the reader's consciousness of mask and reality (or is it another mask underneath the first?) to add to and deepen the effect he is creating. One can almost say, in certain cases, that this interplay between different levels of self-awareness is the whole effect to be conveyed.

In the famous preface to *Beyond Good and Evil*, for instance, which begins 'Supposing truth to be a woman . . .', he first adopts a tone of light badinage. He makes the outrageous comparison of truth to a woman and the philosophers' search for it as skirt-chasing incompetently carried out. She is too much for them and escapes the dogmatists' pursuit. But almost immediately the light-hearted jest becomes a serious analysis of the claim of any judgment to have validity – the time is near when all system-building will be seen to be a childish delusion, constructed out of superstition (the superstition of the soul, or its modern form, the superstition that there exists a subject, an ego to do the philosophizing) or perhaps out of mere verbal and grammatical falsities. He goes on to compare dogmatic philosophy to astrology in earlier times, which at least displayed more erudition and scholarly dedication than most sciences and left the world some very fine buildings! Examples of dogmatism include Vedanta in Asia and Platonism in Europe, and against the latter Nietzsche inveighs with scorn, stigmatizing Plato's 'invention' of 'pure spirit' and the 'good in itself' as the most pernicious errors ever passed off as 'truth'. All this is hard-hitting polemic, deliberately exaggerated and made as theatrical as possible, preparing for the switch to the present and Nietzsche's view of the philosopher's task today, which is to awaken us from our long dogmatic slumbers, and the imagery shifts with a jerk to a picture of doctor and patient and a series of questions is posed. Where did the illness come from? Was it Socrates who misled Plato? But Nietzsche does not linger here, he moves on swiftly to a grandiose image of the forces long repressed by dogmatism (Platonism, or Christianity, which is its popular form) as a bow fully stretched, ready to shoot far. This stretched bow, the 'Spannung des Geistes', has been felt as oppressive, and various attempts have been made to reduce the tension. Jesuitism was one, the democratic Enlightenment another. The latter was carried by a free press and the spread of newspapers (and here Nietzsche slips in a small joke – the Germans invented gunpowder and all honour to them, but they cancelled this by inventing the press!). But we good Europeans are not taken in by this, we need the tense bow and will shoot our arrow to its target.

It is apparent that Nietzsche is building up an extremely subtle effect here. The enormous over-simplifications, the highly tendentious judgments, have to be put into our minds in such a way that, even as we reject them (if we do), they leave an aftertaste, a predisposition to accept the general position from which they spring. And this he does by introducing the whole thing as a joke, then very swiftly making it quite clear that he is deadly serious and really believes the grotesque things he is saying (or at least wishes to have them accepted as genuine counters in the debate), and then moving on to an almost apocalyptic style at the end with his programmatic vision, but again with a joke to show that he is really a buffoon after all. We are, of course, not taken in, nor are we meant to be.

And we are not persuaded either, but our minds have been led to an openness and elasticity which will be utilized by Nietzsche during the course of the book. This is not strictly polemical writing at all, as one might think. Nietzsche is seeking here not so much to persuade us (though if we are persuaded that is of course an added bonus) but rather to achieve in us a state of half-agreement. Our minds are amused, then tickled, then engaged, leaving us in the sceptical, anti-dogmatic state that is Nietzsche's fruitful soil for the planting of his ideas. His mask here is that of the comedian, but he has taken very good care that it is only half on, and we are aware of the deception.

Much of this self-masking of Nietzsche's takes the form of buffoonery, though always carefully adjusted so that the seriousness is never lost to sight, but there are many other modes of presentation in which an underlying pathos is very much emphasized. Very near the end of *Beyond Good and Evil*, for instance, there is a passage (section 289) in which Nietzsche sees the philosopher as a hermit (perhaps a gold-digger, living in a cave), in whose writings can be heard 'something of the echo of the desert, something of the whisper and shy vigilance of solitude', in whose loudest cries there resounds a dangerous kind of silence. Such a man, living by himself, talking to himself, year after year in his labyrinth or gold-mine, will have thoughts which become twilit, smelling of decay, cold to the passer-by. Nietzsche goes on:

> The hermit does not believe that any philosopher – assuming that philosophers have always been hermits first of all – ever expressed his real and final opinions in books: does one not write books precisely to conceal what lies within one? – indeed, he will have his doubts as to whether a philosopher *can* have 'final and real' opinions at all, whether behind each of his caves there does not and must not lie a yet deeper cave – a more extensive, stranger, richer world beyond the surface, an abyss behind every ground, beneath every 'grounding' ['Begründung']. Every philosophy is a foreground-philosophy[. . .] Every philosophy also *conceals* a philosophy; every opinion is also a hiding-place, every word also a mask.

We do not need to know very much about Nietzsche's life and his personal character and circumstances to realize how deeply felt is his sense of isolation, how much the iron has entered his soul, and how close all this comes to a cry in the darkness, yearning for an answering voice. As always when he talks of the philosopher he means himself (just as for instance his portrait of Schopenhauer in the *Untimely Meditations* is largely a portrait of himself). But the element of self-pity here is not allowed to dominate. The lightness of touch passes all this off as an agreeable fancy, and the concreteness of the imagery takes the reader well beyond the level of sympathetic engagement to a real insight into the 'perspectivism' which is Nietzsche's fundamental attitude. It is the nature of philosophical thinking which is being described here, quite as much as the isolation and self-distrust of the thinker. And, of course, the basic insight into that nature is well characterized in the image of the labyrinth which has no end, or the gold-mine where the digging stopped at a certain point quite arbitrarily.

There are many examples in all Nietzsche's works of a similar technique. He is fond of isolating some aspect of his thinking, giving it a stature and personal reality of its own, and then addressing it directly, or playing it off against himself, creating a tension whereby his thinking becomes a dramatic contest with the reader as spectator and, as it were, judge. Or, sometimes, it turns into a grandiose play within a play, with a carefully constructed mask being apparently ripped off for the reader's delight and satisfaction with further revelations and puzzles to follow, so that all is left shimmering and only half expressed. The penultimate section of *Beyond Good and Evil* (II, 754f), the famous passage on 'the genius of the heart', proceeds thus, with the very long first sentence, slow and highly rhythmical, a sort of Dionysian dance of words, leading to a short dialogue with the reader, a teasing semi-jocular appeal to his intelligence – you do know who I mean, don't you? – and the pretended revelation of the identity of Dionysus. This is followed by a long characterization of him, full of reservations, guesses and a hovering sense of the danger of unveiling a mystery, finally culminating in a mock-dialogue between Nietzsche himself and the god, and the god's command to be 'stronger, more evil and more profound', with Nietzsche's ironical comment at the end that the god could learn from us human beings. The whole is a most beautifully adjusted piece of theatrical masking and unmasking, Nietzsche himself is several different *personae* at once, deadly serious throughout, yet exploiting to the full the opportunities his chosen form gives of playing with his thinking, creating a tension between expectation and reality, between logic and fancy, between self-revelation and self-concealment.

Immediately following this exalted lingering on the heights, and forming the last section of the whole book, Nietzsche addresses his own thoughts (II, 756):

Alas, what *are* you then, you my written and painted thoughts! Not long ago you were still so gaily coloured, young and malicious, so full of thorns and secret spices that you made me sneeze and laugh – and now? You have already cast off your novelty, and some of you, I fear, are on the point of becoming truths: so immortal they look already, so heartbreakingly worthy, so boring! And has it ever been otherwise? What objects do we then write of and paint, we mandarins with our Chinese brushes, we immortalizers of things which *allow* themselves to be written, what alone are we capable of portraying? Alas, always only what is about to wither and beginning to lose its fragrance! Alas, always only the departing storms that have blown themselves out, only sere and yellowed feelings! Alas, always only the birds that have grown weary and lost their way, and now let themselves be caught in the hand – in *our* hand!

We immortalize that which cannot live and fly much longer, none but weary and over-ripe things! And it is only for your *afternoon*, you my written and painted thoughts, that I have the colours, many colours perhaps, many gaily-coloured tendernesses and fifty yellows and browns and greens and reds: – but no one can guess from these how you looked in your morning, you sudden sparks and miracles of my solitude, you my old beloved – *wicked* thoughts!

This is all, of course, persiflage. The philosopher's thoughts are likened to birds which have reached the end of their activity and can now be caught and captured in the written word, but the life has gone out of them. It is all given a sad and resigned colour, as though the expression of a thought were already the admission of its death. One is reminded of one of Schiller's most touching and affecting insights: 'When the soul *speaks*, then alas! what speaks is no longer the *soul*.' [*Spricht* die Seele, so spricht ach! schon die *Seele* nicht mehr.]

But Nietzsche carries all this in a lightly woven web of fancy, with himself (the philosopher) as the mandarin painting in the calm and seclusion of his study, choosing his colours to bestow eternal life on his subjects and aware even as he touches them in that they are ossified, decayed, dead. At the end the heavy play with the idea that these are *afternoon* thoughts, which have outlived the freshness of their morning, cannot obscure the resigned melancholy of his recognition. The last sentence, of course, with the insertion of the word 'wicked' ['schlimm'], is blatantly a *non sequitur*, but again quite deliberate. Nietzsche is leading us on a path of his own, bidding for our sympathy and then challenging us to withdraw it in the face of his special pleading. This technique – and the number of examples of it in Nietzsche's works make it clear that it is a deliberate technique – of sailing as near as possible to the edge of the reader's sympathy, and daring him to disagree and reject the often outrageous views expressed, is a large part of Nietzsche's armoury. When it is expressed, as here, in a semi-ironic tone and sometimes in the manner of a buffoon, it leads to a most subtle and highly sophisticated kind of argumentation, which leaves the reader both amused and touched, and more willing to accept the underlying presuppositions of the argument than the intellectual cogency of what is expressed would otherwise allow.

A comparison of Nietzsche's later works, especially those written after *Zarathustra*, with the earliest productions, such as *The Birth of Tragedy*, leads to the strong impression that the 'masking' we are study-

ing, the adoption of a 'role' and a particular voice in a particular context, of which we have seen several instances, is a technique which he
uses more and more frequently, and with ever greater complexity, as
he develops. Some indication of this is given in the series of prefaces
he wrote for his earlier works for the 1886 edition, looking back on
them from his standpoint then after completing *Zarathustra*. In the
Essay in Self-Criticism which he wrote for *The Birth of Tragedy* he castigates
the book as badly written, sentimental, overlaid with imagery and
rhetoric, logically muddy, arrogant and emotional. And he goes on
(1, 12):

> The voice that spoke here – one confessed this to oneself with
> curiosity as well as distaste – was at all events a *foreign* voice, one that
> belonged to the disciple of a still 'unknown god', who was hiding
> himself for the time being in the cowl of an academic scholar,
> hiding behind the heaviness and the dialectical cheerlessness of the
> Germans, even behind the bad manners of a Wagnerite; [. . . and
> here he drops the name Dionysus . . .] what spoke here was some-
> thing like a mystical and almost maenadic soul, painfully and wil-
> fully stammering as if in a foreign tongue, barely certain whether it
> wished to communicate or to secrete itself. It should have *sung*, this
> 'new soul' – and not spoken!

Nietzsche is here clearly being wise after the event, imputing to his
earlier self a complexity and indirectness of statement which is hard
to discover in the original work. But it is significant that he here makes
a deliberate attempt to defend the book with the argument that his
writing then involved a process of 'masking'. This process seems by
now to have become so much a part of his method of self-expression
that he can hardly look at his earlier work without detecting the same
thing there.

In other prefaces written at the same time a similar process is
apparent. In the new preface to *Human, All-Too-Human*, vol. 1, for instance, Nietzsche opens with a long self-scrutiny. He has been told, he
says, that his works all contain challenges to reverse traditional conceptions, they encourage distrust of morality, they are a school of
suspicion and scorn. And, he agrees, nobody has been more suspicious
than he. But, he goes on, anyone who has understood the pains and
frustrations of total isolation will also understand his urge to take
refuge

in some kind of hero-worship or antagonism or piece of scholar-
ship or frivolity or foolishness: and also why, where I failed to find
what I *needed*, I had to extort it artificially, to forge it, to fabricate it
(– and what else have poets ever done? and what might all the art
in the world be there for?). But what I always needed most of all,
for my own cure and self-restoration, was the conviction of *not*
being so alone, not *seeing* so alone – an enchanting suspicion of some
kinship and likeness in glance and desire, a moment of relaxation in
the assurance of friendship, the shared blindness of two companions
with no mistrust or question-mark, a delight in foregrounds, in
surfaces, in what is near and next to hand, in all things that have
colour and skin and apparency (I, 437f).

This passage is a very sad summing-up of his intellectual life, but very
striking in the combination of a basic honesty, which is utterly uncompromising, with a recognition of the necessity – for him at least –
for deception of one sort or another, not only in his expression but in
his very thinking itself. And not only deception of others, of his
readers, but of himself as well. The basic need to overcome, or come to
terms with, his isolation, has driven him to this. And a half-hearted
(deliberately half-hearted?) justification is attempted with the paren-
thetical assertion that all art is, at bottom, an identical process. The
call for sympathy is most beautifully balanced with the strong assertion of privilege. He goes on to admit that this overwhelming need
for deception and the comfort of at least an answering voice has
on occasions led him astray; it led him, he thinks, to misinterpret
Schopenhauer badly, to overlook Wagner's incurable romanticism,
as though it were a beginning and not an end, to misunderstand the
Greeks and even the Germans, and perhaps a whole lot of other
things. He ends in high pathos:

but supposing all this were true and justifiably held against me,
what do *you* know, what could you know of how much cunning of
self-preservation, how much prudence and higher surveillance is
contained in such self-deception – and how much duplicity I still
need if I am to be permitted to keep on fashioning the luxury of *my*
truthfulness? – Enough, I am still alive: and life, say what you will,
is no invention of morality: it *wills* deception, it *lives* by deception –
but there I go again, don't I, and do what I have always done, old
amoralist and bird-snarer that I am – and speak immorally, extra-
morally, 'beyond good and evil'? (I, 438).

One could hardly have a clearer revelation of Nietzsche's deepest recognition of the nature of his thinking and writing, and one must accept that to be so fully aware of his own tortured self-questioning requires a high degree of courage as well as a rare clarity of vision. But it is clear that the admission, or rather proclamation, that his work is based on counterfeiting, is held sternly against, and totally subordinate to, the assertion of his basic belief, the 'luxury of *my* truthfulness'. This he cannot, will not, relinquish. It is as though he is challenging the reader, not merely bidding for his sympathy, challenging him to penetrate the various masks, disentangle the various misconceptions and deceptions, and excavate the hard nugget of naked honesty and truth lying beneath them. And, curiously, the effect of the parade of self-accusation is to predispose the reader not to reject what is to be asserted but precisely to welcome it, to take for himself the credit of discovering it and thus to make these apparently hard-won recognitions his own.

It is the contention of these pages that this technique of Nietzsche's, which may well have begun (I do not mean chronologically, but logically) as a defence-mechanism against accusations of wrong-headedness or simple error, develops more and more as he goes on, and especially from 1886 onwards, as a deliberate part of his armoury. It becomes a way of setting up between himself and his reader a sort of shadow-play, starting with a teasing 'How serious do you think I am?' and moving on to 'Do you really believe that I believe this?' and 'If this is not my real view, can you guess what is?' and so on, culminating in a conspiracy between writer and reader to entertain any sort of outrageous suggestion and examine its consequences, thus in the end entering a realm of thought which is free of all presuppositions, all received opinions.

In the very next section of his preface to *Human, All-Too-Human*, vol. 1, Nietzsche considers one of his main ideas, that of the 'free spirit ['freier Geist'], and it is immediately apparent that this too is a *persona*, a mask which he has assumed, not an expression of his deepest nature. He is quite uncompromising about this:

> And so it was that once, when I found it necessary, I also *invented* those 'free spirits' to whom this gloomily courageous book called 'Human, All-Too-Human' is dedicated: such 'free spirits' do not exist, never have existed, – but at that time, as I say, I needed them for company, so as to keep a good heart in bad circumstances

(sickness, isolation, exile, *acedia*, inactivity): as brave fellows and sprites with whom one chats and laughs when one feels like chatting and laughing and sends to the devil when they become boring, – as my compensation for lack of friends (I, 438).

And although he goes on to say that such people may well be coming in the future, it is quite clear that the whole concept of the 'free spirit' is a fabrication of his mind, a 'hermit's shadow-show' ['Einsiedler-Schattenspiel'] as he calls it, a wish-dream of his own which he has created to comfort himself in his solitude. There is a poignant and moving recognition here of his utter humility, very different from the common notion of his arrogance and dictatorial authoritarianism, which should make us revise our view of his mental life. But beyond this, of course, and far more important, is the hint, or rather the clear statement, that the whole conception of the 'free spirit' is a mask and not a fundamental reality. When one reflects that this conception is the basis of a large part of Nietzsche's thinking, certainly in the central part of his life, the time of *Human, All-Too-Human* and *The Joyful Science*, one can judge how far one must take his most programmatic utterances at anything but their face value.

For the 'free spirit' is the epitome for Nietzsche of the intelligence operating entirely on its own terms, unhindered by tradition or morality, or even logic, the ideal of pure mental activity unswayed by passion or loyalty or any other extra-intellectual motive. And this has been the basis of his whole attack on falsity, on pretence, hypocrisy, self-delusion. It is in the service of this ideal that he has for years laid about him so zestfully, destroying the shibboleths of the past, toppling down the old tablets, calling in question all mankind's most cherished beliefs. If now we are to see that noble ideal as merely another mask, created to help him bear his solitude, does this mean we discard it, and return to our comfortable illusions? Clearly, such a conclusion would be quite repugnant to Nietzsche, who is, after all, writing a preface for his own earlier book enshrining the ideal. And yet, why call it in question in this way, why cast this sort of doubt on it? The answer to this question must surely be two-fold. First, we have Nietzsche's unswerving passion for honesty in his self-scrutiny, for what he calls 'Wahrhaftigkeit' ['truthfulness'], which will not allow him to erect a pretence without at the same time affirming that it is a pretence. And this we must not under-estimate. But second, and to my mind more important, we must accept that his whole notion of truth is a relativistic one, that truth and error, honesty and deceit, reality and mask, are so intertwined and bound up with one another than one cannot and must not attempt any unequivocal separation of them. Later he will elaborate a whole theory of what he calls 'perspectivism' to attempt to make sense of this apparent paradox, but one can see that already in 1886 he is on the way to this and has grasped the essentially questionable nature of all assertions. Not only has he grasped this basic limit to all our thinking but he has, I think, devised a way of intimating this, albeit indirectly, to his reader. And the complex masking process which we are discussing is a powerful weapon at his disposal in this effort.

In his preface to the second volume of *Human, All-Too-Human* he emphasizes once again the suffering he underwent in his isolation and the very complicated responses he cultivated in order to retain his grip on life, the common effort of pretence, the assumption of a mask of gaiety and strength to disguise his real state. At one point, indeed, he puts his finger on the truth:

> so I forced myself, as doctor and patient in the same person, into a diametrically opposite, untried *climate of the soul*, and in particular into a journey of withdrawal to strange parts, to strangeness itself, into a new curiosity about every kind of strange thing . . . (I, 742).

It is this seeing himself as doctor and patient in one person which gives, I think, the truest insight into one of the fundamental reasons for the masking we are discussing, and it adds weight to the contention that the whole process may well have started as a sort of psychological defence-mechanism on his part. It should be noted that in the books from the central period of his life, from *Human, All-Too-Human* onwards, where there is a great emphasis on the isolation of the philosopher deprived of any answering voice, where, as we have seen, a common image of himself is that of the hermit or gold-miner, where the first part of *Human, All-Too-Human* ends with the grandiose image of the wanderer in the desert, there are also a large number of visions of a state of perfect bliss, a release from tension and worry, a calm and still experience of joy. At one moment, for instance, he speaks of the 'free spirit' still experiencing the temptation of metaphysics at rare moments of ecstasy in artistic experience, hearing Beethoven's Ninth perhaps (*Human, All-Too-Human*, vol. I, section 153; I, 548). And this whole section, subtitled 'Of the Psychology of Artists and Authors', is full of such comfort, as for instance in the long analysis of the classical ideal in art as manifest in the Greeks, in the French, and in Goethe (section 221; I, 577ff). Or often it is not art which is the comfort, but the delicious sense of pursuing the truth for its own sake. One section of this book ends with a long rhapsodic celebration of the 'path of wisdom' in which his joy bursts out:

> If so, thou hast not yet learnt that no honey is sweeter than the honey of knowledge, and that the hanging clouds of affliction must yet serve thee as an udder from which thou shalt draw the milk for thy refreshment (I, 624).

In *The Wanderer and His Shadow* a beautiful example of such visionary illusion is section 295 entitled 'Et in Arcadia ego'. It is remarkable in the use Nietzsche here makes of the visual imagination, describing in full detail a (presumably) Swiss scene, with meadows and trees bordering a lake, flowers and grass, cows in the evening light, the bull standing in a stream, two children as herdsmen, boy and girl, rocky hills and snowfields above, two icy peaks on one side, everything still and bathed in light.

> So much beauty gave rise to a shuddering amazement and to the silent worship of its momentary revelation; involuntarily, as if nothing could be more natural, one set Greek heroes into this pure and sharply delineated world of light (which knew no longing, no anticipation, no forward or backward glance); inevitably one felt as Poussin and his pupil had felt: the heroic and the idyllic were here at one (I, 993f).

And Nietzsche ends his idyllic vision with the envious assertion that men once really did live in such peace and bliss, and quotes Epicurus as an example. This is a most interesting passage. It starts with the clear assertion that Nietzsche is describing an experience of his own, and one can believe that there were occasions when such was the case, but gradually we are led to an awareness that, as so often in his works, he is indulging in a pose, seeing himself as he would like to be, and finally, with the mention of Epicurus (who is one of the eight kindred spirits mentioned in the famous 'journey to the underworld' passage, *Human, All-Too-Human*, vol. 2; I, 869f) it is clear that the whole idyllic scene was an opportunity for Nietzsche to don yet another mask. The note of bitterness at the end is a clear indication of the gap between reality and appearance.

The passages quoted, and there are many more similar ones scattered about all Nietzsche's works, are indicative of his urge to rest from himself, to escape his solitude and frustration, by constructing comforting visions of a better state. It is not denied that he did experience such states. His descriptions of the moments of insight accompanying the composition of *Zarathustra*, or his famous account of the process of inspiration in *Ecce Homo*, for instance, are abundant evidence to the contrary, ringing true as they do, if not to the facts of the matter, certainly to the mental state he is portraying. But it would seem that many of his flights in the same direction are extensions of reality, flights of fancy composed (and very carefully and consciously composed) to be a counterpoise to his innate melancholy. He is truly at such moments doctor to his own patient.

In the preface to *The Dawn of Day* he begins with a beautifully written, fanciful picture of himself as a mole, burrowing ever onwards after the truth, cut off from light and air, and one must admire the way in which the image is summoned up and developed in a very few lines. He goes on:

> Does it not seem that some faith is guiding him, some comfort recompensing him? That perhaps he *wants* to have his own long darkness, his incomprehensible, hidden, mysterious things, because he knows what he is to have in addition: his own morning, his own redemption, his own *dawn of day*? (1, 1011).

It is noteworthy that Nietzsche is fond of such animal-images, and frequently casts himself in such roles. The most obvious examples are of course the snake and the eagle, with which he makes such play in *Zarathustra* and the *Dithyrambs of Dionysus*, but there are many others. One has the feeling that they are all parts of a most complicated technique of self-projection, designed to present his own thoughts and feelings in a variety of guises, always indirectly, always with an element of make-believe which is part of, as well as being a cloak over, his intensely serious honesty of mind.

And there are a number of cases where the search for truth or self-knowledge is dramatized and presented in a highly theatrical way which amounts in the end to the donning by Nietzsche of yet another mask which we are implicitly invited to penetrate. The passage in *The Dawn of Day* entitled 'A Fable' (1, 1198) describes what Nietzsche calls the 'Don Juan of Knowledge', who has no love for the things he knows but is inspired solely by a love of the chase. He pursues his quarry to the very end, the very heights of knowledge and insight, until finally

nothing is left for him to hunt except 'the absolute *pain* of knowledge';
he is like a drinker who is finally driven to absinthe or acid, and at the
end he yearns for hell itself, since this is the last knowledge which
seduces him. And perhaps even that will disappoint him; then he
would stand for ever, a stone guest, yearning for a last supper of knowledge which will never be his, for the whole world has no crumb left
for him.

Clearly there is positive and negative here. Nietzsche is seeing himself in a glamorous role, that of the folk-hero and Mozart's hero, but
also we have the sad recognition of ultimate sterility in the image of
the stone statue. 'The chase itself, not the prize' – there is heroism and
nobility here, with an echo of Lessing's famous preference for the
search for truth over truth itself. But there is also an element of buffoonery, just as there is in the passage mentioned above likening truth
to a woman and the philosopher to a philanderer. The ambivalent
attitude to what is after all Nietzsche's dearest activity, at once glori-
fying it and at the same time making gentle fun of it, is entirely typical
of the process we are considering. Add to this the movement onwards
where the philosopher is reduced, in imagination, to the imbecilities
of a broken-down drunkard and at the end to the lifelessness of
Mozart's statue, and one can see how subtle and ambiguous is
Nietzsche's self-projection.

In the fifth book of *The Dawn of Day*, in the first section entitled 'In
the Great Silence', Nietzsche again describes a moment of total still-
ness and bliss, this time by the sea, away from the noise and disturbance of the town 'at the crossing of day and night'. But this time the
emphasis is on the silence of all. The sea cannot speak, the sky is
beautifully coloured, but it cannot speak. The cliffs and coves cannot
speak. The beauty everywhere is dumb.

Her tied tongue and the suffering joy in her countenance are a trick
to mock your sympathy! – So be it! I am not ashamed to be the butt
of such powers as these. But I do pity you, Nature, for having to
keep your silence [. . .]. Behold, it grows stiller yet, and once again
my heart swells: it shudders at a new truth, *it too cannot speak*, it joins
in the mockery when the mouth calls out something into the
midst of this beauty, it too delights in its sweet malice of silence.
Speaking, even thinking becomes abhorrent to me: for do I not
hear behind every word the laughter of error and vain imagining
and the spirit of delusion? Must I not mock my own sympathy?

Mock my mockery? – O sea! O evening! You are evil teachers! You teach man to *cease* being man! Should he abandon himself to you? Should he become as you now are, pale, glittering, dumb, vast, resting upon himself? Uplifted over himself? (I, 1219).

These final lines make typical play with the reader, summoning up a shadow-world of ambiguities, in which Nietzsche sees himself in double perspective, with every assertion containing an error or a delusion, provoking finally only derision, which itself is to be decided. This is more than the sad recognition, as we have seen it before, that the act of speaking is itself a sacrifice of truth; Nietzsche pushes his disillusion a stage further, his very thinking itself is beset with the knowledge that ultimately there is a circularity in it which must destroy it, must lead to questions which are themselves questionable. And, in this *persona*, he visualizes total silence as the only dignified posture, yet cannot escape the conviction that this negates the whole nature and drive of man, who is above all the *speaking* animal. The beauty of nature cannot communicate, man must communicate, otherwise he ceases to be human. Yet the more he tries the more he is led to the circle of self-doubt, and to the realization that all he says is self-contradictory. Seldom is Nietzsche's tragic awareness of his help-less isolation more openly and poignantly expressed than here. But we can see that the roots of his suffering do not lie simply in the ab-sence of an audience, an answering voice in his solitude, but are deeply involved in his own consciousness, his own penetration into himself. And the movement of the passage, from the sunny blissful opening to the frenzied doubt and questioning at the end, betrays the insecurity which underlies all the 'idyllic' moments of perfect ease and insight of which Nietzsche makes so much and so often.

In another of the prefaces written in 1886, that to *The Joyful Science*, Nietzsche develops a line of thought totally opposite to the various 'heroic' masks he has treated us to, of the philosopher pursuing the search for truth at all costs, coming instead to the conclusion that art, rather than truth, is his business. But the matter is not nearly so simple as it might appear, and Nietzsche's handling of the argument is worth examining. The passage opens with a grandiose picture of a man re-cuperating from a long sickness, feeling new-born, with a finer appre-ciation of all the joys of life, a new innocence, a new delight in all good things, 'at once more childlike and a hundred times more ingenious'. And the more obvious and vulgar enjoyments are now distasteful to him, the whole 'cultural' achievement of the times now seems horrible, the art of the people is so much self-indulgence. If he needs art at all, he needs a different art, delicate, light, satirical, fleeting – an art for artists, an art of 'serenity' ['Heiterkeit']. So far there is no difficulty and we can follow the line of thought easily. But at this point Nietzsche introduces a new note, with the assertion that this delicate artists' art contains the imperative of forgetting our know- ledge: 'There are some things which by now we know too well, we knowing ones: oh, how we now learn instead to forget well, to be good at *not*-knowing, as artists!' Having planted the seed, he goes off for a time to speak of Egyptian youths determined to discover the secrets of the temples, and then resumes:

> No, this bad taste, this will to truth, to 'the truth at any price', this youthful frenzy in the love of truth – it has lost all its savour for us: we are too experienced for that, too serious, too merry, too scorched, too profound. . . . We no longer believe that truth remains truth when the veils are drawn aside; we have lived too long to believe that. Today we regard it as a matter of decency not to want to see everything naked, to want to be a witness to everything, to want to understand and 'know' everything. 'Is it true that God is present everywhere?' a little girl asked her mother: 'but I think that's in- decent' – a hint for philosophers! One should have more respect for the *modesty* with which nature has concealed herself behind riddles and colourful uncertainties. Perhaps truth is a woman, who has good grounds for not disclosing her grounds? Perhaps her name is, to put it in Greek, *Baubo*? . . . Oh, those Greeks! They understood how to *live*: what is needed for that is to stop boldly at the surface, the fold, the skin, to worship appearance, to believe in forms, in tones, in words, in the whole Olympus of appearance! Those Greeks were superficial – *out of profundity*! (II, 14f).

It is not so much the sentiments expressed which are noteworthy – indeed we have seen similar things often before. The passage quoted at the beginning of this paper makes the comment about decency, and the image of truth as a woman is not uncommon in Nietzsche, while the general conclusion that it is better that certain things be not known is a familiar one. But two things are important here. First, the explicit playing-off of truth against *art* is a pointer to Nietzsche's very carefully worked-out theories of art in general which fill so much of his later works, and which are implied by the throw-away judgment of poets as liars in so many places. And second, we should watch carefully the way Nietzsche here expresses his argument, moving with reasonable logic from the notion of a return to health to the awareness of a new need, and from that, with a small joke put in to soften the blow, to the full-blooded claim that the search for truth at all costs is wrong, that is to say that all his own efforts in that direction are misconceived. Such a conclusion is clearly no more than just another pretence, and we are not taken in by it, but we have to take account of the move-ment of a mind which skips so lightly into such paradox. The Cretan who said 'All Cretans are liars' was a simple-minded child compared to the dexterity which Nietzsche exhibits here. The uncomfortable revelation that truth does not remain 'true' when it is stripped of its covering is programmatic and, of course, logically self-negating, but it is intimately bound up with the deepest recognitions of Nietzsche's thinking and gives us more grounds than ever to apply just such qualifications to all that he says of his own feeling and thinking. We can legitimately infer that the 'mask' which he continually constructs is at once a direct projection of what he feels must be kept hidden and at the same time an invitation to the reader to penetrate it, to expose what is beneath it, which of course may well be just a further mask.

The problem raised by all Nietzsche's thinking about art is the problem of sincerity, 'Wahrhaftigkeit'. All is subject to the blanket judgment: 'Poets lie too much' ['Die Dichter lügen zu viel']. And it is often seen by him in terms of play-acting. In a later passage in *The Joyful Science* (ii, 234) he treats explicitly of the nature of the actor. This, he says, has always fascinated him, and he links it to the problem of art generally.

> Falseness with a good conscience; the delight in dissimulation bursting out as a force that sweeps one's so-called 'character' aside, flooding it, at times extinguishing it; the inner craving to enter a role and a mask, to put on a *show*; a surplus of all kinds of adaptive-ness that can no longer be satisfied in the service of the most im-mediate and narrowest utility: perhaps all this defines not *only* the actor as such?

He goes on to talk about this same quality in the life of ordinary people and in such professions as the diplomatic service, ending with the general observation that the Jews have this trait in large measure, and finally, that women by their very nature are actresses every moment of their lives. The whole development is very finely balanced, with the ironic semi-humorous note dominating at the end and the reader unable to decide whether Nietzsche is approving or condemning. We can all guess at what he has in his mind – Wagner, perhaps, whom he roundly condemns on several occasions as basically a play-actor, showman and charlatan. Or perhaps, we are uneasily aware, himself. Certainly the suggestion that it is by understanding the actor that one can come to grips with the problem of art leaves no doubt that all this is very far indeed from a general condemnation.

In *Beyond Good and Evil* and the books which follow it, the habit of writing little dramatic scenes, with short dialogues, in which Nietzsche, so to speak, splits himself in two to portray more vividly his contentions, becomes more and more frequent. He has used this technique before, of course, and sometimes in a most elaborate way, as in the section of *The Joyful Science* entitled 'The Madman' (II, 126ff), where the consequences of the death (or murder) of God are theatrically demonstrated. But now such small scenes and dialogues become much more common. One of them is worth our attention (*Beyond Good and Evil*, 278):

> Wanderer, who are you? I see you go on your way, without scorn, without love, with unfathomable eyes; moist and sad as a plummet that has returned from all the depths unsated to the light – what was it seeking below? – with a breast that does not sigh, with a lip that conceals its disgust, with a hand that now grasps but slowly: who are you? what have you been doing? Take your ease here: this place makes all men welcome – refresh yourself! And whoever you may be: what is your pleasure now? What will serve to refresh you? Only name it: all that I have, I offer you! – 'To refresh me? To refresh me? Oh, you inquisitive one, what are you saying! But give me, I beg you –' What? What? Speak out! – 'Another mask! A second mask!' . . . (II, 747).

This, of course, is simply a small *jeu d'esprit*, but it is significant that once again the concept of masking is very much in Nietzsche's mind, and allied here to the familiar *persona* of the wanderer. But here there is a double perspective, since the wanderer, whose bearing and behaviour puzzles his interlocutor, explicitly unmasks himself and demands a second mask. Nietzsche could hardly reveal his essential meaning more clearly.

In *The Genealogy of Morals* the tendency to dramatize his thinking in dialogues, sometimes amounting to fairly elaborate discussions, is carried further. A good example comes in the fanciful and entertaining account (first treatise, section 14; II, 791ff) of how ideals are constructed, in which Nietzsche envisages a guide showing his visitor round the underground factory and asks him to describe what he sees, once his eyes have become accustomed to the murky light. And then, stage by stage, a mock-serious description of the process is given in the form of a dialogue between the two. The visitor speaks:

> 'Weakness is here to be twisted into a *virtue*, there can be no doubt – it is as you said' –
> – 'Go on!'
> – 'and impotence which does not retaliate into "goodness"; cowardly baseness into "humility"; submission to those whom one hates into "obedience". . . .'

and so it goes on, with the guide urging the visitor to describe the monstrous process of deceit and trickery by which all the weak and miserable qualities are transformed into blessedness and humility, until finally the visitor protests at the foul air and begs for release. The whole is a spirited attack on 'morality' and particularly on Christian notions of God and the state of humanity, but dramatized in such a way that the savagery of the indictment is associated with a satirical vision of a conveyor-belt for morals and the discomfort of foul and stinking air.

There are many self-analyses in the later books, especially in *Ecce Homo*, which decline into a shrillness and vulgarity that removes them from serious consideration, but even here there are nevertheless clear indications of the perceptiveness of Nietzsche's self-knowledge and the conscious way in which he manipulates his various *personae*. At a relatively simple level, for instance, we can see the 'self-revelation by opposites' coming clearly into focus as an effective piece of presentation in the passage in *Ecce Homo* beginning 'Apart from the fact that I am a *décadent*, I am also the opposite of one' ('Why I am so Wise', section 2). What follows is a description of the essence of decadence (always choosing what will do most harm, cultivating ill-health, and so on) but shot through with the counter-portrait of its opposite. As the passage proceeds, this second comes more and more to over-weigh the first, and the first-person narration gives place to an account in the third person. Finally, we read of the 'healthy' man:

> He believes neither in 'misfortune' nor in 'guilt': he knows how to dispose of everything, of himself and of others, he knows how to *forget*, – his strength is such that all things *must* redound to his advantage. – Very well, I am the *opposite* of a decadent: for I have just described myself (II, 1072f).

The swing from describing himself to describing a notional ideal and then abruptly in the last line, back to himself, is a highly effective piece of self-projection, enabling Nietzsche to claim all sorts of virtues, strengths, insights which he perhaps knows are not really his, but to do so without alienating the reader and forfeiting his sympathy. One can find many other examples in these later books of the same technique.

It should be emphasized that we have considered only a small number of examples in this study. Wherever one turns in Nietzsche one can find the same tendency to disguise himself while letting the reader know that what is being shown is in fact a disguise. One cannot escape the conclusion that all Nietzsche's works are 'confessional', but that his presentation of himself, of his deepest and most heart-felt emotions, is contrived in a far more ambiguous and teasing way than is commonly understood. Whether, as I believe, the whole process began in the 1870s as a defence-mechanism, a self-consolation for his loneliness and isolation, or whether it was a trick learnt perhaps from Wagner, is for our purposes immaterial. We have seen many different versions of it, from the simple adoption of a fictitious *persona* to the most complicated play with the reader, donning mask after mask, inviting us to penetrate his pretences and setting us guessing as to what lies below them.

It remains to assess the effect of all this on our understanding of his work. It is clear that his position has been so frequently misconstrued and misrepresented partly at least because his interpreters have been far too prone to take his statements at their face value. And of course by selective quotation his support can be claimed for all sorts of beliefs and opinions that are very far from his real meaning and are often absurdly contradictory. He was a great student of Pascal in whom he saw an enemy with whom it was an honour to do battle, and indeed one can detect an affinity between the two men so that when he is ostensibly fighting Pascal, it is essentially within himself that the combat lies. This comes out also, I suggest, in the manner of his self-masking, the revelation by opposites, which we have studied, and

which can be likened to what Pascal called the 'renversement con-
tinuel du pour au contre'. The dialectic which Nietzsche continually
sets up in his thinking leads to the 'perspectivism' which is the back-
bone of his final position. One can see this throughout his work, and
not least in his singling out of great figures on which to pour his
scorn and vituperation, but with which he so often betrays a more
than superficial sympathy, so much so that one can guess on many
occasions that it is himself, at the deepest level, that he is attacking.
Such figures as Rousseau, Pascal and Socrates spring to mind here.
And of course the violence of his attack on Christianity betrays a
hidden affinity with it, as on occasion he was ready to admit.

It is of immense importance, therefore, that one pay attention always not so much to what is being said as to the *tone* in which it is
uttered, to the carefully built-up tension which is created between the
ostensible meaning and the real significance. This we have studied in
a few examples, but one must have it in mind always in reading
Nietzsche. Only thus is there any hope of understanding the astounding paradoxes his thought entails. That a man should devote so much
of his strength to clearing away illusions, should strive heroically a
whole life long to rid the world of pretence and humbug in all
spheres of thinking, and should believe in the depth of his heart that
'truth' itself was an illusion, that the whole of life was founded on
illusion – this paradox has to be held close to our mind before we can
come at him. And there are many others, equally fundamental,
equally frightening. There are, of course, psychological contradictions – that such a gentle man should preach such ruthless and
authoritarian doctrines – which have been exhaustively studied and
explained. But the paradoxes I have in mind are not of this nature,
they are not a matter of a surprising gap between what the character
of the man would lead one to expect and what he actually says, rather
they are at the root of his thinking itself, internal to his mental and
emotional life not external to it. They have presented a puzzle to all
students of Nietzsche, and I suggest that a full realization of the matters discussed in this essay may go some way towards helping us to
come to terms with it. As Nietzsche himself says in *Ecce Homo* ('Why
I Write such good Books', section 1): 'I am one thing, my writings are
another'.

5

NIETZSCHE AND THE IMAGERY OF HEIGHT

F. D. Luke

In studies which, like the present one, devote particular attention to the literary devices by means of which Nietzsche expresses his philosophical thought, it is often assumed or implied that Nietzsche's achievement as a philosopher or thinker or psychologist is equalled or even excelled by his achievement as a literary artist. I should prefer it to be clear at the outset that I share neither this view nor its corollary that *Thus Spake Zarathustra* (with which we shall of course here be chiefly, though not exclusively, concerned) is his greatest or most representative work. Nietzsche is, to be sure, *sui generis* and a black sheep in any fold, whether philosophic or literary; I doubt however that his prose is at its best when it approaches the nature of poetry; he is certainly at his worst when writing verse.

Nevertheless I think that *Zarathustra*, whatever its merits and demerits as a work of literature (or for that matter as a work of philosophy), still offers some interesting possibilities of study from the point of view of the general theory of imagery and the psychology of its use; and this is especially the case if *Zarathustra* is considered against the background of Nietzsche's other more prosaic writings. In the interesting study of the language of *Zarathustra* by Michael Landmann,[1] which includes some account of Nietzsche's poetic or pseudo-poetic technique of endless self-propulsive image-association and word-association, it has been pointed out that in *Zarathustra* the linguistic devices are often not so much the means to the expression of the thought, but that the thought becomes merely the occasion for the

use of the devices, and Nietzsche's language is here, independently of
its discursive function, itself a direct expression of his metaphysics.
The Nietzschean world of Eternal Becoming is reflected in the perpetual flux of Zarathustra's word and image patterns, which are, as
Professor Landmann puts it, 'the faithful rendering of a world in
which everything glides gradually over into everything else'. Nietzsche has converted his aphoristic style into a strange, Protean music,
appealing perhaps to an infantile and archaic level of the mind which
finds perpetual movement and change intrinsically fascinating (Landmann mentions in this connection the performances of shamans or of
Mickey Mouse). It may here also be remarked that the development of
chains of verbal association based merely on sound and not on sense
(so-called 'klang-association') is recognized by psychopathologists as
a characteristic symptom of hypomanic states; thus there is a connection between Nietzsche's tendency to approach mere klang-association (often embarrassingly close, as when Zarathustra breaks into
rhyming prose in 'The Second Dance Song') and the elated, euphoric,
near-manic mood which is so important a factor in his thought and
imagery.

I wish here to concentrate on one particular language-device,
namely that which can broadly be called imagery, and, unlike Landmann, to extend the inquiry into this beyond the limits of *Zarathustra*.
There thus arises, of course, the need to apply some principle of
selection to the material to be studied. But here we are at once in a
difficulty, out of which no conventional method of classification will
help us. The associative inter-attraction of Nietzsche's images is so
strong that it is useless to try to isolate any one of them for the special
study of its function in his work as a whole. If we choose, for example,
the image of a ship or ships (or let us say, the idea or motif or theme of
sea-faring) and try to follow up Nietzsche's use of it, we soon find that
it is closely associated with the image of migrating birds (an alternative
vehicle for the idea of bold adventurous intellectual or spiritual exploration); this involves reference to a whole complex of imagery of
bird-flight and flight in general; this, with Nietzsche, is quite impossible to isolate from the ideas of dancing, climbing and the ascent of
mountains; and in any case one cannot without artificiality separate
Nietzsche's unexplored seas from his desolate wildernesses or his bold
mariners from his bold mountaineers. Similarly, the idea of height
cannot be separated from that of depth and distance and scope and
spaciousness generally. In short, Nietzsche's images must be explored

not singly, but in clusters or complexes; and the word 'height' in my title is in fact intended only as a *faute-de-mieux* designation of such a complex.

It is also of course necessary, for the reasons already pointed out by Landmann, to effect a compromise between the attempt to group Nietzsche's images according to their 'vehicles' and the attempt to do so according to their 'tenors'; no neat choice between these methods is possible. In *Zarathustra* the same image can express several ideas, or the same idea suggest a number of images; and the image often seems to be more important to Nietzsche than the idea. If we then look at his use of the same or related images in earlier works, a curious development may be observed, which is that of language passing from a more discursive into a more poetic function – of words becoming toys rather than tools. From their beginnings as occasional conventional figures of speech or straightforward similes (in the early books such as *Untimely Meditations* or *Human, All-Too-Human*) certain images attain to a status of relative prominence (in *The Joyful Science*, for example) in which Nietzsche appears to enjoy them for their own sake and to feel impelled to revert to them; and then when, in *Zarathustra*, he adopts a more decidedly 'poetic' manner and the devices of extended allegorical narrative and an allegorical spokesman, these favourite images can be used not only as metaphors but also as allegorical events or activities. Thus Nietzsche who elsewhere states 'I cannot think of anything that a philosopher's mind would rather be than a good dancer' (II, 257), also makes Zarathustra walk 'like a dancer' or invite his followers to a dance in his cave (II, 512). Or the images can operate on two levels simultaneously: thus Zarathustra declares 'In the mountains the shortest route runs from peak to peak . . . maxims should be peaks: and those to whom they are addressed should be tall and of giant stature' (II, 306) (the metaphorical level); and in addition (on the allegorical level) we find that Zarathustra himself, when he is not speaking, spends most of the time mountaineering. Or Zarathustra delivers a speech comparing mankind to 'a rope over an abyss', and as he does so an acrobat begins walking along a high tightrope. The incident is a transcription of the metaphor, introduced especially for the purpose of reinforcing Zarathustra's use of the metaphor, or perhaps indeed merely in order to give him occasion to use it (II, 281). The procedure, in this and other cases, savours strongly of artificiality. To promote a metaphor-image to the status of an allegorical event is not necessarily to effect a literary improvement. Only very occasionally is Nietzsche able to achieve authentic *poetic* language in which the image or vehicle has become virtually autonomous. More often, in *Zarathustra*, we are embarrassed by a kind of rhetorical debauch of images which did better service as prose metaphors in the aphoristic works and which tend to revert in the post-*Zarathustra* period to this more respectable role.

In the selected 'complex' of imagery which I am here roughly indicating by the word 'height' but to which all the foregoing examples belong, this process of *allegorization* can be especially clearly seen, and I have taken this as evidence that this particular imagery is *characteristically* Nietzschean – i.e. that it has a significance for him which is in some way personal and not entirely accounted for by convention (as a 'topos') or literary habit and the tendency to revert again and again to a literary trick which has already proved serviceable. Why serviceable to him, and why the habit? I think, in fact, that it may be permissible to talk not only of a cluster or 'complex' of 'height-imagery' in Nietzsche's writings but also psychologically, of a 'height complex' in Nietzsche's mind. We have only to remind ourselves of how closely and constantly the idea of 'height' associates itself, in various ways, with the most central conceptions of Nietzsche's philosophy of values, to realize that this metaphor, although commonplace and almost dead, is nevertheless a metaphor and alive enough to irritate the purely philosophic reader's demand for maximum clarity and abstractness of thought. To talk of 'ascending' or 'descending' vitality ('decadence') or of life 'raising' itself to 'higher levels' of intensity, or of 'higher' men, the superior or 'sovereign' individual, the 'super-' or 'overman', and so forth, is to use a metaphoric image – normally it is scarcely a live metaphor at all, but Nietzsche makes frequent determined attempts to galvanize it into life. In the light of these attempts (chiefly, but not only, in *Zarathustra*) we are inclined to look afresh at the metaphoric element in many of his more abstract trains of thought. His violent repudiation, for instance, of all forms of egalitarianism, of the principle of distributive utility and utilitarian ethics in general, of any principle or ideal (whether socialistic and humanitarian or Christian and theological) that would tend to 'level out' mankind – all this, if visualized, suggests a scenery of vast dramatic contrasts: it is, as it were, a bathy-orographical vision. Mankind, or what Nietzsche more abstractly calls 'the human type', is to be valued not by any average of achievement but solely by the great exceptions, 'the highest specimens' – as an artist's stature is judged by his greatest works or the height of a mountain-range by its highest peaks. Human life can remain significant after the 'death of God' only by aspiring to ever loftier summits of proud and astounding distinction. When we consider the world of Nietzsche's thought, the idea of a mountain-landscape easily suggests itself; and not only because he lived at Sils-Maria and wrote part of *Zarathustra* there. In any case, mountain-imagery is only one element in the 'height' or 'height-depth' complex. Let us consider, as a further example of how closely this complex is associated with Nietzsche's leading doctrines on human culture, the very revealing aphorism from *The Joyful Science* entitled 'Hohe Stimmungen' ['Elevated Moods'] (II, 167f). Nietzsche here refers to certain states of intellectual elation, peaks of self-confidence, 'hohes Gefühl' ['elevated feeling'] – moods which are all too rare and transitory even in the elite of today, but which represent to him the possibility that at some time in the future, when more favourable cultural and eugenic conditions have been created, men will be born in whom this ecstasy will be a normal and constant experience: 'the man of a single high feeling, the embodiment of one unitary grand mood. . . .' This is, of course, one among a number of preformations of the 'superman' conception in Nietzsche's aphoristic and earlier works, though the word 'Übermensch' does not seem to occur before *Zarathustra*. According to Hans M. Wolff in his illuminating study of Nietzsche's thought,[2] Nietzsche is in this aphorism not only expressing the essence of the 'superman' idea, but also – by implication though not by direct reference – relating it to his other central doctrine, that of the eternal recurrence of all things: inasmuch as it is precisely the recognition of life's perpetual recurrence that creates an inescapable alternative of absolute despair or superhuman elation, and so the necessity of clinging to the latter in order to avoid the former. If this interpretation is correct (and it is in any case true, as we shall see, that Nietzsche elsewhere appears to define the superman as the being who can endure the thought of eternal recurrence) then the aphorism we are considering is doubly at the centre of Nietzsche's thought: and whether or not this is so, it is evident that Nietzsche attaches great theoretical importance to the 'elevated mood' which he describes at the end of the aphorism with (and this is the point to which I wish to draw attention) the following imagery: 'a perpetual movement between high and low, and the sensation of high and low, a continual feeling that one is climbing stairs and at the same time resting on clouds.'

It is difficult to read this passage without suspecting that the exhilarated euphoric state here described (evidently the manic phase of a manic-depressive temperament, both aspects of which are later fully expressed in *Zarathustra*) is an experience upon or around which much of Nietzsche's metaphysics, ethics and metabiology is built up. And what of the images – height and depth, stair-climbing and cloud-like hovering – by means of which he feels he can best evoke this experience, and which are all embodied later in Zarathustra's allegorical activities? When we reflect that in the language of dreams 'stair-climbing' and 'floating in the air' have been found to be common ideational equivalents of sexual excitement, we must acknowledge that, despite Nietzsche's own occasional recognition of an erotic element in the 'Dionysian' euphoria,[3] there must have existed in his thought a level of association and fantasy of which he was himself quite unconscious.

To confirm this we have his own remarks on his own frequent dreams about flying and hovering. In a long aphorism of *The Dawn of Day* in which he attempts to develop a neurological theory of human instincts, and suggests (anticipating Freud to some extent) that the function of dreams is to provide partial compensation for the frustration suffered by one or more of the sleeper's instinctive wishes during the day, Nietzsche cites his own dreams by way of examples: 'Why do I, in one dream, enjoy music of inexpressible beauty, why in another do I *hover and soar with an eagle's delight towards distant mountain peaks*?' (I, 1094; my italics). Nietzsche never advanced very far towards a Freudian metapsychology or *Trieblehre*, and his formulations tend to cling to physiological assumptions now outdated, but he possessed a degree of intuitive self-knowledge which made possible not only the famous aperçu of *Beyond Good and Evil* 'the degree and nature of a man's sexuality reaches up into the loftiest peak of his mind' (II, 626), but also enabled him to recognize a similar pervasiveness in what, in another very important aphorism from the same book, he calls our 'dream-habits': 'Quidquid luce fuit, tenebris agit: but also the other way round', he begins, and goes on to suggest that our dream-experiences are an essential factor in our total psychic economy – we are 'guided a little, in broad daylight and even in the clearest moments of our waking thought, by the leading-strings of our dream-habits'. And, once again, he refers to his own dreams of flying, this time as *habitual*, deeply satisfying and deeply influential personal experiences:

Suppose someone has often flown in his dreams, so that finally as soon as he starts dreaming he becomes conscious of a power and art of flight as if it were his special privilege, and his most personal and enviable form of happiness: someone confident of being able on the slightest impulse to describe any kind of arc or turn, who knows that particular sensation of a divine levity, that movement 'upwards' without tension or constraint, or 'downwards' without condescension or abasement – without *heaviness*! – would not a man with such dream-experiences and dream-habits be bound in the end to find that the word 'happiness' had a different colour and definition in his waking hours too? Would he not have a *different* kind of – desire for happiness? 'Elation' as the poets describe it must seem to him, by comparison with such 'flight', still too earthbound, muscular, strenuous, still; too 'heavy' (II, 651).

To the above quotations we need only add the following from as early a work as *Human, All-Too-Human*:

The man who has grown tired of play, and has no new needs and therefore no reason to work, is sometimes seized with longing for a third condition which stands in the same relation to play as hovering to dancing, as dancing to walking – longing for a blissful, calm mobility; this is, for artists and philosophers, the vision of happiness (I, 716; cf. CM, vii, 55).

and with this example of Nietzsche's use (here in a simile) of the motif of dancing (and of how, as so often, he thinks of it as one of a progressive series of locomotive achievements culminating in flight) we have completed the list of the main elements in what I am here trying to exhibit as an essentially indivisible complex of ideas, prominent in his literary imagination, rooted partly at least in his unconscious desires (as 'for artists and philosophers, the vision of happiness'), and having a strong influence on the development of his more abstract thought. These inter-associated ideas or images include, as we have seen, (1) climbing in general and mountain-climbing in particular; (2) flying and hovering, and in particular the flight of birds; (3) leaping and dancing. Of these activities, 1 and 2 are specifically mentioned by Nietzsche as having been manifest-contents of his dreams, and this in itself is sufficient to establish them as ideas of personal psychic importance to him. There is strong presumption that he also dreamt of dancing, at least in so far as the phrase 'being able to describe any kind of arc or turn on the slightest impulse' may be interpreted as referring to the sense (often experienced in dreams) of being able to take immense flying strides in easy defiance of gravity ['ohne Schwere']. The folklore equivalent of this fantasy is of course the possession of seven-league boots, which would make one's legs long enough to leap (as Zara-thustra demands) 'from summit to summit'.

To this basic list (climbing, flying and dancing) it is necessary to add the following secondary or subsidiary elements: (4) seafaring, as al-ready mentioned; (5) the attainment of exceptional height by *growth* (aristocratic tall stature) ['Hochwüchsigkeit'], tall trees with deep roots, tall mountains rising from deep seas); and perhaps also (6) the height of the sky and the stars, and the ascent and descent of the sun. The inadequacy of the description 'imagery of height' grows clearer as we consider all these features, which include horizontal as well as upward and downward movement – the complex suggests, in fact, a sense of vast freedom and *scope*, in any direction. Moreover, although these images are not all kinetic, the idea of height as a *state* is less prominent than that of *ascent* to a height. In my supposition that this literary 'complex' is not merely (though of course partly) a matter of the proliferative power of inter-associating words and convenient clichés, but that a consistent psychological tendency underlies it, I have been emboldened by finding that precisely such a psychological 'complex' was some years ago postulated for study by an American clinical psychologist in a quite non-literary context – though Nietz-sche's *Zarathustra*, significantly enough, is mentioned in passing as a parallel literary example. I refer to a paper entitled 'American Icarus' by Professor H. A. Murray of Harvard, which is a report on the case-history of a Harvard undergraduate.[4] The author describes and names a psychic complex or 'constellation' which he considers to be not only an influential factor in the latent personality of the subject of the report, but also a fairly common psychic pattern: it consists of

> the wish to overcome gravity, to stand erect, to grow tall, to dance on tip-toe, to walk on water, to leap or swing in the air, to climb, to rise, to fly, or to float down gradually from on high and land without injury, not to speak of rising from the dead and ascending to heaven.

This may also take 'emotional and ideational forms' such as

> passionate enthusiasm, rapid elevations of confidence, flights of the imagination, exultation, inflation of spirits, ecstatic mystical up-reachings, poetical and religious. . . . The upward thrust of desire may also manifest itself in the cathection of tall pillars and towers,

of high peaks and mountains, of birds – high-flying hawks and eagles – and of the heavenly bodies, especially the sun.

For convenient reference to the totality of these tendencies, Murray proposes the term *ascensionism*; and although I have preferred to avoid this expression in my title, it would be true to say that what I am attempting to do here is to give some account of the 'ascensionist' element in Nietzsche's imagery. As a more picturesque alternative to 'ascensionism' Murray also uses the phrase 'Icarus complex'. In the present setting it might be more appropriate to talk of a 'Euphorion complex'. This designation not only suggests the more or less pathologically euphoric character of the moods which Nietzsche's ascensionist imagery usually expresses, but will serve to remind us that his use of such imagery is also partly a matter of literary tradition and not unconnected, perhaps, with his admiration for Goethe's *Faust*, allusions to which and quotations from which are scattered throughout his works. Faust himself, it will be remembered, is frequently either flying through the air or expressing a desire to do so, and his euphoric son is a boy who grows up very quickly, dances and leaps, climbs up precipices, and finally perishes in the attempt to launch himself like a glider. The fantasy of light-footed leaping transforming itself into flight is extremely prominent in Nietzsche's euphoric imagery; Zarathustra evidently succeeds where Icarus and Euphorion failed: 'Zarathustra the dancer, Zarathustra the light, he who beckons with his wings, poised to fly, beckoning to all the birds, poised and ready, blessed in the ease of his levity' [ein Selig-Leichtfertiger'] (II, 530). And indeed, the study of *Zarathustra* shows that if, within the complex of imagery we are here considering (whether we call it imagery of height, ascensionist imagery, or perhaps imagery of elation) any one image occupies a leading or central place, it is that of flight. For Nietzsche the idea of flight is evidently a culmination and meeting-place of several different lines of associative development, an idea which he has approached from several different directions and which he finds peculiarly satisfying. Flight is an activity of which the dancer, seafarer and mountaineer have always unwittingly been in search: 'And all my wandering and mountaineering: it has been sheer necessity and a crutch for my clumsiness – all that my whole will wills is *to fly* . . .' (II, 415).

The detailed analysis of which I am here giving a necessarily rather compressed report has the aim of exploring the relations and associations between the flight-image and the other (in a sense subsidiary) elements in this height, height-and-depth, or height-and-motion complex; it attempts to show in what ways these images are represented in Nietzsche's work as a whole, to what tenors they are related as vehicles at different times, and to what extent and in what contexts they take on a more personal (as distinct from merely conventional) character. The analysis operates partly on what may be called vehicle-level, in a manner analogous to an account of the recurrences, developments and inter-relations of themes or motifs in music; and partly on tenor-level where it bears upon the interpretation of some of Nietzsche's philosophical or moral ideas. In what follows, it has been necessary in the present compass to forgo a detailed presentation of the material, and I must confine myself to summarizing a few results. For convenience of exposition I shall deal with mountain and climbing imagery first, and then go on to imagery of leaping, dancing, and flying.

As constantly recurring elements in Nietzsche's presentation of the theme of mountains we may distinguish (1) the idea of pure, rarefied, stimulating, uncontaminated *mountain air*, and (2) that of the wide *view from the mountain-tops*; both these being connected with (3) the idea of an *aristocratic élite* living 'on the heights'. This in its turn gives rise to the secondary motif of (4) *descent* from the heights. Finally (5), it is to be noted that an especially characteristic use of climbing and mountain imagery occurs in association with Nietzsche's doctrine of the need for *self-exploration, self-creation and self-transcendence* ['Selbstüberwindung'].

In connection with (1) and (2) it is noticeable that in the earlier Nietzsche the emphasis tends to fall on a strictly *scientific* ideal: the pure Alpine air signifies the absence of befogging illusions (1, 325), the mountains are 'mountains of truth' ['Gebirge der Wahrheit'] and the task of the sage is simply to climb up and up (1, 861, 873). In the later Nietzsche scientific truth ceases to be an absolute value. The images, however, of the 'Höhenluft' ('mountain air', as the atmosphere proper to the intellectual élite) and of the vast 'open view' or 'distant view' ['Freiblick', 'Fernblick'] of the philosopher, remain till the end (cf. for example the chapters 'Of the Rabble' and 'On the Mount of Olives' in *Zarathustra*, the aphorism 'Our Air' in *The Joyful Science* (II, 171f) and certain passages in *Ecce Homo* (II, 1066, 1134)).

It is interesting to observe that the elated élite of the heights – 'elevated' ['erhoben'], 'superior' ['vornehm'], 'a higher, brighter humanity' (III, 461) – are conceived as a class but do not form a community. The 'friends' invoked by Zarathustra in 'Of the Rabble' are a rhetorical fiction; he is essentially unrelated to anyone. But his attitude to solitude is ambivalent: he alternates between withdrawal into ever more rarefied seclusion, and the desire to have at least a pedagogic contact with mere mankind – to 'descend' into the valleys, like an overflowing sun descending into the sea (his mountain sometimes appears to be an island) – or to attract visitors up to his summit. And yet when the visitors come (*Zarathustra*, Part IV; cf. also the poem 'On High Mountains')[5] they are allegorical repudiation-figures, received only to be derided.

Versions of the idea (5) of 'climbing up to oneself by climbing above oneself' may be found in the early work (I, 290), but it is more characteristic of Nietzsche's later pragmatism or existentialism, which (to put the matter very briefly and crudely) subordinates 'knowledge' to 'life'. When the stoic 'freethinker' or 'wanderer', has become transformed into 'Zarathustra', 'knowledge' is sought not as an end, but 'in order that the superman may one day come into being' (II, 282). The supreme task is the discovery of personal truths, of 'one's own' truth – the creative, transforming exploration and indeed *invention* of the personal self. This task is conceived also as an enrichment of culture in general, a discovery of new human values and a 'heightening' of the human type; it is a deeply individual and yet more than individual matter: the species as a whole, 'Life' itself is involved: 'to rise, and in rising to overcome itself, is the will of *Life*' (II, 359). Climbing is the usual metaphor, though we occasionally encounter that of ripening fruit, and frequently of course that of *growth*. Here the process is dialectical: for 'the human plant' (III, 468) to be bred tall, his roots must strike deep: 'what is highest must come to its height from the lowest depths' (II, 405; cf. also II, 307 ('Mankind is like a tree . . .' etc.) and III, 520 ('With every increase in man's stature . . .' etc.)). This idea (the height-depth or ascent-descent paradox) is prominent in the important chapter 'The Wanderer' in which Zarathustra meditates about self-transcendence while climbing a sea-surrounded mountain. There is here no longer the simple positivistic ascent to enlightenment: Zarathustra must discover 'his own summits' before he can gaze down into the abyss of truth; he must go down into the darkest suffering before he can reach the heights of his real self and view 'the ground and background of all things'. This 'self-seeking' ['Selbstsucht'], then, is no naïve or uncomplicated egoism: as well as euphoric self-affirmation it contains an element of tragedy and sacrifice. The chapter 'The Wanderer' fully reflects a tragic, manic-depressive temperament in bathy-orographical imagery.

The idea of self-transcendence also enters into the complex of ideas associated with imagery of light-footed leaping, dancing, soaring and flying, though not so prominently as in the case of climbing-imagery. The chief theme here is that of the bold, free, rapid and exhilarated movement of the creative philosophic intellect. Both in earlier and later work, Nietzsche never tires of reverting to the comparison between the light-footed intuitive genius and the timid-stepping pedant, the intellectually air-borne and the intellectually earth-bound (e.g. I, 187f) – between those who can dance or fly and those who can merely crawl or flutter (like bats or butterflies, as contrasted with birds of prey) (I, 325, 338, 745, 747 'bat-like souls') or who have lost their capacity for exhilaration and aspiration (II, 309, 428). Light-footedness becomes for him a divine attribute and clumsy-footedness a favourite term of abuse, especially for the Germans, who have 'actually no feet at all, they have only legs' and who have not learnt 'the art of dancing with one's feet, with one's concepts, with one's words' (II, 988). There is, as I have already mentioned, often a *series* of locomotive achievements to be learnt progressively: standing, walking, running, leaping, climbing, flying (II, 442)-and flight is always the most impressive accomplishment, the most expressive image. Those who can still only climb envy bitterly those who have learnt to fly (II, 308, 327). One wonders whether something of the immense psychic importance, during early childhood, of the processes of learning to stand and walk had not remained in Nietzsche's mind as an unconscious determinant of his choice of imagery.

In accordance with this conception of flight as the culmination of the series, there is a tendency in the imagery to replace mountain-climbing (as well as dancing) by flying – the tenor remaining the same: thus instead of 'Fernblick' ['vista'] we have 'Vogelumblick' ['bird's-eye view'] (I, 441) or (with a characteristic wordplay) 'Vogelschau' (meaning also the prophetic view drawn from augury) (III, 690); similarly, the idea of 'Höhenluft' becomes detached from that of mountains and associated with bird-flight, or the mountain air is a stimulus to flight (II, 172, 849f). Nietzsche also sometimes includes the idea of a *transformation* of climbing into flight in the imagery itself. We have already noticed that the dancer, like Euphorion, is an incipient Icarus; but so, too, is the mountaineer. In 'Of the Rabble' Zarathustra finds his laborious climbing ('painfully my spirit ascended steps') miraculously transformed into flight which carries him to the summit: wings have sprouted from his 'disgust': the Wanderer has become the Bird.

He was, as a matter of fact, already 'Prinz Vogelfrei' before he became Zarathustra. This untranslatable pun – a stroke of genius – condenses the idea of aristocratic immoralism ('Prince Outlaw') with that of a bird's complete detached mobility, its freedom to move at any moment in any direction. These motifs, and that of the bird's-eye view, are prominent in the 1886 prefaces and preface-sketches (cf. I, 441, 742, etc.), and the bird as a symbol of emancipation from traditional values occurs in *Human, All-Too-Human* (e.g. I, 473) as well as in *The Joyful Science* (e.g. II, 173), as an appendix to which the 'Prinz Vogelfrei' poems were reprinted (having already appeared as 'Idylls from Messina'). In one of these poems (II, 263) we again have the theme of bird-flight being *learnt* as a supreme, and un-German, achievement; and in addition, the theme of bird-flight *across the sea*. It must here again be mentioned in passing that the Seafarer is another prominent variant of Nietzsche's Wanderer (cf. I, 1224; II, 166, 168, 362, 410; III, 478, etc.); and it is to be noticed that migrant birds easily serve him as an alternative for questing ships (see for example the concluding aphorism of *The Dawn of Day*[6]). Ships, too, become birds; sea-faring is yet another apprenticeship to the final conquest of gravity.

The Nietzschean bird *par excellence*, however, is not one of a migrating flock, but the large proud solitary bird of prey, flying usually over mountains, a free and sublime observer, able to reach and maintain vast heights and gaze piercingly into vast depths; fierce and rapacious, like a Renaissance prince or a blond 'Raubtier'; in fact, the eagle. It is no accident that Zarathustra is accompanied by one; with lions and eagles he is equally at home, and he shares the appetite of the latter for 'the flesh of lambs' (II, 439; cf. 534f and 789). Nietzsche not only compares the qualities of the free thinker to those which he attributes to savage animals, but also derives the former from the latter by way of sublimation; intellectual 'courage', for example (II, 538). The eagle braves the terrible solitude of the emancipated spirit, it scorns to fly in company (III, 562). It is the motif of 'courage', combined with that of piercing vision from a height, that leads Nietzsche to his most significant use of the eagle-image:

Courage also annihilates all vertigo at the abyss . . . like the eagle

who gazes long, long and fixedly into abysses, into *his* abysses . . .
You are no eagles: . . . and whoever is not a bird should not lodge
over abysses . . . Whoever sees the abyss, but with eagle's eyes –
whoever *seizes* the abyss with eagle's claws: that man has courage
(II, 407, 534f, 362, 524).

This association of the eagle with the 'abyss' is a significant parallel
to the coupling of high mountains with deep seas, tall trees with deep
roots, etc. The 'abyss' in its most typical uses, represents the dark and
tragic element that haunts Nietzsche's conception of knowledge:
'where could man ever stand save on the brink of abysses? Is not the
very act of seeing – the seeing of abysses?' (II, 407). This element is also
represented, in certain passages of Zarathustra, by the image of a
black snake: the snake is thus associated with the abyss, and this, I
think, casts additional light on the choice of a snake as the second of
Zarathustra's two animals, the eagle of the heights and the snake of
the depths[7] (though this aspect of the snake is not, in fact, made
explicit in the context of its function as Zarathustra's companion).
The 'black snake' or 'abysmal snake' passages to which I refer are both
connected with the theme of the eternal recurrence, the thought to
which Nietzsche reacts with manic-depressive ambivalence. The snake
('a black heavy snake', 'eine schwarze schwere Schlange') crawling
into the sleeping shepherd-boy's mouth (in the chapter 'Of the Vision
and the Riddle') represents (as we learn in the chapter 'The Convalescent') the horror of this thought ('the most abysmal thought')
entering Zarathustra's mind, and the action of the boy in biting off the
snake's head represents the superman's supreme conquest of 'the
nausea of knowledge', of the 'abysmal' truth. There is an explanatory
paralipomenon to *Zarathustra* in which the following words contain the
whole ambivalent programme of Nietzsche's philosophy: 'We have
created the heaviest thought – let us now create beings for whom this
thought is light and blissful.'[8] The vision here is of a mind and personality in which the maximum positive valuation of life is synthe-
sized with the maximum tragic nihilistic insight – the latter constantly
endangering and thus constantly compelling the euphoric affirmation. The shepherd, transformed after biting off the snake's head,[9] is
a personification of this triumphant synthesis, which at other times
Nietzsche identifies with the superman or with Zarathustra himself,
or with the god Dionysus – different names of a being who exists
simply to meet the challenge offered by the truth to the possibility of

his existence. In Nietzsche's descriptions of this being, height-depth imagery is frequent, and we also encounter a further significant use of the image of dancing, which here appears in association with the idea of a difficult achievement – the conquest of nihilism, the 'trotzdem' or 'defiant assertion'. We are prepared for this use by the many passages in Nietzsche's works in which the dance is presented not as mere light-footed leaping in preparation for flight, but as a highly skilled acrobatic feat.[10] I must omit detailed discussion of the examples here, and shall merely mention that Nietzsche more than once uses the idea of *dancing in chains*, for which he also characteristically supplies a flight-imagery equivalent (flying with weighted wings) (I, 932; II, 690 (here also sword-dancing); I, 1239, etc.); and that we also more than once encounter the tightrope-walker ['Seiltänzer']; who is of course the dance-imagery equivalent of the eagle poised over the abyss (II, 213, 710, and the episode of the acrobats in the Prologue to *Zarathustra*).

In *Zarathustra* and other later works, with the increasing emergence of the euphoric element, Nietzsche lays less and less emphasis on the theme of *difficulty* (as represented in the earlier dancing, flying and mountaineering imagery) and insists more and more on that of godlike ease, 'die göttliche Leichtigkeit, Leichtfertigkeit im Schwersten' (III, 441). This is one of the essential differences between Zarathustra and the earlier 'free-thinker'. *Zarathustra's raison d'être*, his programme, is to be 'the creature for whom the heaviest thought is *light and blissful*'. Heroism is not enough, sublimity must become grace, mastery must become child's play, the camel and the lion must become the divine child (cf. the chapter 'Of the Three Transformations'). Ease is divine, lightfootedness is divine; to be a god is to be lightfooted, as Zarathustra remarks in the chapter 'Of Reading and Writing' – 'I would only believe in a god who knew how to dance'. In developing this theme Nietzsche makes characteristic play with the double meanings of the German words *leicht* and *schwer*, and in particular he evolves the highly significant (and untranslatable) concept 'der Geist der *Schwere*'[11] – Zarathustra's arch-enemy, the negative counterpart of the dancing god, the personification of the depressive phase – the Spirit of Heaviness, of Difficulty, of Gravity: and here 'gravity' must be understood not only as *Schwerkraft* but also as the opposite of 'levity', which is an essential element of Nietzsche's conception. It is at this point that his imagery of ascending motion directly rejoins the euphoric mood. In 'Of Reading and Writing' we read: 'Not by wrath does one destroy, but by *laughter*. Come then, let us destroy the Spirit of Heaviness!'

When the shepherd-boy in Zarathustra's vision spits out the head of the snake – the dark, heavy, 'abysmallest' thought – he laughs, and it is this laughter that transforms him into a god or superman: 'no longer a man, one transformed, one transfigured ['ein Umleuchteter'], who *laughed*'. This vision – the Nietzschean counterpart to the story of the transfiguration of Jesus – follows immediately upon Zarathustra's dialogue with the Spirit of Heaviness (his 'devil') personified as a mole-like dwarf who sits on his shoulder and mocks his ascent with allusions to Newton's law. Zarathustra defies him, invoking the 'courage that can kill vertigo at the edge of abysses', and goes on to expound the 'abysmallest thought' (the eternal recurrence); he then tells the story of the shepherd, and comments: 'my longing for this laughter gnaws at me'. The sequence of thought is essentially the same as in 'Of Reading and Writing', where for instance the aristocratic levity is described as follows:

> I look down, because I am exalted. Who among you can laugh and be exalted at once? He who climbs upon the highest mountains laughs at all tragedies, tragic plays and tragic realities ['Trauer-Spiele und Trauer-Ernste'].

In fact, the whole complex of ideas and images here under consideration is largely anticipated in this important earlier chapter. The way in which this whole complex is related to the image of the *eagle* is now clear: to have courage is to defy the macabre tragedy of life, to laugh at the Abyss, to achieve levity and overcome Gravity, to conquer the snake, to be raised up like an eagle, to hover effortlessly, to dance lightly through the sky like a god.

An essential element in this condition is what Nietzsche calls self-love – 'He who would be light and as a bird must love himself: this is *my* teaching' (II, 440). The implication is that a true pagan delight in the self, owing to the prevailing debilitating Christian ideal of self-denial, has become something difficult to learn: a discipline of self-emancipation from established values is necessary for the achievement of true egoism, 'hale, healthy self-seeking': but to the euphoric Zarathustra this too has become blessed ease, for he is 'the elastic persuasive physique, the dancer, whose likeness and distillation is the self-delighting soul' (II, 438).

In the concluding perorations of Part IV ('Of the Higher Man')

Zarathustra's vision of pagan joy is expressly associated with his repudiation of Christianity as a morbid plebeian religion of self-denying gloom. Jesus, he declares, was the enemy of laughter ('Woe to those who laugh here!'): such fanatics have heavy feet, do not know how to dance, do not understand the lightness of the earth; but the light-footed can dance even over quagmires of 'Schwermut' and sloughs of despond. Zarathustra, the high of head and light of heart, recognizes no authority above himself. He is his own value-giver and self-consecrator: 'I myself placed this crown upon my head, I myself consecrated my laughter.' This speech contains the repeated exhortation to his disciples: 'Lift up your hearts, my brothers, high, higher! And forget not your legs!'

Dancing is here no longer merely a metaphor in Zarathustra's utterances, but also a real activity with significance on the more general level of the allegory. Like climbing, it now embodies the theme of self-transcendence and the creation of human value: 'not one of you has learnt how to dance as one should dance – how to dance out and away beyond yourselves! What does it matter that *you* miscarried? How much is still possible!' And laughter, the sacred laughter, is now plainly identified with dancing as a mode of locomotion:

> Learn then, how to laugh out and away beyond yourselves! Lift up your hearts, you good dancers, high, higher! And forget not the right laughter! . . . You higher men, I say to you, learn how to laugh![12]

It is pointed out by Karl Schlechta 'that talking about laughter does not amount to actually laughing; nor does feeling it to be one's duty to talk about laughter' (III, 1447). Nietzsche's thought (as Wolff, Schlechta and others have shown) is inescapably nihilistic, its positive 'life-affirming' superstructure strained and hysterical. A self-critical sense of the ludicrous does not appear to have been part – or at least, not a well-functioning part – of his mental equipment, despite all his protestations about learning to laugh and even (as, for instance, in the first aphorism of *The Joyful Science*) about learning to laugh at oneself. The unfortunate combination, in Nietzsche's case, has been described by Thomas Mann in his essay on Nietzsche (*Neue Studien*, pp. 111f) as 'ghastly facetiousness' and 'embarassing would-be humour'. A sense of embarrassment marks the sensitive reader's perception of a pathological quality in this humourless Zarathustra-euphoria or verbal mania - his perception of Nietzsche's own *lack* of perception of this quality. The creative mind cannot, indeed, be expected to be excessively self-analytical, and Nietzsche, no doubt, if certain things had not remained unconscious and inaccessible to his passionate introspection, would neither have dreamed his nightly dreams of flying 'like an eagle, towards distant peaks', nor seen his central vision of a 'higher' humanity, poised eagle-like and triumphant above the abyss of despair. The present-day reader, however, aware of the phallic significance of such images as climbing and dancing and flying and hovering and birds and (in many contexts) snakes, and aware also of certain literary developments in the generation or two since Nietzsche, must be inclined to reflect more than fleetingly, even when reading *Zarathustra*, on the tendency of humanism-turned-vitalism to move to its logical conclusion as phallus-worship (witness Hauptmann, Rilke, Lawrence and others).[13] Is there not an element of primitive castration-fear (the secret weakness of Thomas Mann's phallic daemon Peeperkorn) in Nietzsche's shrill protesting demand for fullblooded life and unemasculated thought? The Freudian analysts have shown that phallic significance (and consequently castration-fear) can attach itself to even something so incorporeal as the intellect – to the erect head, the shameless penetrating activity, the jealously guarded human (and especially masculine) prerogative, of which Christianity demands the *sacrificium*. In what light is 'the free spirit' here revealed?[14]

The question, however, of the extent to which one may justly base a negative assessment of a writer on the unconscious aspects or potentialities of his work, is even more difficult to answer than the question of how much blame should be attached to Nietzsche for his adoption by Nazi ideologists. The sympathetic reader will wish to end by forgetting the psychological as well as the political approach to Nietzsche, remembering instead the rich stimulation of his thought, its value as a corrective or even as a negative object-lesson, and the occasional splendour of his imaginative apprehension. 'We must have chaos within us, if we are to give birth to a dancing star' (II, 284).

NOTES

1 Michael Landmann, 'Zum Stil des Zarathustra', in *Geist und Leben* (Bonn, 1951); originally published in *Trivium*, no. 2 (1944).

2 Hans M. Wolff, *Nietzsche. Der Weg zum Nichts* (Bern, 1956).

3 Cf. for example the descriptions in III, 755f (where Nietzsche also draws attention to the interassociative character of his own imagery), and III, 785.

4 Published in *Clinical Studies in Personality* (edited by A. Burton and R. E. Harris, New York, 1955), pp. 615–41.

5 In this poem (II, 757ff), which was written at about the same time as *Zarathustra*, Part IV (1884–5), honey is mentioned as an enticing item of the solitary mountaineer's intellectual fare; cf. the first chapter of Part IV ('The Honey Offering') in which Zarathustra, fishing for men, baits his hook with honey. A variation on the theme of fishing from a sea-surrounded mountain appears in the *Dithyrambs of Dionysus* (II, 1253). Nietzsche's rather frequent and personal use of imagery concerned with sweetmeats and other foodstuffs, eating, drinking, swallowing and being swallowed, sucking, biting, chewing, voracious animals, etc., is perhaps matter in itself for a separate study. This might be described as an 'oral' category of imagery, as distinct from the 'phallic' category which I am considering here.

6 I, 1279; cf. also the sequence of imagery in the last three sections of the chapter, 'The Seven Seals' in *Zarathustra*.

7 Cf. also the phrase 'this man's-courage with eagle-wings and snake-wisdom' (II, 538). The legendary 'wisdom' of snakes is no doubt connected with the phallic significance both of snakes and of the intellect itself (cf. the sexual meanings of words such as 'knowledge' and 'Erkenntnis').

8 *Werke* (Taschenausgabe, Leipzig, 1906), vol. VII, p. 487. This posthumous note also explains the relationship between the story of the shepherd and the chapter 'The Convalescent' ('Suddenly the terrible chamber of truth is opened . . . the calling-up of truth out of the grave', etc).

9 In view of the phallic significance of snakes, there is possibly some unconscious echo here of primitive phallo-phagic practices designed to incorporate the strength or manhood of a defeated enemy.

10 An important early use of the dance-image in this sense is the aphorism 'Parable of the Dance' (I, 617f) in which dancing stands for the synthesis of scientific and aesthetic values.

11 Cf. a slightly different but revealing use of this phrase in a posthumous passage (III, 794); also the phrase 'specific gravity' in II, 255.

12 The laughter-theme undergoes a further development in Book IV when, turning the wheel of his associations full cycle ('laughter – courage – dancing – flight above abysses – eagle – bird of prey – beast of prey') Nietzsche arrives (II 519) at the fantasy of the 'laughing lion'. This image is both more extravagant and more personal than those of the courageous eagle and the wise snake; it is translated into allegorical narrative in the final chapter ('The Sign').

13 Illuminating remarks on the phallic element in modern literary religiosity, are to be found in E. C. Mason's *Der Zopf des Münchhausen* (Einsiedeln, 1949). In this connection Thomas Mann's emphasis on the concealed erotic element in Schopenhauer's philosophy (*Adel des Geistes*, p. 374, etc.) is also interesting. Although Nietzsche differentiates himself with so much fuss from Schopenhauer, their philosophies are basically similar: it is merely that Schopenhauer's vitalism is negative, Nietzsche's positive or would-be positive. An ambivalent coexistence of nihilism and euphoria is perhaps an inherent tendency of vitalistic and naturalistic systems. Even Goethe, as Mason points out, gave indications that he thought Mephistopheles was perhaps right after all. D. H. Lawrence was content with the 'pointlessness' of the cosmic 'natural curve' (*Letters*, edited by A. Huxley, Harmondsworth, 1954, p. 15).

14 The possession or assertion of phallic attributes (wings, seven-league boots, *esprit fort*, etc.) is probably to be regarded as compensatory to a repudiated view of oneself as small and weak (impotent, castrated, infantile).

6

NIETZSCHE'S USE OF MEDICAL TERMS

Malcolm Pasley

I

The overriding concern of Nietzsche's early years was to offer an effective critique of the culture of his day, in the hope of contributing to its improvement. He first turned his guns on that aspect of German culture which he knew best, the educational system, in particular the way in which the classics were studied in grammar schools and universities. He deplored both the lack of aesthetic sensitivity and the absence of any vigorous, unified, inspiring philosophic vision: the academic world seemed to him dominated by blinkered professionalism, undiscriminating fact-worship, and small-mindedness generally (cf. his *Introduction to the Study of Classical Philology* and *On the Future of our Educational Institutions*). And when he looked beyond the academic walls at other cultural institutions and at social manners, he was only confirmed in his view that he was living in a 'Pseudokultur' (III, 258), whose forms were borrowed garments covering an inner emptiness rather than the product of lively culture-forming drives or needs. The typical specimen of this pseudo-culture was not the truly cultivated man, but the 'degenerate man of learning' ['entarteter Bildungsmensch', III, 259], a kind of smug and knowledgeable donkey whom he pilloried with great panache. His ideal of what might constitute, by contrast, a true culture was drawn from ancient Greece.

Following Schiller and Hölderlin, often echoing their very phrases, he depicted the culture of ancient Greece as the shining example of that 'wholeness' of which man was capable. Its positive attributes are contrasted with the negative attributes of modern German culture according to the usual Romantic scheme (simplicity/complexity, harmony/discord, youth/age, vigour/weakness, instinct/reflection, originality/imitation, the complete man/the specialist, etc.). In the 1860s and early 1870s he seems often to be merely reiterating the commonplaces of German Hellenism and *Kulturpessimismus* which had gained currency in the late eighteenth century: 'The Greeks are, like the genius, *simple* . . .' (Mus. II, 346[1]); 'Modern man is torn in pieces . . .' (*Ibid.*); 'The Greeks were no scholars, but they were not mindless athletes either. Are we then so necessarily bound to choose one side or the other? Can it be that Christianity has produced here a split in human nature, of which the people of harmony knew nothing?' (letter to Carl von Gersdorff, 6 April 1867). We notice, however, that as a general term of approval for the (pre-Socratic) Greek way of life, Nietzsche is far more inclined than his Romantic predecessors to choose the word 'healthy'. Already in 1867 he describes the Greeks as 'a healthy people' (Mus. I, 282), while in 1873, in a most prominent place, he asserts that the Greeks, as the 'truly healthy ones' ['die wahrhaft Gesunden'], provide the supreme authority for what is to be called healthy in a people (III, 353).

This choice of 'healthy' as a cover-term of approval – and the special, though still unformulated conception of health which it carried – indicates that what Nietzsche found worthy of glorification in ancient Greece was in fact very different from what Schiller had found there. First of all, he refused to associate the Greeks with the idea of some original, unspoilt moral purity of mankind, an idea which he emphatically rejected: 'healthy', in so far as the term scarcely brought moral connotations along with it, was at least suitable on that score. But second, he turned his back on the notion that the Greek attitude to life was serene and unclouded ['heiter'], holding on the contrary that they were uniquely prone to mental suffering and deeply in need of artistic and philosophical consolation (*The Birth of Tragedy*); and third, he was convinced that their great achievements were no products of easy growth and painless development but rather the outcome of intensely energetic struggle and competition. In other words, they were not the 'people of harmony' after all, but the people of superlative vigour. The term 'health' would only do as a designation of the glory of Greece if it was understood in a rather special way. If the term was to serve Nietzsche's purposes in his campaign for cultural improvement, it was essential that it should be taken to imply

much more than the absence of abnormality, or the unimpaired
functioning of an organism, or the maintenance of a state of balance
in any self-regulating system. It had to mean, above all, a high degree
of vitality or organizing power, and the capacity to cope triumphantly
with all manner of checks and challenges. He had to make it clear that
cultural 'health', in his mouth, meant something very different from
the anaemic brand of health claimed by his despised contemporaries,
the 'degenerate men of learning' or *Bildungsphilister*. These learned folk,
he says, have 'agreed among themselves to invert the nature and
names of things, and to speak henceforth of health where we can
recognize sickness, of sickness and extravagance where true health
confronts us' (I, 195). 'You may fall upon a past age in your thousands',
he exclaims to them elsewhere (CM, IIIii, 274), ' – you will still starve as
you starved before, and can pride yourselves then, if you wish, on your
own brand of health-acquired-through-abstinence ['angehungerte
Gesundheit'].'

In both the above contexts Nietzsche quotes from Tacitus's *Dialogue
on Oratory* (ch. 23): 'illam ipsam quam iactant sanitatem non firmitate
sed ieiunio consequuntur' – which appears to mean: 'even that condition of health which they boast of, they owe to fasting (or dieting)
and not to any robustness of constitution.' This passage, which was
clearly important to Nietzsche, distinguishes neatly between one kind
of cultural 'health' which is defensive and restrictive and another kind
which is marked by abundant strength and vitality. The passage
continues:

> Porro ne in corpore quidem valetudinem medici probant quae
> nimia anxietate contingit; parum est aegrum non esse, fortem et
> laetum et alacrum volo. Prope abest ab infirmitate in quo sola
> sanitas laudatur.

> [Why, in dealing with the human body, doctors have not much to
> say in praise of the patient who only keeps well by worrying about
> his health. Not being ill doesn't amount to much; I like a man to be
> strong and hearty and vigorous. If soundness is all you can com-
> mend in him, he is really next door to an invalid.]

What interests us is not simply Tacitus's recourse to the medical
simile, such a stock simile among philosophers and theorists of culture
in the ancient world, when he wished to lament the decline of Roman
oratory and of late Roman culture in general, but that in doing so he

should distinguish between a *positive* (dynamic, energetic) concept of health on one side and a *negative* (static, valetudinarian, conservative) concept of health on the other. The distinction served Nietzsche well in his campaign to contrast the admirable, vigorous 'health' of the cultural leaders in ancient Greece with the despicable pseudo-'health' of his contemporaries.

But there was one characteristic of his admired pre-Socratics which was not easy to subsume under the heading of health: namely, their (supposed) extreme sensitivity or 'Reizbarkeit'. Robustness is, after all, normally associated with a certain measure of *in*sensitivity. Yet the Greeks were 'a people of such sensitive feeling', and hence 'so uncommonly exposed to *suffering*' [jenes so reizbar empfindende . . ., zum *Leiden* so einzig befähigte Volk', I, 30] that they were forced to conjure up their wonderful visions of divine harmony in order to find life tolerable at all. In a later context Nietzsche asserts: 'For the truth is that the Greeks had anything but a *sturdy* [or 'robust', 'vierschrötig'] kind of health' (I, 572).

To sum up the foregoing: Nietzsche pronounced his own culture 'sick' by contrast to a kind of 'health' for which ancient Greece set the standard, but he made it clear at the same time that his ideal of cultural health combined exuberant energy with deep sensitivity, and had nothing to do with the 'golden mean' or the anxious preservation of a neutral condition, nor with the dull self-satisfaction of the thick-skinned.

II

Let us now consider how Nietzsche – still in his pre-1876, 'idealistic' phase – begins to develop his basic metaphors of cultural health and sickness. Which aspects of the body's workings does he find most useful as analogies? He seizes above all on the *digestive system*, and on the body's *response to poisons*.

'Just as the body increases by means of food, so our mind increases by means of ideas,' declared Herder (*Ideen*; Suphan, vol. XIII, p. 184), 'indeed, we observe in the case of the mind the same laws of *assimilation*, of *growth*, and of *production*, only they operate in a way special to the mind and not in a physical way.' Nietzsche found this parallel profoundly attractive. One of his chief criticisms of German culture was that it failed to cope satisfactorily with the past, and an obvious way of expressing this medically was in terms of the digestion. Too much chewing over of the past, he declares in his essay *On the Benefits and Dangers of History for Life* (I, 213), 'damages and ultimately destroys a living system, whether it be a human being or a people or a culture.' Modern man carts around with him a load of indigestible rocks of knowledge in his belly; alternatively he is like a snake which has swallowed more whole rabbits than it can deal with (I, 232). 'The excess of history has affected the formative ['plastisch'] power of life: it no longer knows how to make use of the past as a strengthening nourishment' (I, 281). What he calls the 'historical sickness', although sometimes referred to as a fever, is diagnosed essentially as a condition of acute dyspepsia. Speaking of the younger generation of Germans – the Wagner enthusiasts on whom he still pins his hopes – he asserts that the 'sure symptom' of their 'more vigorous health' is their conviction of the presence within them of 'an active, combative, excretory and resolving force at every good moment of the day' (I, 283). No doubt such language came easily to a man who suffered from chronic indigestion himself, but we need not suppose that he was yet thinking in much detail of the biological processes which served him as analogies. That came later, as we shall see. At this stage he is content to suggest that a healthy mind, and by extension a healthy culture, is like a sound digestion in that it knows what is good for it, being able to discriminate with almost unerring instinct between what is useful to its own system and what is not, and to assimilate the former while ruthlessly rejecting the latter.

It was one thing to diagnose the sickness of the age in such terms, another to prescribe the proper treatment. Was it enough simply to encourage a change of intellectual diet, of 'Geistesnahrung'? Or was the trouble so severe that the application of drugs was indicated, the instilling of foreign modes of thought and feeling? Was it even possible – an alarming thought which never ceased to nag him – that the modern mind and modern culture had become so constitutionally enfeebled, so irreversibly degenerate, that they were no longer capable of responding to treatment at all? At all events the physician was already nominated: he was 'the philosopher as cultural doctor' ['Der Philosoph als Arzt der Cultur', title of a treatise attempted in 1873]. In his notes for this treatise, sketched when he was still under Wagner's spell, Nietzsche states that where a culture is enfeebled the restorative power can flow only from great artistic achievements. The task of the philosopher-physician is a preparatory one: by destroying one tendency, moderating another, and releasing a third from inhibition he prepares the sick body of culture to receive new life from the artistic genius. However, the medicines which this cultural doctor carries in his bag are dangerous; his antidotes are themselves toxic and must be judiciously applied. In the *Benefits and Dangers of History* the remedies proposed are a dose of forgetfulness ['das Unhistorische'] and a dose of belief in what is eternally unchangeable ['das Überhistorische'], and he tells us not to be surprised to find that these are the names of poisons which can cause distress in their turn (I, 281).

From 1875 onwards this pharmacological language becomes obtrusive. Poisons and antidotes, pain-killers and stimulants, injections and inoculations take a strong hold on his imagination. Increasingly, he visualizes ideas and cultural habits as agents which enter the bloodstream of individuals or groups – whether as drugs taken or as infections caught – and which either enhance the vital activity of the organism by the challenge they offer, or alternatively dull it and deaden it. Already in *The Birth of Tragedy* he had recourse to the imagery of drugs. He even says there, gloomily enough, that the whole of human culture is merely a compound of the various irritants or stimulants ['Reizmittel'] which man has prepared for himself in order to counter the depression he must feel as he contemplates existence (I, 99). Not only is science, the pursuit of knowledge, such a 'stimulant'; so is art, so is music, so are myths and religions. All these things are 'stimulants': it is still a crude pharmacology. But by 1875/6, during the crisis of his disenchantment with Wagner, Nietzsche is ready to start refining it, to distinguish between stimulants proper on one side and mere pain-killing drugs of no positive effect on the other. Religion is now clearly just a pain-killer, but so apparently is art as well. Both are 'Betäubungen' [analgesics], and as such represent a low or primitive stage of the healing art (CM, IVi, 161f; 1875): 'it has to be shown', he adds, 'how even the highest achievements of mankind hitherto have developed on the basis of this primitive kind of medicine.' This note is not one of his random fireworks, for he reformulates it in the following year (CM, IVii, 418) and then expands it to figure prominently as his first aphorism on the religious life in *Human, All-Too-Human*, vol. I (I, 517), adding rather offensively that priests have always made their living from the narcotizing of human ills. (The parallel with Marx's dictum that 'religion is the opium of the people' should not mislead us; for Nietzsche was chiefly worried about the effect of this 'drug' on highly cultivated men, with their supposedly refined capacity for mental suffering.) Similarly he suggests that poets, in so far as they too aim to relieve the pains of life, 'soothe and heal but temporarily, but for the moment', indeed, by neutralizing and bringing to palliative discharge the 'passion of the dissatisfied' they even deter man from working towards a real improvement of his condition (I, 547). However, he does not adhere for long to the notion that the drug of art is essentially narcotic in function, like the drug of religion; instead he reverts to his original conviction that art is (or can be) a powerful 'Reizmittel' which stimulates intense and subtle delights. Religion, on the other hand, continues to be seen as a mere palliative for the sick, or as actively damaging when administered to the healthy. 'I conceive religions as narcotics,' he notes in 1875 (CM, IVi, 134), 'but if they are given to tribes like the Germans they are pure poisons.'

From the examples so far given it appears that Nietzsche's use of medical language, up to 1875, remains essentially figurative. However much he may enliven the ancient metaphors of cultural or spiritual 'health' and 'sickness' by his references to digestive ailments or to the effects of drugs, they still remain metaphors, which we can accept as the poetic or rhetorical devices of an enthusiastic cultural reformer. But at this point an insidious change sets in, namely that progressive confusion of medical figure and medical fact which concerns us in the present essay. To take one preliminary instance: when he asserts, in the passage just quoted, that the Christian doctrine had a 'poisonous' effect on the German tribes in the early centuries, we can still safely regard this as a metaphor. But when, three years later, he expands and reformulates the idea (I, 824), we can no longer be quite so sure:

> to implant the doctrine of sin and damnation into the heroic, child-like and animal soul of the primitive German was *quite simply* to poison it; the result was bound to be a *quite monstrous process of chemical fermentation and decomposition*, a turmoil of feelings and judgments, a proliferation of the most extravagant forms, and thus in due course *a fundamental weakening* of such barbarian people (my italics).

It is from this stage that Nietzsche's use of health/sickness terminology becomes a problem, as he begins to couch his general theory of man's cultural development – from which his moral, aesthetic and political theories are derived – ever more exclusively in physiological and medical terms. It is not just that he begins to regard all man's sentiments, ideas and cultural activities as symptoms of physical states or processes; he begins to suggest, further, that his own physio-psychological explanations of individual cultural behaviour can also be applied, literally, to the 'organisms' of advanced human societies and cultural groups. In other words, as his semi-scientific interest in the physical basis of man's higher activities grows, so he transports (starting with *Human, All-Too-Human*) the metaphorical 'bodies' of social units into the context of his amateur physiological-medical theorizing. Thus in the first aphorism of the section 'Symptoms of Higher and Lower Culture' (1, 583f), entitled 'Refinement (or ennoblement) through degeneration', he argues that when a stable and unified cultural community runs the risk of stagnation, the 'weaker', less confident and more non-conformist individuals perform an invaluable service by 'loosening things up and inflicting from time to time a wound upon the stable element of a community'. 'Precisely at this injured and weakened point', he goes on, 'the total system is so to speak *inoculated* with something new; but its strength as a whole must be great enough for it to accept this new element into its blood-stream and assimilate it.' The drift of his argument in this passage is that the 'body' of a community (or of a people, or a race, or a tribe, or a cultural group – he makes no serious distinctions) positively requires the stimulus afforded by local damage if it is to 'grow stronger' and 'progress'. It responds, so he avers, exactly as the body of an individual man responds to the challenge of wounding and partial weakening.

This extended aphorism is doubly important for us. First, it shows us Nietzsche on the brink of taking his metaphor of a cultural 'body' literally, of pursuing his analogies between biological processes and cultural developments so far and in such technical detail that the mental reservation of the inverted commas is abandoned and forgotten. Let us glance at one instance of what happens when he does go over this brink:

> The disintegration of established custom ['Sitte'], of society, is a condition in which the new *egg* (or a number of *eggs*) emerge – eggs (individuals) as germs of new societies and units. The emergence of individuals is the sign that *a society* has attained *the capacity to propagate itself*: as soon as this sign appears the old society dies out. This is not a simile (CM, vii, 449f).

Here (in 1881) he draws an alternative and equally colourful biological picture in explanation of cultural or social change and renewal – but this time he insists that it is 'not a simile'.

Second, the importance of the 'Refinement through degeneration' aphorism lies in the actual argument which he puts forward, namely, that the *partial* weakening or impairment of a basically healthy organism – caused by some wounding or infection or injection – has *positive value* for that organism, provided only that the whole possesses sufficient inherent vitality to assimilate the weakness of the part. This notion becomes absolutely central to his later thinking. Sickness is conceived as *a desirable challenge* to a healthy body, stimulating its powers and leaving it – once the sickness has been coped with, 'overcome' by incorporation – in a 'higher' and 'renewed' state of health, with its vitality not merely enhanced but somehow refined. Certainly this idea collides, not infrequently, with the Romantic idea of a primeval, perfect, untainted state of health, untouched and untroubled by the 'Fall' into sickness; certainly it brings him now and then, as he pursues its consequences, awkwardly close to Christian assumptions and doctrines; but in the end it was solely this positive assessment of sickness, as an agent promoting health, as the necessary stepping-stone to a higher and finer condition of health, which he could find acceptable. And the chief reason for this is perhaps not far to seek. For the theory that an organism *needs* to be damaged if it is somehow to be enhanced in strength and quality reminds us of the fact that Nietzsche was himself an invalid, engaged in a constant battle against ill-health and increasingly preoccupied with self-diagnosis and self-treatment. Before going further, let us approach our topic from this angle of his personal medical history.

III

Bad health dogged him throughout his career. At school he was 'often troubled by shifting headaches' (Schulpforta medical records). During his brief spell as a medical orderly in the Franco-Prussian War he contracted dysentery and diphtheria, which 'sufficiently ruined' him (letter to Rohde, 23 November 1870): digestive disorders came to join his headaches and ensured his almost continuous discomfort. At the end of 1875, the year in which his condition became really serious, he complains of 'my chronic misery, which seizes me for almost two whole days every two weeks, and sometimes for longer periods' (to von Gersdorff, 13 December 1875). In the following autumn he tells his sister: 'to use my eyes is impossible' (1 August 1876), and to Wagner he writes: 'this neuralgia goes to work so thoroughly, so scientifically, that it literally probes me to find how much pain I can endure, and each of its investigations lasts for thirty hours' (letter of 27 September

1876). In the spring of 1877 we hear the same tale from Sorrento (letter to his sister of 25 April), and later, from a Swiss resort, he declares that despite the mountain air 'I lie sick in bed here as in Sorrento, and drag myself around in pain, day after day' (to Malwida von Meysenbug, 1 July 1877). After a year of specially severe bouts in 1879 he writes: 'My life's terrible and unremitting martyrdom makes me thirst for the end, and there have been some signs which allow me to hope that the stroke which will liberate me is not too distant' (to Malwida von Meysenbug, 14 January 1880). The same desperate note is struck in a letter from Sils Maria of September 1881: 'Pain is vanquishing my life and my will. What months, what a summer I have had! My physical agonies were as many and varied as the changes I have seen in the sky . . . Five times I have called for Doctor Death, and yesterday I hoped it was the end – in vain' (to Overbeck, 18 September 1881). These lines were written in Latin, as if to mask the unspeakable confession of the defeat of his will to live. The next year, 1882, seems to have brought some respite: 'on the whole I have the right to talk of recovery, even though I am often reminded of the *precarious balance* of my health' (to Overbeck, September 1882). But it was a respite only: 'Things are very bad indeed. My health is back where it was three years ago. Everything is kaput, my stomach so much so that it even refuses the sedatives – in consequence of which I have sleepless, terribly tormented nights . . .' (to Overbeck, 22 February 1883). And so the story of his struggle with sickness continues. In May 1884 he believes he may be 'over the hill' (to Overbeck, 2 May 1884), but again in September we hear: 'one good day in ten – those are my statistics, the devil take them!' (to Peter Gast, 2 September 1884). In March 1885: 'I have not been well the whole winter. . . . But that is an old story' (to Malwida von Meysenbug, 13 March 1885); in July: 'My health, disturbingly uncertain – some cardinal danger or other' (to Gast, 23 July 1885). In July 1887, six months before his mental collapse, he writes to Gast of 'a physiological constraint which has given me for the past year, without exaggeration, not a single good day', and declares: 'The extremely bad attacks are so frequent that I feel tomorrow could be a return to the same old state of things' (letter of 18 July 1887).

Enough has been said to indicate that his physical health was sufficiently bad, at least from 1875 onwards, to have affected all that he thought and did. We may leave aside the notoriously disputed question of what his ailments really were, of their correct medical diagnosis. What interests us is how *he* interpreted them, how *he* reacted to them, and how he understood their relation to his intellectual and spiritual life.

Naturally, he wanted to get better, whatever value he might be inclined to attach in theory to sickness. But how was he to set about it? When the need to take remedial action first became acute he placed his trust in physical treatment, assuring Hans von Bülow, for instance (2 January 1875), that his daily cold plunges offered him the prospect of never being ill again, and taking a cure at Steinabad that summer under the dietician Josef Wiel. There is little evidence, at this stage, of his fancying that the cold baths needed to be reinforced by intellectual 'cold baths', or that the little-and-often dietary regime which he devised for himself on Wiel's advice required as its supplement an equivalent cultural 'diet', some new and salutary regimen of thought. In August, however, he does tell Malwida von Meysenbug (11 August 1875): 'People like us never suffer just physically – it is all deeply entwined with spiritual crises, so that I have no idea how medicines and cookery can ever make me well again'; and at the end of the year he tells von Gersdorff (13 December 1875) that his physical health will not become more reliable 'until I *deserve* it, until I have found the state of soul which is, as it were, my promised land. . . .'

It was just at this time that he began (in *Human, All-Too-Human*) to lay great stress on the physical basis of the human personality, so that we might have expected him henceforth to seek the roots of his bad condition in such things as unsuitable diet, unsuitable climate, infections, or organic troubles, and to look for remedies or palliatives appropriate to such findings. But that is not quite what happens. It is true that he does, by way of self-treatment, seek out for the rest of his life the 'right' climate and diet for himself (though he seems to avert his mind from the possible need to cope with organic disease), yet for all that he continues to speak as if his ailments were primarily psychosomatic, i.e. caused by disturbances of the mind or soul, as in the two letters just quoted. Thus, in a letter to Mathilde Maier of 15 July 1878, he declares: 'That metaphysical befogging of all that is true and simple [. . .] this matched by a baroque art of over-excitement and glorified extravagance – I mean the art of Wagner; both these things made me more and more ill'. The paradox is partly resolved if we notice the concrete, physical way in which he now makes a habit of describing the non-physical influences which affect him. In the above self-diagnosis he does not attribute his sick condition directly to his reading of certain metaphysical philosophers and to his acceptance of their arguments or his adoption of their habits of thought; instead he uses a climatic metaphor, 'that metaphysical *befogging*' ['Vernebelung'], suggesting that he had been suffering from the effects of an unhealthy intellectual 'climate'. The letter continues thus:

> I wish you could now feel like me how it is to live, as I do *now*, in such pure *mountain air* ['reine Höhenluft'], in such a gentle mood vis-à-vis people still inhabiting the haze of the valleys, more than ever dedicated, as I am, to all that is good and robust, so much closer to the Greeks than ever before [. . .]. I became fully aware of this at Bayreuth that summer. I fled, after the first performances which I attended, fled into the mountains.

The expressions 'mountain air' and 'haze of the valleys' refer back directly to 'metaphysical befogging', so we assume that they, too, are metaphors. But since the letter comes from the Bernese Oberland we realize that they are meant literally *as well*, which is confirmed by the reference to his literal 'flight into the mountains' in 1876 (from Bayreuth to Klingenbrunn). By using such terms as 'climate', 'diet', 'infection', etc., together with their related terms, now in a metaphorical sense, now in a literal sense, and now *in a pseudo-literal sense which was unacknowledgedly metaphorical*, he succeeded in blurring all distinctions between physical and mental modes of self-treatment for his ills. When he notes, in the summer of 1878 (CM, IViii, 352): 'A cold-water cure seemed to me necessary,' we are obliged to read on in order to discover whether he means the application of cold to his body, or the application of 'cold' ideas to the 'hot' ones which he had previously entertained. (In this case he meant the latter.) Thanks to the ambiguity of such terms he could persuade himself that a crisp mountain walk, for example, and the reading of some crisp sceptical maxims were interchangeable remedies for his general pathological condition, or that his switch from German to Italianate cookery on the one hand, and his switch to lighter and more elegant intellectual and artistic 'fare' on the other, were merely two aspects of the same course of self-treatment to which he was being guided by a profound and mysterious instinct. 'I feel', he notes in 1878 (CM, IViii, 403), 'as if I had recovered from a sickness; my thoughts turn with inexpressible sweetness to Mozart's Requiem. Plain dishes taste better to me.' In a striking letter to Rohde (15 July 1882) he calls the books which he had written since 1876 (i.e. *Human, All-Too-Human, The Dawn of Day*, and *The Joyful Science*) 'my prescription and my home-brewed medicine against weariness with life', and he goes on: 'If even my physical health re-appears, whom have I to thank for that? I was in all respects my own doctor; and *as a person in whom nothing stands separate*, I have had to treat soul, mind and body *all at once and with the same remedies*' (my italics). Similarly to Overbeck (31 December 1882): 'I simply am not mere mind or mere body, but yet a third thing beyond these. I always suffer from the whole and within the whole.'

Let us consider one of the remedies which he had been applying to his 'soul, mind and body all at once' since 1876, that mountain air just mentioned. He sought this out in a variety of places, notably in the Upper Engadine. What he felt (and was told by his medical advisers) that he needed was a rarefied atmosphere and a clear sky, and count-less letters during this period testify to his sense of greater well-being when he found them. 'High mountain altitudes have always had a beneficent influence on me,' he cheerfully tells Malwida von Meysen-bug from Rosenlaui (1 July 1877), pointing out that it is 4,000 feet above sea level. And even when his bodily pains persist, he experiences at such altitudes 'so many happy exaltations of thought and feeling' (to Rohde, 28 September 1877). Literal exaltation (i.e. being several thou-sand feet up) and metaphorical exaltation of the spirit become curiously intertwined. While seeking his own healing in the literal mountain air of the Swiss Alps, he dreams of doctoring others by leading them into the figurative 'mountain air' of his own elevated thoughts. 'I observe the patients who come to the mountain air of the Engadine,' he notes in 1878 (CM, Iviii, 348), 'I, too, send my patients into *my* mountain air . . .' Nietzsche's patients might reply by inquiring whether the 'mountain air' of his bracing philosophy will alone suffice for their cure, or whether they need – like him – to reinforce a metaphorical 'climatic' treatment by actually proceeding to an Alpine resort.

The fact that his physical sufferings and his mental sufferings both came to a head at the same juncture – during the period of the Wagner crisis in 1875/6 – encouraged him to develop a *unitary* concep-tion of personal health, embracing the whole personality. He came to regard himself as an inseparable, homogeneous body-soul unit, and set about doctoring himself on that assumption. It is not just that he assumed a direct, rather than an inverse, relation between the health of his body and the health of his mind or soul (the idea of an inverse relation was still toyed with in summer 1876 – 'the sick man is often healthier in his soul than the healthy man' (CM, Ivii, 394) – but was soon firmly rejected as a Christian or anyhow unGreek aberration); he came to believe that both body and soul are controlled, in joint harness, by 'yet a third thing beyond these', a 'dictatorial something' as he later calls it (II, 694; cf. I, 740), the master of all our drives and appetites and the informer of our total 'taste' ['Geschmack'].

We need have no quarrel with the idea that both the literal mountain air of the Alps on the one hand, and the metaphorical 'mountain air' of emancipated ideas on the other, might have a tonic and restorative effect on his entire system, on 'soul, mind and body all at once'. The confusion only enters when he begins to persuade himself, misled by the concreteness of his own imagery, that the Alpine air and the new set of ideas somehow amount in reality – on the basis of some undisclosed mystical assumption – to the *same remedy*.

His new conviction of the 'indivisibility' of personal health ran him, furthermore, into serious difficulties in his own case. For his much-vaunted series of mental/spiritual 'recoveries' ['Genesungen'] – see for instance his Preface (1886) to *The Joyful Science* – ought by rights to have been accompanied by a marked improvement in his bodily condition. Yet, as we have seen from the above sketch of his medical history, there was depressingly little sign of this happening; on the whole, the 'physiological constraints' which made his life a misery obstinately refused to go away; only rarely, it seems, was his growing mental exaltation in the 1880s so matched by a sense of physical well-being that both could be taken together as a symptom or expression of some 'total healthiness'. Nevertheless, he certainly did his utmost to believe – and to 'live' the belief – that in all matters pertaining to health and sickness his body and soul were not enemies, but inseparable allies: if he had been sick 'as a whole', he could only achieve health 'as a whole' – and this was true whether he envisaged his achievement of health as a 'recovery', a balance recovered after disturbance, or as an 'ascent' (on the shoulders of sickness, so to speak) to a 'higher' condition than the original, lost one.

IV

After 1875 medical terms multiply and become the common coin of Nietzsche's writing. He no longer uses them simply to illustrate his thinking on cultural topics, such as the origin of tragic art or the dangers of an excessive preoccupation with the past; instead, matters of health and sickness become themselves a main object of his reflections, and medical or pseudo-medical categories come to furnish the very framework of his thinking. Indeed by the final stage, by 1888, one can almost say that there *are* no other topics, that the question of health has swallowed up everything else.

This development was bound up, no doubt – as suggested in the previous section – with his recognition of the overriding need to attain to health in his own person, and in particular with his new conviction that health for him, as a 'person in whom nothing stands separate', was something indivisible. But we can scarcely suppose that it was his own experience of ill-health alone which taught him to speak and conceive of health and sickness generally in the ways that he now did. It was hardly just the introspection and self-therapeutic experiments of an invalid which led him to attach so much credence to medicine in the widest sense of the term. Perhaps, indeed, we should rather put it the other way round, and declare that his attempts at self-doctoring were so many attempts to confirm the truth of his emergent monistic, naturalistic philosophy. At all events, this philosophy of his, which he tries at once to propound in theory and to live out in practice, is henceforth based (or, more exactly, *claims* to be based) on physical science, above all on physiology, medicine and anthropology. The question which now arises is how far this claim was misleading, and if so, to what extent this was due to Nietzsche's oscillating use of physiological and medical terms – now in the literal sense appropriate to the natural sciences, and now in the metaphorical sense appropriate to poetry.

Before we examine this question by looking at some post-1875 texts, a further consideration is in place. During all Nietzsche's most formative years, both as a student and as a professional scholar, he had been sufficiently steeped in Greek habits of thought for these to have acquired an abiding power over his mind. Until he left Basle, his academic work kept him in daily contact with that interaction of philosophical and medical viewpoints which is such a striking feature of ancient Greek writings. In studying Plato or Aristotle, for instance, he met the recurrent interplay of medical notions with ethical and political theory; in reading, say, the plays of Aeschylus he imbibed a poetic mode of thought which made no sharp distinctions between disorders of the mind or soul and disorders of the body. The *Prometheus Bound* serves well to bring out the latter point, since Nietzsche's deep admiration for this play is attested: he called it 'the most sublime poem of human culture, hovering like a rainbow over the millennia' (CM, IVii, 490).

Prometheus is presented by Aeschylus as the founder of 'all the arts of men' (line 522), and he regards the foremost of these as the art of medicine. He makes his greatest boast of having 'discovered gently tempered medicines/To shield men from all manner of disease . . .' (lines 514f). But this opponent of the tyrant Zeus has brought men not only cures for their bodily ailments, he has also brought them a cure for the 'disease' of foreseeing their own deaths (a cure for Greek pessimism, Nietzsche might call it), in the form of the 'drug' (*pharmakon*, line 251) of blind hopes. Prometheus is evidently not just the inventor of the skills of physical medicine, but the first 'doctor of souls' as well. As the mythical first healer he has come to remedy the human condition in two senses, one of which – at least from our modern point of view – is only metaphorically medical. Furthermore, Prometheus as doctor of men lacks the skill to rid himself of his own personal torment; we learn that he is like a sick physician who cannot find the drugs to heal himself (lines 472–5) – another element in the story which encouraged Nietzsche to identify himself with this heroic challenger of divine authority.[2] But how are we to understand this torment [*nosos*] from which the self-appointed healer of human ills suffers in his own person? Is his torment a sickness of the body, or a 'sickness' of the soul? Certainly he suffers pains of the body, and it is of these that the Ocean Nymphs think, but he also suffers – even more acutely – from a tormenting hatred of the gods (lines 977f). It is hard to determine how far such terms as *akos* [remedy], *pharmakos* [drug], and *nosos* [disorder, disease or torment] were meant literally or metaphorically in texts like the *Prometheus Bound*. What we can say for certain is that Nietzsche was thoroughly accustomed to a pervasive and suggestive ambiguity in their use.

With *Human, All-Too-Human*, in his new dress as a 'scientist', he sets out to inspect man's higher activities from a psychological point of view. As he engages in his 'reflections about what is human, all-too-human – or, as the learned expression goes: psychological observation' (I, 475), he begins to concern himself directly with the body, with literal feeding habits, literal climatic effects, literal diseases. When he speaks of the 'dietetics of health', for instance, as a field of inquiry in which 'unshakable' scientific truths can gradually be established (I, 464), he means quite simply rules for bodily care. It is true that his remarks about what constitutes sound diet have little to do with science in any rigorous sense (cf. the section 'Against bad diet' in *The Dawn of Day*, I, 1151), but the fact remains that he now regards such things as falling very much within his purview as a philosopher.

However, this does not mean that he ceases to use medical terms in a metaphorical manner: on the contrary, his metaphorical uses of them proliferate, they become increasingly specific and technical, and through mixing them with literal uses he insinuates the idea that they can be understood literally as well.

> To have a thought of revenge and carry it out means getting a violent attack of fever, which passes however: but to have a thought of revenge without the strength and courage to put it into effect means to carry a chronic disorder ['ein chronisches Leiden'], a poisoning of body and soul, around with one (I, 492).

Or: 'active ambition is a skin-disease of the soul, it expels all noxious substances (CM, IVii, 466; late 1876). He frequently suggests that the emotion of pity is not merely associated with bodily disorders, but may actually be one. 'There are people who through sympathy and concern for another person become hypochondriac; the form of compassion ['Mitleiden'] which thus arises is nothing other than a sickness' (I, 484). Regular sympathizing can, it appears, through its effect on the hypochondria (which according to ancient medicine was the seat of melancholy), become itself a literal sickness. Such suggestions are still made in a fairly tentative way – in his comments on the doctrine of tragic *katharsis* (I, 571f) he admits that pity cannot be connected with the need of any particular organ of the body to relieve itself through discharge. 'Mitleiden' may *sound* in German like a physical disorder ('ein Leiden'; cf. the 'Ohrenleiden' or 'ear-trouble' by which Nietzsche accounts for the *daemonion* of Socrates, I, 529), and indeed the term itself derives ultimately from an imaginative transfer or identification (*pathe* denoting at once strong emotion, and sickness of the body). But this does not mean that by reversing the imaginative transfer, or repeating the imaginative identification, Nietzsche is getting us back to natural fact, back to base. His use of medical language. in other words, often merely remits us to pre-scientific theories of the natural world. So long as he restricts himself to exploring the dependence of mind on body, and the interaction of both, we may concede that in principle he is thinking 'scientifically' (even if some of his theories, such as that of the effect of eating beans or rice on one's philosophical outlook, may seem crude and unconvincing). But when, going beyond this, he presses his structural and functional *analogies* between mind and body (e.g. 'skin-disease of the soul'), suggesting that mind and body are mysteriously prone to the *same* disorders and responsive to the *same* remedies, he is pursuing a poetic mode of philosophizing behind a mere smoke-screen of scientific terminology.

The 'philosopher as cultural doctor' has now extended his duties. No longer does he content himself with prescribing beneficent changes of intellectual 'diet', or the instilling of stimulating ideas *as if* they were drugs; now he actually prescribes, at the same time, for the bodily health of his patients – and invites us to believe that both prescriptions are at bottom identical. We are encouraged in the same breath to abstain from Christianity and alcohol ('the two great European narcotics', as he later calls them, II, 984; cf. II, 137), or from Wagner's music and richly seasoned food. Let us consider the following passage from *Human, All-Too-Human*, vol. 2, entitled 'Intellectual and physical transplantation as a remedy' (I, 950):

> Different *cultures* are different intellectual climates, each one of which is mainly injurious or mainly salutary for any given organism. *History* as a whole, conceived as knowledge of the different cultures, is the *science of remedies* ['Heilmittellehre'], but not the science of healing itself. A *doctor* is still most definitely required, who will make use of this science of remedies in order to send each individual into precisely that climate which is beneficial to him – temporarily or permanently. To live in the present, within a single culture, will not suffice as a general prescription, for in that case too many extremely useful kinds of men, who cannot breathe properly ['gesund atmen'] in their own culture, would die out. By means of history one must give them *air* and seek to preserve them; even the men of retarded cultures have their value. – As a counterpart of this mental cure, mankind in bodily respect must strive to discover, by means of a medical geography, which forms of degeneration and which sicknesses each quarter of the globe gives rise to, and conversely which remedial factors it offers: and then, gradually, peoples, families and individuals must be transplanted, over a sufficiently long and unremitting period for their inherited physical infirmities to be mastered. The whole earth, in the end, will consist of a sum of staging-posts for health.

It is easy to smile at this tourist agent's dream of whole populations on a permanent health trip, but the implications of the passage, and the habits of thought which it confirms, deserve to be taken seriously. In the first part of the passage Nietzsche develops one of his favourite medical metaphors, that of intellectual 'climates' (cf. for instance the section entitled 'Zones of Culture' in *Human, All-Too-Human*, vol. 1; 1, 591f); in the second part he moves on to consider the effects of literal climates. The question is how these two parts relate to each other.

He argues first that the historical study of different cultures can be beneficial to us all, provided we select those cultures which are suitable to our particular intellectual and emotional requirements, and that such a preoccupation with past cultures may be quite essential for those whose minds are dissatisfied and repelled by the age in which they live. In order to argue this, he uses such an elaborate and persuasively concrete medical simile, based on the metaphor 'intellectual climate', that we almost forget that he is really talking – as in his essay of 1874 – about the benefits and dangers of history. Having thus deluged us with medical terms, used in a figurative sense, he now switches to a medical question proper: the effect of different climates on the human body. And his remarks on this matter are by no means based, independently of what has gone before, on strictly scientific considerations; on the contrary, his practical suggestions for climatic treatment of the body are derived straight from his poetic notions about the 'climatic' treatment of the mind. Indeed the one is the 'counterpart' of the other: we are encouraged to think that the analogy must hold good at all points.The passage provides an example of Nietzsche's insidious and growing habit of taking metaphors literally. We have already noticed how – in respect of the 'climate' metaphor especially – he performs this trick in private, in the way that he writes about and conducts his personal self-treatment; here we see him doing it publicly, as part and parcel of his philosophical thinking, and it leads him into such speculations as the following: 'Perhaps the Germans have simply got into the *wrong* climate! There is something in them which could be *Hellenic* – it awakens upon contact with the south – Winckelmann Goethe Mozart' (CM, VIIii, 52; 1884). As an afterthought he adds: 'The *nourishment* of the Germans, too, was their disaster: philistinism' (*Ibid.*). At the risk of labouring the general point about his confusions of medical figure and medical fact, let us now look in more detail at his use of terms connected with man's diet and man's digestive functions.

V

In *Ecce Homo* Nietzsche's first boast, in the chapter called 'Why I am so Clever', is that he has managed to discover which kinds of food and drink suit him best. He has learned, for example, that tea only suits him in the mornings, and that English food – he implies here as usual that Englishmen live exclusively on underdone roast beef – is repugnant to his system. The 'question of *nourishment*' ['Frage der *Ernährung*'] which he discusses in this chapter is a question of literal nourishment, nourishment of the body. And the line of thought is straightforwardly, if crudely, materialistic: 'all advantages come from the intestines' (II, 1085). Thus German thought, or 'the mind of Germany' ['der deutsche Geist'], has emerged from sluggish German bowels ['aus betrübten Eingeweiden'], a consequence of eating soup '*before* the meal', overboiled meat, greasy vegetables, pudding to finish, and washing the whole lot down with liquid afterwards in a 'positively beastly' manner.

In the course of his diatribe against the German cuisine and its supposed intellectual consequences he suddenly switches to metaphor: 'The German mind is a case of indigestion, it is never done with anything' ['Der deutsche Geist ist eine Indigestion, er wird mit nichts fertig']. From asserting that our ways of thought are *dependent* on our digestive system he moves on to suggest that the mind actually *works in the same way* as the digestive system, that it is a kind of 'digestive system' itself. This metaphor of 'mental indigestion' had previously been one of his great favourites. In *The Dawn of Day*, for instance, the section called 'The nourishment of modern man' begins: 'He knows how to digest a great deal, indeed almost everything – it is his kind of ambition: but he would be of a higher order if digesting everything was precisely what he *couldn't* do; *homo pamphagus* is not the most refined of species' (I, 1128). All this is plainly metaphorical: 'nourishment' is a metaphor, 'digestion' is a metaphor. The same is true in *Beyond Good and Evil*, section 282 (II, 748):

We have probably all of us, at one time or another, eaten at tables where we did not belong; and precisely the most spiritual among us, who are the most difficult to nourish, know that dangerous *dyspepsia* which comes from a sudden insight and disillusionment about our food and table-companions – the *after-dinner nausea*.

When he says, earlier in the same book (II, 695), that the mind is really like nothing so much as a stomach, and speaks of the mind's power to assimilate experience as a 'power of digestion', he still puts the phrase in inverted commas and explicitly declares it an image ['im Bilde geredet']. But this image has certainly taken an obsessive hold of him; it has become a controller of his thinking; further than that, it is presented with so much insistent physiological detail that it clamours to be understood literally. What are we to make of the following note of 1881, for instance? 'People speak of those with gastric complaints ['Magenkranken'] and mean those who suffer from their digestion – as if the stomach were the sole digesting organ!' ['als ob der Magen allein das Verdauende sei!' CM, vii, 428]. At such points, it appears, a real identity is being proposed between the assimilative power of the mind and that of the stomach.

It is left to Zarathustra the poet, released from the inhibition of scientific thought, to assert roundly the identity of mind or spirit and stomach:

> Because they have learned badly and the best things not at all, everything too unripe and too hastily: because they have *eaten* badly, – that is how they came by that ruined stomach, –
> – for their spirit is indeed a ruined stomach: *it* counsels death! For truly, my brothers, the spirit *is* a stomach!
> Life is a spring of delight: but from whomsoever a ruined stomach speaks, the father of affliction, for him all wells are poisoned. (*Thus Spake Zarathustra*, Book III, 'Of Old and New Law-Tables', section 16; II, 452).

Nietzsche carries over this assertion of real identity from his poetry into his philosophical arguments. In *The Genealogy of Morals* he declares that a man who has lost the capacity to close his mind from time to time to new impressions 'is comparable to a dyspeptic (*and not merely comparable to one*)' (II, 798; my italics). The path to this identification is smoothed by techniques of linguistic *Gleichschaltung* which are characteristic of the later work: thus the essential oneness of the two 'digestive processes' is insinuated by the coining of the word 'Einverseelung' ['inmentalization'] as an exact counterpart of 'Einverleibung' ['incorporation'] (*Ibid.*).

Later in the *Genealogy* he is anxious to emphasize (II, 870) that while mental 'indigestion' may indeed often be a *consequence* of physical indigestion, he is not simply making a materialist point:

A strong and soundly-constituted man ['wohlgeratner Mensch'] digests his experiences (deeds and misdeeds included) just as he digests his meals, even if he has some tough morsels to swallow. If he 'cannot cope' with an experience, then this type of indigestion is every bit as physical as the other – and often, in fact, merely one of the consequences of the other. – Between ourselves, one can hold such a notion and still be the sternest opponent of all materialism....

He seems to argue that both mind and stomach, as they carry out their more or less successful digesting activities, are obeying a single 'will to assimilate' which stands behind them both. We are reminded of his remark to Overbeck quoted above: 'I simply am not mere mind or mere body, but yet a third thing beyond these.'

If we return to *Ecce Homo* with these passages in mind we look with more suspicion on the phrase 'the German mind is a case of indigestion'. We now recognize that 'mental indigestion' claims to be more than what it normally is (and what it was for Nietzsche, too, when he wrote his essay on history), more, that is, than a lively metaphor with a metaphor's distinct but limited usefulness. And equally we recognize that the items of literal food and drink, in the effects of which he seems to be taking a straightforward medical interest, have secretly taken on a 'deeper', mystical significance. For by this stage the terms 'nourishment' and 'digestion' have acquired a free pass to all areas, and can move between them unchallenged by the censorship of reason and without having to declare what they carry. When he gives, in 'Why I am so Clever', the following working formulation of the 'question of nourishment': 'how have *you* personally to nourish yourself in order to achieve your maximum of strength, of *virtù* in the Renaissance style [. . .]?', the answer can indeed be supplied in the form of a literal diet-sheet – but alternatively it can be supplied as a list of ideas to be coped with or stomached.

However, Nietzsche's attempt to lump mental and physical nourishment together landed him in difficulty. For while his real stomach demanded easily digestible foods, the 'stomach' of his mind or spirit felt a heroic or perverse urge to seek out *in*digestible ideas. As far as he was concerned, the items on his mental diet-sheet had to be arranged – if he was to achieve his 'maximum of strength, of *virtù* in the Renaissance style' – precisely in ascending order of their disagreeableness and difficulty to stomach. The hardest thing of all for him to swallow and digest, the 'heaviest thought' of the eternal recurrence, was also what was *best* for his mind-alias-stomach, provided only that he could 'overcome it' by incorporating it fully.[3]

In calling the mind a stomach Nietzsche intends to bring out something basic about the nature of both. Yet it is hard to impute heroism to a real stomach: if a stomach could speak, it would probably declare, in a most un-Nietzschean manner, that it was interested in maintaining its normal functions, and in sending messages of refusal when threatened with something really nasty. On the other hand, it seems to be natural to *minds* of a certain type (to the 'higher' type, Nietzsche would say) that they actively seek out what disturbs them for the purposes of their self-improvement. And it is these 'higher' minds or souls, these compulsive seekers after invigorating new challenges and dangers, which he is inclined to regard as the truly healthy ones.

VI

These considerations bring us back to the central question of how Nietzsche tried to define health and to clarify its relationship with sickness or sicknesses. As more and more things fell, by a kind of linguistic landslide, into the province of medicine, so it became at once more urgent and more difficult for him to do this. Already by 1873 he had declared a general hygienics of life necessary, a 'Gesundheitslehre des Lebens' (I, 282), but his projected 'Untimely Meditation' on the subject of 'Health and Sickness' (see CM, IVi, 264) came to nothing. The harder he tried to work out general principles of health – 'one hour each day: theory of health', he notes in 1878 (CM, IVviii, 454) – the more impossible it seemed.

The first problem was whether he was personally equipped to do it, whether as a sick man – for by 1875 at latest he had accepted the fact that he was indeed sick – he had the right perspective on the matter. Did his own disturbed and uncomfortable condition qualify him to be a medical theorist in the widest sense, or was it instead a disqualification? Should the sick physician of mankind, in the interests of his task, resist his natural inclination to become well? Would he, if he found health himself, cease his efforts to define it and promote it? Reflections of this kind preoccupied him during the middle period of his career. In the autumn of 1879 he notes (CM, IViv, 487): 'Aegrotantium est, sanitatem cogitare: medicorum autem aegritudinem. Qui sani sunt nihil cogitant.' (It is for the sick to reflect on health: for doctors [presumably sick doctors] to reflect on sickness as well. The healthy reflect on nothing.) This first draft of an aphorism for *Human, All-Too-Human*, vol. 2, certainly puts the dull, intellectually unproductive healthy folk in their place; but the formulation did not satisfy him. The second version runs (CM, IViii, 474): 'Aegrotantium est sanitatem, medicorum aegritudinem cogitare. Qui vero mederi vult et ipse aegrotat, utramque cogitat.' [It is for the sick to reflect on health, for doctors [presumably healthy doctors] to reflect on sickness. The man who really wishes to heal, and is sick himself, reflects on both.] The 'man who really wishes to heal and is sick himself' requires no further introduction. As a man painfully conscious of his own unhealthiness, Nietzsche turns his eyes to an ideal of perfect soundness; at the same time he incorporates, as a philosopher-healer, the living urge to identify and remedy what has gone wrong with mankind in general. Only a man like Nietzsche, so the revised aphorism implies, only an invalid with an overmastering desire to improve the souls and the culture of men, can grasp the true relationship between health and sickness.

If there were any general laws of health and sickness perhaps he was well placed to discover them. But did they exist? This was the second, more serious problem which confronted him. For between the Wagnerian certainties of the pre-1875 period and the Zarathustrian certainties of the post-1881 period the strain of radical scepticism in his thought was strong. He doubted whether the uniqueness of existing phenomena could ever be comprehended by any general theory, and he was inclined to deny the possibility of formulating any grand principles of health and sickness whatsoever:

> For there is no health as such, and all attempts to define anything in that way have been miserable failures. Even the determination of what health means for your *body* depends on your goal, your horizon, your energies, your drives, your errors, and above all on the ideals and phantasms of your soul. Thus there are innumerable healths of the body; and [. . .] the more we put aside the dogma of the 'equality of men', the more must the concept of a normal health, along with a normal diet and the normal course of an illness, be abandoned by our physicians. Only then would the time have come to reflect on the health and sicknesses of the *soul*, and to find the peculiar virtue of each man in the health of his soul: in one person's case this health could, of course, look like the opposite of health in another person (*The Joyful Science*; II, 123f; cf. CM, vii, 379).

According to this view it makes no sense to generalize about health and sickness at all, whether of body or soul: health is simply the condition that happens to suit each particular individual (or tribe, or culture). During the years 1876–81, when the question of finding his own personal route to health was very much in the forefront of Nietzsche's mind, he often subscribes to such thoroughgoing medical scepticism; it is tied up with his conviction that each man is in practice his own best doctor because he alone knows just what works in his case. As he had explained much earlier, there was 'no general recipe for how each man is to be helped' (letter to von Gersdorff, 6 April 1867), and in 1882 he admits to Rohde that 'others might perish' by using those same remedies which he has been applying successfully to his 'body, mind and soul all at once'.

But we should not be misled by this, for even during his most sceptical period – that of *Human, All-Too-Human, The Dawn of Day* and *The Joyful Science* – he continues to grope for a generally valid definition of what true health is. Is it to be understood as a state of balance, a neutral condition to be protected from disturbance and restored thereafter, or should it rather be conceived dynamically as a capacity to *use* disturbances for the purposes of self-furtherance and growth? In the latter case, sickness or disturbance becomes a welcome and perhaps a necessary ally of health; in the former it remains a tiresome enemy, to be kept at bay or countered. Before his Wagner-crisis Nietzsche opted firmly, as we have seen, for the latter, dynamic conception: cultural 'health', with which he was still exclusively concerned, was recognized in the vigorous search for fresh stimuli and fresh obstacles, and in the power to make triumphant use of them. This heroic idea of health, as self-increasing, all-conquering vigour in action, was certainly the one which he in due course made emphatically his own. However, in the years immediately following the Wagner-crisis it was temporarily pushed into the background by the competing, classical notion of health as a balance.

During this interlude he is inclined to speak of both cultural health, and the health of the individual soul, in terms of the moderation of extremes, the correction of excess, the approximation to a golden mean. In the aphorism 'Music and sickness', for instance, he declares (1, 796) that even the 'moderate and noble man' is liable to drink a few drops too much from the enchanting cup of modern music, and he goes on: 'This minimal over-indulgence, constantly repeated, can however in the end bring about an even more profound disturbance and undermining of one's spiritual health than any single, crude debauch [. . .]'. Temperance, temperateness, self-restraint and the right measure are for the time being key-words in Nietzsche's vocabulary, and whether he is dealing with the emotional or moral health of the individual, or with the 'healthiness' of a work of art or of a culture or of a political system, his temporary assumption is that health resides in a proper equilibrium. At this juncture his general notion of health seems to reflect his need to palliate his own disturbed condition, by applying cold to counteract fever, by seeking dry air to counteract the effects of damp fogginess, etc. In retrospect he may have interpreted this pursuit of coldness and dryness as just one more stage in his search for the stimulatingly unsuitable (see his 1886 prefaces to the works of the middle period), but at the time he conceived arid frigidity simply as a necessary counter-balance and restorative. If it was the care of his own body, above all, which determined his thinking about health between 1875 and 1882, the sweet reasonableness which this care seemed to enjoin could not satisfy him emotionally for long: on the contrary, that heroic and dynamic notion of health, to which he had always been instinctively drawn and which could only with difficulty be related to physical medicine, soon reasserted itself. The concept of health derived from medicine proper was not inspiring enough for his taste:

> There is no health; Physitians say that wee,
> At best, enjoy but a neutralitie.
> And can there be worse sicknesse, than to know
> That we are never well, nor can be so?
>   (John Donne, *An Anatomie of the World*).

The idea of balance was finally quite unacceptable to Nietzsche. Even in *Human, All-Too-Human*, indeed, what is required for health often sounds less like a balance than a schizophrenic oscillation between extremes, a precarious leaping to and fro across chasms: 'A higher culture must, then, provide man with a double brain, so to speak with two cerebral ventricles, one to receive science, one to receive non-science: lying side by side, without confusion, separable, capable of being sealed off; this is a requirement of health' (I, 601).

In the post-*Zarathustra* work we no longer find even lip-service paid to the idea of health as a balance or a golden mean. Instead, health is conceived in two alternative ways, which are hard to reconcile: either it is something inextricably interlocked with sickness, something that requires sickness as its precondition, its partner, its eternally stimulating and eternally re-forming antagonist, – or else it is a condition of perfect wholeness, unimpaired strength. These two notions of health are uneasily juxtaposed: unspoilt pre-sickness health, and health-in-the-teeth-of-sickness (or health as 'self-overcoming'); on the one side health as undisturbed, pristine vigour, and on the other, health as a 'higher' kind or degree of vigour which thrives on damage and triumphs over damage – what he calls the 'great health' [*die grosse Gesundheit*, e.g. II, 258]. It seems plain that neither notion was derived – as was perhaps the notion of health as a balance – from strictly medical considerations or from biological studies. The latter one is the essentially Nietzschean one, but for all that he could never quite dismiss the Romantic dream of an original, immaculate soundness. Indeed, the images of spotless, 'innocent' strength come crowding in during his last phase – the blond lion, whose history is traced elsewhere in this volume, being the most notorious among them. We encounter in his final works a whole stage-army of *Wohlgeratene* ('soundly constituted' specimens, specimens which have turned out well). In modern times, especially in Europe, which Nietzsche now likens to a gigantic hospital, there is no logical room for these 'rare cases of magnificence in body and soul' (II, 863); yet still he paints their cheeks and puts them on parade. 'It is not inherently impossible', he muses (II, 935), that there may still be, somewhere in Europe, *remnants* of stronger races, of typically untimely human beings ['typisch unzeitgemässer Menschen'].' True, he fails actually to spot any such specimens of unspoilt health, but he has the nagging feeling that they *ought* to exist somewhere. And if they *do* exist, these paragons of health, miraculously untainted with the 'disease' of (Christian) morality, then they should be firmly protected from the sick all round them (II, 863).

VII

The fundamental idea that health cannot do without sickness, that it actually resides in the power to respond positively to the challenge offered by sickness, runs right through Nietzsche's work. Already in the early 1870s he had envisaged the cultural 'health' of the ancient Greeks, as we saw at the outset, not as some serene immunity from disorders but as their capacity to suffer from them and transcend them. No 'sturdy souls' they ['Vierschrötige des Geistes', II, 12], any

more than was Nietzsche himself, whose 'richly variable' condition
(*Ibid.*) he projected upon them: their skill lay in transforming sicknesses into agents promoting culture ['grosse Hilfsmächte der Kultur',
I, 572]. Even in the *Human, All-Too-Human* period, when – as we have just
noticed – he tried to impose on himself a calmer notion of health, the
challenge-and-response pattern is still clearly in evidence (cf. the
section 'Refinement through Degeneration' discussed above). In *The
Dawn of Day*, for instance, he complains that 'no thinker hitherto has
had the courage to measure the health of a society or of individual men
according to the number of parasites which they can stand' (I, 1151).
Later, in his preface to *Twilight of the Idols*, he declares (II, 941) that his
motto has long been *increscunt animi, virescit volnere virtus*;[4] in *The Wagner
Case* he repeats that sickness itself can be a stimulus to life, provided
that one is *healthy* enough for this stimulus (II, 913); but the classic
formulations occur in the Prefaces of 1886. In the preface to *Human,
All-Too-Human* he speaks of 'that immense, overflowing certainty and
health, which indeed has no wish to dispense with sickness, as a means
and a fish-hook of knowledge', of that 'superfluity of plastic, healing,
re-forming and restorative powers which is the very sign of *great*
health . . .' (I, 440f). In the preface to the second edition of *The Joyful
Science* he writes (II, 12f):

> Life – that means for us constantly transforming all that we are into
> light and flame; including everything that wounds us, we *cannot* do
> otherwise. And as for sickness: are we not tempted to ask whether
> we could get on without it? Only great pain is the ultimate liberator
> of the spirit [. . .].

And in the epilogue to *Nietzsche contra Wagner*, taking up the same passage, he states:

> And as far as my own long sickness is concerned, am I not infinitely
> more indebted to it than to my health? It is to my sickness that I owe
> a *higher* health, a kind of health which grows stronger on whatever
> does not destroy it! – *I also have it to thank for my philosophy.* . . .

'A kind of health which grows stronger on whatever does not destroy it!' . . . So even the most heroically healthy system has its limits
of tolerance; there are some things which even it cannot transform
and which ultimately bring it low. What are these things, both for
Nietzsche himself, and for humanity at large, whose history he re-
constructs in the image of his own?

Obviously, some physical wounds and poisonings are fatal even to the strongest constitution; some physical agents, at least, are absolutely harmful and destructive to living systems. Does the same apply to the most damaging non-physical agents that Nietzsche can think of in his last years – all of them connected with Christianity and the Christian ethic? When we come to those 'contagions' or 'infections' or 'poisons' such as a pessimistic view of the world (cf. I, 442), or a belief in sin (cf. I, 912), or a bad conscience (cf. II, 829), or the sentiment of pity or altruistic moral doctrines (*passim*), the question arises whether even these most dreaded and accursed 'sicknesses' can be regarded as the allies of health, in that they stimulate an individual or culture to attain to a 'higher' or 'grander' level of well-being. Should even those doctrines, thoughts and feelings that he personally finds most sick-making be allowed their status as good servants, willy-nilly, of the great Ascent of Man? This problem becomes acute in *Beyond Good and Evil* and *The Genealogy of Morals*: it is one of the most maddening problems of his last two sane years.

'The greatest and most uncanny malady ['Erkrankung'] of all, of which mankind has to this day not been cured', he says in the *Genealogy*, is 'man's *suffering from humanity*, his *suffering from himself*: brought on by the violent severance from his animal past' (II, 825f). Since then, i.e. since his very beginnings, man has been 'the animal soul turned in upon itself, taking arms against itself'; he has been the unhappy creature suffering from the malady of self-division, the creature with a 'bad conscience' [*schlechtes Gewissen*]. Looking at the matter from this height (gods would be needed fully to appreciate the spectacle, he says), we recognize sick humanity as the successor of healthy animality, and as the forerunner – perhaps – of superhealthy superhumanity. Man is '*the* sick animal' (II, 862), the species which is necessarily at odds with itself because it has had to turn its most basic self-assertive instincts *inwards*. Yet, although our enforced self-division may be disgusting to contemplate, we can take heart, he suggests, from the fact that it is only a sickness in the sense that pregnancy is a sickness (II, 829). Bad conscience, that malaise inseparable from humanity, can only be cured by mankind's giving birth to the superman. So the argument runs; but what is the role ascribed to Christianity within this large framework? It is the Christian doctrine, so it seems, which has brought this 'sickness' to 'a most terrible and sublime peak' (*Ibid.*), by deliberately feeding man's curious taste for self-denigration and self-torture. Does this mean therefore – to pursue the image – that Christianity, that '*one* will [which] has dominated Europe for eighteen centuries, the will to make of man a sublime *abortion*' (II, 624), may turn out, contrary to intention, to be precisely what stimulates the birth-pangs and hastens the delivery of the superman? Taking a bird's-eye view of human history – or looking at it 'with the mocking and unconcerned eye of an Epicurean god' (II, 624) – it seemed possible to assign a positive function *even* to Christianity, even to that most insidious poison ever taken by man: for ultimately the 'body of mankind' ['Leib der Menschheit', II, 781] might prove its fundamental health by assimilating and transforming even that. In practice, however, Nietzsche was quite unable to maintain such a divinely superior and detached view of the matter. He was only too deeply engaged in his immediate struggle against Christian sentiments and doctrines, in the interest of his own sanity and of the 'sanity' of European culture. And from this, immediate point of view he normally declared Christianity the one disastrous and fatal poison, which dried up the very sources of life, the one malady that could not put us on our mettle, the one damaging agent that even the healthiest individual or culture could not use in order to magnify itself through the combat.

Previously he had sometimes thought otherwise: 'If in earlier times the smallpox provided a test of the strength and health of one's physical constitution [. . .] so now perhaps the religious infection can provide such a test for the strength and health of one's mental constitution' (CM, IVii, 439; 1876). Exposure to Christianity might be actually beneficial to those strong enough to deal with it. But usually he was inclined to deny the possibility that (Christian) theism, and the moral values associated with it, might engender anything positive: as we have already seen, he envisaged it as a narcotic for the sick and suffering, and as a 'pure poison' for the not-yet-sick, i.e. as something that could only have a rotting and paralysing effect on them, never a stimulating and productive one (cf. I, 824). Hence he found it needful, in the general interest, to issue his vituperative condemnations of Christianity and all its works, culminating in the *Antichrist*, his dread warnings to us to keep clear of *this* disease at all costs. And yet . . . had he not personally imbibed the Christian poison to the full and demonstrated his 'superior' kind of health by his capacity to synthesize it and go beyond it? Even in the *Antichrist* there are passages which suggest that men *ought* to have sufficient inherent heroic vigour to absorb Christianity and deal with it.

That the strong races of northern Europe have not repudiated the Christian God certainly reflects no credit on their talent for religion – not to speak of their taste. They *ought* to have been able to cope [*fertig werden*] with such a sickly and decrepit product of *décadence*. But there lies a curse on them for not having coped with it: they have absorbed sickness, senility, contradiction into all their instincts – and since then they have *created* no new god' (II, 1178).

One line of Nietzsche's thought, in this last period, runs as follows: Christianity, in that it teaches man to vilify his natural impulses, to turn his eyes towards another (unreal, supernatural) world, and – so far as this world is concerned – to exhaust his energies in sympathizing with the 'bungled and the botched', is a 'sickness' which has an absolutely destructive effect on individuals, on cultures and on humanity at large. It is the great, contagious product and agent of decay which must be eliminated at all costs if possible; at least, those who are still unaffected, still 'healthy', must (if they exist) be protected from its dire influence.

According to a secondary line of thought, however, Christianity is the 'sickness' which provides an indispensable test and stimulus of human vigour.

I have declared war on the anaemic Christian ideal (along with all those things closely associated with it), not with the intention of destroying it, but simply to put an end to its *tyranny*, and to clear the ground for new ideals, *more robust* ideals . . . The continuance of the Christian ideal is one of the most desirable things there is [. . .] – Thus we immoralists need the *power of morality*: our instinct for self-preservation wants our *enemies* to stay strong, – it justs wants to achieve *mastery over them* (CM, VIIIii, 189).

The idea that Christianity as the prime threat to unbroken, *pre-sickness health* is something to be cut out and stamped on, lies awkwardly alongside the idea that it is at once the enemy and the secret ally which makes *great health* possible.

VIII

In this last period, 1887 to 1889, the very terms 'health' and 'sickness' become a burden and a trial to Nietzsche. Their ambiguity and their awkward interconnections frustrate him, and prevent him from announcing with effective simplicity which types of men, of thought, and of cultural activity he favours. He falls back instead, for preference, on the more fundamental biological terms: *ascending* and *descending life* [*das aufsteigende/das niedergehende Leben*], or alternatively *rich life* and *impoverished life* [*das reiche/das verarmte Leben*]. 'The man who is poor in vitality, the weak man, impoverishes life itself: he who is rich in vitality, the strong man, enriches it' (III, 780); there is only one apparently unambiguous concept, and that is 'exhaustion' [*Erschöpfung, Ibid.*] or 'weariness' ['Ermüdung', *passim*]. This simple distinction seems to provide a release from earlier complexities: all that now seems needed is to assign to everyone and everything a place either on the up-escalator or the down-escalator of 'life':

> Every individual may be examined to see whether he represents the ascending or the descending line of life. [. . .] If he represents the ascending line his value is indeed extraordinary – and for the sake of life-as-a-whole ['das Gesamt-Leben'], which in him takes a step *forward*, it may even be right to expend extreme care on the preservation, on the creation, of optimum conditions for him. [. . .] If he represents the descending development, decay, chronic degeneration, sickening (– sicknesses are, broadly speaking, only the consequences of decay, *not* the causes of it), then he can be accorded little value, and elementary justice demands that he *take away* as little as possible from the soundly-constituted. He is no better than a parasite on them . . . (*Twilight of the Idols*; II, 1008).

But it is not clear that much is gained by substituting these more basic biological terms for the medical terms 'health' and 'sickness'. The old problems still remain. Above all, how do the rising and falling parts or organs relate to one another, either within the literal organism of the individual human being, or within one of Nietzsche's (metaphorical) 'macro-organisms' such as a society, or a culture, or a people, or mankind itself, or perhaps even the world?[5] We cannot dispose of decay, certainly, but how should we react to its particular manifestations? Should we preserve what strength we may have by cutting them out or averting our eyes from them, or can we alternatively wax stronger by battling with them and 'absorbing' them, or in some other way turning them to our advantage? We are back, in fact, to the old question of *pre-sickness health* and *health-in-the-teeth-of-sickness*.

Décadence itself is not something *that should be opposed*: it is absolutely necessary and something that belongs to every age and every people. What *has* to be opposed with all strength is the introduction ['Einschleppung'] of this contagion into the healthy parts of the organism (III, 820; cf. III, 779).

The 'healthy parts of the organism' are evidently those which still enjoy pristine soundness. How does our 'physician of culture' propose to protect them from the spread of decay? By erecting some kind of *cordon sanitaire*? (But this would, on the *health-in-the-teeth-of-sickness* model, deprive the healthy parts of precisely the stimulus they need.) Or should we, more actively, hasten the total dissolution of the decaying parts, or even get out the knife?

> *A moral code for physicians.* – The invalid is a parasite on society. In a certain state it is indecent to go on living. To vegetate [. . .] ought to entail the profound contempt of society. Physicians, in their turn, ought to be the communicators of this contempt – not prescriptions, but every day a fresh dose of *disgust* with their patients . . . [. . .] Finally, a word of advice to *messieurs* the pessimists and other *décadents*. We have no power to prevent ourselves from being born: but we can rectify this error – for it is sometimes an error. When one *does away with* oneself one does the most estimable thing possible [. . .] . . . Society – what am I saying! *life* itself derives more advantage from that than from any sort of 'life' spent in renunciation, greensickness and other virtues – one has freed others from having to endure one's sight, one has removed an *objection* from life . . . (*Twilight of the Idols*, II, 1010f).

And as far as the knife is concerned, he declares in *Ecce Homo* (II, 1126) – repeating his constant complaint that we overvalue altruism at the expense of egoism – that *physiologists* know what to do with 'altruistic' organs:

> When within any organism the smallest organ begins to slacken, however slightly, in the complete certainty of its urge to preserve itself and assert its strength, in the certainty of its 'egoism', then the whole organism degenerates. The physiologist demands the *excision* of the degenerate part, he rejects any kind of solidarity with what is degenerate, he is utterly remote from feeling any sympathy with it. But the priest actually *desires* the degeneration of the whole, of mankind: that is why he *conserves* what is degenerate . . .

Nietzsche's last published works contain many such passages which suggest that men of altruistic mind (or in his language: men infected with the disease of Christian morality) should be literally extirpated – as centres of corruption, as corrupt and corrupting organs within a larger 'organism' – from the human community to which they belong.

At least by this stage it should have become clear that the question of how far Nietzsche may have misled and entrapped both himself and others by using the vocabulary of health and sickness in the ways that he did, is far from being a merely academic question. Where there has been talk, since his day, of a 'sick' or 'decadent' culture or society, and where this talk has been understood literally, the call has often come for radical surgery, for the excision of the 'diseased' or 'degenerate' or 'poisonous' or 'infected' parts of the 'organism'. When Plato (*The Statesman* 293A) aired the view that the rulers of the 'body politic' were justified in treating the 'organs' of such a 'body' – provided they were acting for its betterment and 'in accordance with science' – just as a doctor treats the bodily organs of an individual patient, e.g. by cutting out, burning, etc., he did not forget that he was making a comparison; but Nietzsche drew such parallels so close that the lines often converged.

Whenever he throws in – as he frequently does in his late works – the phrase 'as every doctor knows' or 'as every physiologist knows', then the time has come for us to prick up our ears. For it means that he is talking, not about the literal bodies which are the concern of physicians and physiologists, but about one or other of his metaphorical 'bodies', which he is now persuaded must work exactly as a human body works, or – to be more precise – exactly as he supposes his own body to work, the pain-racked yet somehow triumphant body of Herr Dr Friedrich Nietzsche.

We have seen that the medical terms which pervade Nietzsche's writings are used to begin with largely as conventional metaphors, but that after 1875 changes set in. First of all, the medical imagery which he uses to illuminate his discussion of cultural matters becomes more obtrusive and is elaborated in more concrete detail; he develops his analogies more precisely, referring frequently to specific diseases and cures; and in doing so he begins to imply that some of his metaphorical statements, for instance those concerning poisons and antidotes, might be understood literally. Secondly, we now find him paying attention, not only in his private documents but in his philosophical works as well, to medical questions proper, questions of diet and so forth, and these forays of his into the field of physical medicine have the effect as intended of making his quasi-literal uses of medical metaphor sound more plausible.

It is on this border line between metaphorical and literal statement that Nietzsche sets up his philosophical dispensary. The metaphors which he encourages us to take literally do not rest merely on analogies between the body's workings and the activities of the mind or soul; they are also based on structural and functional analogies between the human body and such larger units as cultures or the world in its entirety. He was well aware – particularly in his middle period – of the dangers of wholesale analogizing, but he also recognized that philosophers are inveterate analogizers and that he could not avoid the habit.

The aim of this essay has been to suggest – no more is possible in the compass – some of the ways in which medical terms and concepts came to dominate Nietzsche's thinking. In proceeding chronologically we have had to move from his relatively amiable twitting of his duller academic colleagues for their (metaphorical) anaemia and dyspepsia, to his rabid assault on altruism conceived as a literal plague of humanity. If that leaves a bad taste in the mouth – to use an appropriate image – it cannot be helped. But if we read him throughout with the sympathy which he affected to despise, we may find that even the most cruel and repulsive of his final statements sound less like encouragements to evil than cries of despair. Irrespective of what has been done in his name he remains a figure as moving as that Philoctetes with whom he felt such obvious affinity.

NOTES

1 The reference is to the Musarion-Ausgabe, ed. R. Oehler, M. Oehler and Fr C. Würzbach (Munich, 1920–9), vol. II, p. 346. Following references to this edition are given in the same form.
2 Sections 251 and 300 of *The Joyful Science* (II, 156 and 176) indicate how closely Nietzsche identified himself with the figure of Prometheus. Already for the title-page of *The Birth of Tragedy* he had chosen a representation of the unbound Prometheus, probably inspired by Shelley's version of the myth, which he admired (see his letter to Rohde of 28 August 1877).

3 Cf. his first note on the subject of the eternal recurrence, written in August 1881 (CM, vii, 392). It takes the form of a menu-card, beginning:

1. The incorporation ('Einverleibung') of the basic errors.
2. The incorporation of the passions.
3. The incorporation of knowledge [. . .].

The last item on this menu for the mind-stomach is the 'eternal recurrence of the same things', the 'thought of thoughts'. 'If you can incorporate the thought of thoughts,' he writes (CM, vii, 394), 'then it will transform you.' To judge from its heaviness it is not bread, but a stone, and requires a superhuman digestive system if it is to be coped with.

4 'Courage grows, strength is renewed through wounding.' From a fragment of the epic poet A. Furius Antias (*Fragmenta Poetarum Romanorum*, ed. Baehrens (Leipzig, 1886), p. 276). Nietzsche was coy about the source of this quotation which Mr Oliver Taplin kindly traced for me.

5 'Let us beware of thinking that the world is a living being. In what direction could it expand? What could it feed on? How could it grow and multiply?' (*The Joyful Science*, II, 115). He issues this 'let us beware' warning precisely because he is himself inclined to apply his organic model to everything.

7

NIETZSCHE'S ANIMALS:
IDEA, IMAGE AND INFLUENCE

T. J. Reed

I

Animal nature is at the centre of Nietzsche's thought. His inquiries belong to the philosophy and criticism of culture but they speak the language of natural history. He regularly refers to man as the 'animal species "Man" ' ['das Tier "Mensch" '], fitting the precise description to the nature of the case. Thus man is 'an animal in the highest degree subject to fear', a fact which explains human laughter as a response to welcomly non-lethal surprises (1 558f).[1] He is a 'fantastic animal' in his need, unique among species, to believe that he knows the reason for his existence (II 35). He is 'the most endangered animal', and therefore developed means to communicate his situation and needs, which in turn became the basis for his reflective self-consciousness (II 219ff). He is 'the not yet fixed animal', i.e. a species still malleable about which evolution has not yet said the last word (II 623). He is 'the cruellest animal', especially towards himself (II 464), and he is 'the bravest animal', having overcome all the others (II, 407). He is, in his aberrations from the path of instinct, 'the sick animal' (II, 862); and yet precisely these aberrations make him 'the most interesting animal' (II, 1174). Indeed, he only became an interesting animal at all, with a 'depth' denied to other species, as a result of one such aberration (II, 778).

The basic proposition is meant literally, in a way the occasional reference to man as a plant species ['die Pflanze "Mensch" ' – II, 606] obviously is not. There is also, it is true, a rhetorical intention, which is to stress Nietzsche's unconventional view and express the mixture of scientific detachment and passionate sympathy he feels for man. But the statements quoted, and the many others like them, are not on that account metaphorical. It is one of Nietzsche's basic beliefs that man is, before all else, an animal being, and that to attribute other origins to him is an illusion. He summarizes this view in a late work thus: 'We have learned to think differently. We have become in all respects more modest. We no longer derive Man from "the Spirit" or "the Godhead", we have put him back among the animals' (II, 1174). Unlike so much in the late writings, the tone here is unassertive, matching the modesty to which Nietzsche lays claim. For the issue is in his eyes a settled one, and it has long been so. What he states as a conclusion has in reality, from his earliest essays on, been an axiom. To this extent Nietzsche is a Darwinian.

The first function of such a belief is, not surprisingly, reductive. Traditional conceptions of man are undone. Nietzsche labels as one of man's two 'fundamental mistakes' the idea that he is 'the astounding exception, the super-animal, the almost-God, the meaning of the Creation' (I, 879). Human history is only the continuation of animal and plant evolution (I, 266). To Nietzsche's penetrating eye human social conventions reveal, as they do to a modern ethologist, patterns of primitive purpose analogous to those of animal instinct; and he accordingly designates 'the whole moral phenomenon as an animal one' (I, 1031f). Humanity may not regard animals as moral beings – but what is 'humanity'? No more than a 'prejudice from which at least we animals do not suffer', so he imagines one of them saying (I, 1199). And in a not readily translatable pun on the German for common sense ['der gesunde Menschenverstand'] he similarly imagines an animal critique of man as a creature which has lost its 'gesunden Tierverstand' (II, 152).

'Humanity' as popularly conceived is thus false in one of two senses. It either overlays man's true nature or – worse – has perverted it. Indeed, the overlaying with spiritual and social concepts is only the ideological superstructure created by the perverting agencies, Christianity especially. Nietzsche's campaign is directed at revealing what has been overlaid and at restoring what has been perverted. For, if the 'animal' argument is reductive, it is only so in a formal sense: the basic animal nature is not seen as of lower value than the false constructs of Western culture, but as the necessary starting-point for a different and healthier culture which it is Nietzsche's ultimate aim to bring about.

Of the two distinguishable tasks, revelation and restoration, the former is the more straightforward. It involves polemicizing against received ideas and against the psychological and historical mechanisms responsible for establishing them. In this part of his campaign Nietzsche is not far from the French *philosophes*, although it is doubtful whether any of them can equal the subtlety of his analysis of Christian values and motivation. The logic with which the terms 'good/bad' of primitive peoples are shown turning into the terms 'evil/good' of those who were too weak to come off well in the primal value-system; or the analogous reversal by which a will frustrated in its operations on the outside world turns in on itself and creates a sour-grape spirituality – these not strictly demonstrable historical suggestions have an intuitive plausibility and a sheer intellectual elegance which goes well beyond the denigratory activities of a socially motivated anti-clericalism.

The task of restoration – of persuading men to return to their animal selves – is more difficult. It requires an image of that pristine state impressive and attractive enough to invite allegiance; and it requires a persuasive account of how a superior culture could then arise from the restored animal basis. This second difficulty is one which in some form would face any cultural philosopher who denied the origins of man's spiritual characteristics in a transcendent realm. He would have to account for man's spiritual and cultural life by a theory of transformation or intensification of purely natural attributes, and he might well find himself correlating (as Nietzsche does) levels of natural vitality with standards of cultural achievement. But Nietzsche's difficulty is greater than just this because of his radical position. He is not merely *accounting* for cultural phenomena, he is *rejecting* the greater part of the culture of past and present in the name of an untried potential – or at least, of a potential untried since the Greeks; and the Greeks themselves only become supporting evidence for his hypotheses when he has subjected them to a revolutionary reinterpretation which is based on the values for which he is arguing, and thus no more readily acceptable than that argument itself.

In other words, Nietzsche is asking modern men to buy a pig in a poke. Clearly, something more magnificent than a pig must be offered if they are to assent. As Nietzsche wrote, it is not enough to prove a thing, one must also seduce people into accepting it' (I, 1199). This is where his characteristic literary method comes in. For, if the consequences of a belief in Man's animal nature for the substance of

Nietzsche's thought are not peculiar to him, the consequences for his literary presentation are unique. The 'animal' thesis gives rise to a whole set of images – of vitality, spontaneity, beauty, cruelty – which dominate the discussions of moral and cultural values, realizing them as a visualizable drama, and setting an emotional tone. This is a central issue of the interpretation of Nietzsche, in the narrower textual and the broader historical sense; for the interaction of thought and image, so unlike the sparseness usual in philosophical exposition, is the essence of Nietzsche's writing, and it was also one source of his immense and problematic influence.

II

Nietzsche had a marked propensity for animal simile and metaphor, even when not treating his central themes. Within the space of the preface to *The Dawn of Day* alone, we find the author presented (implicitly) as a mole busy undermining the ground of moral convention; self-criticism as a scorpion sinking its sting into its own body; and Rousseau as a 'moral tarantula' (I, 1011f). Elsewhere in the same work man is an epistemological spider in a web of deceptive sense-habits on which all his thinking and judging must rest (I, 1092f), and the denizen of a spider's-web of purposes through which the monsters of chance sometimes break (I, 1101). Rome too, though this seems to be a borrowing from Heine,[2] is the great spider, absolute at the centre of her empire (I, 1059). Elsewhere again, man withdrawing his senses from contact with the world in an attempt to live as pure spirit is likened to a tortoise withdrawing into its shell (II, 1174); those rare people who develop their essential nature beneath the second nature of custom and education are called 'snakes enough one day to slough off this skin' (I, 1232); and the source of Nietzsche's philosophy in the warm regions of feeling is put negatively in the statement 'we are not thinking frogs . . . with frozen entrails' (II, 12). There are also numerous references to men in the mass as a herd, or to men singly as sheep (e.g. I, 830; III, 686), which is conventional enough but does produce Zarathustra's epigram on modern conformity and the absence of creative leadership: 'No pastor and *one* herd' (II, 284). Conventional too is the lamb Nietzsche takes over from Christian imagery; but he uses it to make his own anti-Christian position clear by the simple expedient of putting the lamb (and hence Christianity) in its natural place as the victim of fiercer creatures (i.e. tougher *moralinfrei* philosophies):

Then
Suddenly, with a straight stroke,
A plucked flight,
To fall upon *lambs*,
Swiftly down, ravenous,
Lusting for lambs,
Brooking no lamb-souls,
Implacable to anything that looks
Sheep-like, lamb-eyed, fleecy,
Grey, with lambish-sheepish-goodwill!
So
Eagle-like, panther-like
Are the poet's yearnings (II, 535).[3]

With this ravening eagle and the afterthought panther simile, we approach Nietzsche's most important animal. The imagery just reviewed, examples of which could be multiplied, provides so to speak the supporting cast. The central role is played by another beast of prey who carries the main doctrine of Nietzsche's thought on culture and morals. He is, in one of Nietzsche's most celebrated and most commonly misunderstood formulations, the 'blond beast' [blonde Bestie']: that is, the lion.[4]

He appears twice under that title, the first time free and active, the second imprisoned and passive. A careful look at both passages will remove some misunderstandings about what Nietzsche was really saying and implying; but it will also show how his imagery throws the presentation of the argument off balance and, by its own development, is itself conducive to misunderstanding.

The main passage occurs in the first of the three essays that make up *The Genealogy of Morals*, the one which deals with the two value-systems 'good/bad' and 'evil/good' mentioned above. When it comes to pointing out how precisely the 'evil' of the Judeo-Christian system coincides with the 'good' of the more primitive aristocratic morality, Nietzsche confesses that those aristocratic primitives would not be comfortable enemies to have to face:

> Anyone who got to know those 'good' men only as enemies, got to know nothing but *bad enemies*; and the self-same people who are held in check so strictly by custom, reverence, practice, gratitude, and even more by mutual surveillance, by jealousy *inter pares*, and who on the other hand show themselves in their behaviour to one

another so inventive in regard, self-control, delicacy, faithfulness, pride and friendship – these same people, when turned outwards towards alien things, alien *groups*, are not much better than released beasts of prey. They then enjoy freedom from all social constraint, they make up in the wilderness for the tension created by being long enclosed, fenced in, in the peace of community, they *revert* to the innocence of the beast of prey's conscience, as exulting monsters, who perhaps go off after a ghastly sequence of murder, burning, rape, torture, with an elation and equanimity as if they had only committed some student prank, convinced that now the poets will for long have something to sing and celebrate. At the bottom ['auf dem Grunde'] of all these aristocratic races the beast of prey is unmistakable, the magnificent *blond beast* lustfully prowling after booty and victory; this hidden basic layer from time to time needs a release, the animal must out again, must return to the wilderness – Roman, Arabian, Germanic, Japanese nobility, Homeric heroes, Scandinavian Vikings – in this need they are all the same. It is the noble races who have left the concept 'barbarian' wherever they have passed; even in their highest culture there is betrayed a consciousness of this and a pride in it (for example when Pericles in that famous funeral oration tells his Athenians 'our boldness has forced its way everywhere by land and sea, erecting imperishable monuments to itself everywhere, in good deeds *and bad*').

Physical recklessness and a serene pleasure in destruction, victory and cruelty make up this concept of the barbarian, the vandal, the Goth. It finds a modern echo – mistakenly enough, in Nietzsche's view – in the contemporary European reaction to German power:

> The profound, icy mistrust that Germans arouse as soon as they come to power, in our times again – is still a late form of that indelible horror with which for centuries Europe looked on at the raging of the blond Germanic beast (although between the old Germanic race and us Germans there is hardly a conceptual let alone a blood-kinship) (II, 785f).

This last aside would have sufficed, in a world of exact communication, to prevent the misapprehension that Nietzsche's blond beast is the symbol of a powerful and aggressive Germany, of 1870 (to which 'icy mistrust' refers) or of 1914 and later developments (for which he has often been held posthumously responsible). But communication is a chancy business. An image has immensely more power than a corrective aside, especially when the writer becomes more widely known about than actually read – to say nothing of what may happen when his images are taken up by ideologists with aims of their own. For when no surrounding argument is there to limit its implications, the image takes on a cruder meaning than the one it had in its full context.

Yet even there the seeds of misunderstanding are sown by a careless handling of the image, which already begins to blur the sense it was designed to convey. The beast of prey first stood for *one element*, albeit fundamental, lurking in the primitive races and demanding a release which certain occasions licensed. For the rest, the race might have, like the Greeks, a high culture. But the comparison of ancient and modern Germans which follows contains two important shifts. First, 'the blond Germanic beast' now stands for the race as such, no longer explicitly for its destructive impulses – a much easier equation for the imagination to grasp and retain. Second, by placing the adjective 'Germanic' where it is, Nietzsche has altered the function and reference of his image.

To make doubly sure the point that, in its first use, the image did not stand for the Germanic people simply – not even for the ancient one – it has been argued that, if Nietzsche had meant 'blond beast' to apply to them, then the addition of the adjective 'Germanic' second time round would be a senseless pleonasm.[5] But this objection points up what has occurred. Nietzsche should have written 'the raging of the Germanic blond beast'; that would have singled out one from the primitive races he had listed, and left the image intact. But by writing 'blond Germanic beast', he has broken down his own image. For 'blond' now necessarily applies to the entity 'Germanic beast', which means that only 'beast' stands as a metaphor for the race named. The justification for 'blond' is no longer the total image of the lion, but the actual (traditionally assumed) Nordic characteristic. One need only reflect that Nietzsche could never – had he chosen to single out a different exemplar from his list – have written 'blond Japanese beast', to see that his actual formulation has been determined by rhythmic factors and encouraged by the coincidence of original image and ethnic description.

In the second passage on the blond beast, the crudening of the image to stand for a whole human specimen instead of for a distinguishable element in it has become complete. It is the second paragraph of the section 'Improvers of Mankind' in *Twilight of the Idols*. Morality is Nietzsche's target, and he is questioning the assumption that to make moral is to improve:

> Both the *taming* of the beast 'Man' and the *breeding* of a particular species of Man has been called 'improvement': only when we use these zoological terms do we express realities – realities, it is true, of which the typical 'improver', the priest, knows nothing – *refuses* to know anything . . . To call the taming of an animal its 'improvement' is for our ears almost a joke. Anyone who knows what goes on in menageries has doubts as to whether the beast is 'improved' there. It is weakened, made less harmful, the depressive emotion of fear, pain, wounds and hunger are used to make it a *sick* beast. – It is no different with the tamed human being whom the priest has 'improved'. In the early middle ages, when indeed the church was a menagerie more than anything else, they hunted out the finest examples of the 'blond beast' wherever he could be found – they 'improved', for instance, the aristocratic Germanic people. But what did a German look like after he had been 'improved', seduced into the cloister? Like a caricature of Man, like a misshapen creature: he had become a 'sinner', he sat in a cage, they had shut him in with nothing but terrible concepts . . . There he lay then, sick, feeble, malevolent towards himself; full of hatred for the impulses to life, full of suspicion against everything that was still strong and happy. In short, a 'Christian' . . . Physiologically speaking: in the struggle with the beast you *can* only weaken it by making it sick. The church understood that: it *ruined* Man, it weakened him – but it claimed to have 'improved' him . . . (II, 979f).

As in the course of the first 'blond beast' passage, the metaphor has come to mean the primitive race as such, not just a suppressed element within it. The simplification could be explained by saying that Christian morality, for Nietzsche, was directed at taming those crueller impulses for which the 'blond beast' stood in the more discriminating earlier use, and that he is using a rhetorical *pars pro toto*. But that seems an undue rationalization. More plausibly, the nature of the image has pressed towards the simpler equation of beast = man; the subtler psychological understanding on which the image first rested is hard to maintain against this pressure, inherent in any process of talking in images; and the simpler equation makes it easier to create the dramatic situation and its polemical effect. The beast which was so fearsome yet magnificent in his murderous maraudings is proportionately pathetic when confined and denatured.

But the most important feature of this whole development is that we have virtually lost sight of the reason for valuing those aristocratic peoples positively, amid the excitements of an account which concentrates on their destructiveness. To this extent, Nietzsche is an aesthete as he dwells *con amore*, as much fascinated as horrified, on the primitive cruelties whose reality must have been so very unaesthetic. One cannot dismiss the charge of romantic exoticism and immature fancy (the phrase 'as if they had only committed some student prank' gives food for thought here). Why else such glorying in destructiveness? What advantage can it have over the most devitalized denizen of the Christian cage?

This brings us to the second element in Nietzsche's task of restoration: the required account of how a superior culture can arise from animal nature. Immediately following the first 'blond beast' passage, in *The Genealogy of Morals*, Nietzsche tries to explain the positive qualities associated with the beast beneath the skin.

Unfortunately, his explanation takes the form of a lengthy reference to Hesiod on the sequence of cultural ages and is somewhat obscure to the non-classicist reader – especially after the powerful spotlight which has just been directed at the blond beast. The scholar has here taken over from the poet. What Nietzsche says is that Hesiod was embarrassed by the contradictions he found in Homer's poetry – 'the splendid but equally violent, terrible world of Homer'; and the only way he found to solve the apparent contradiction of cultural splendour and primitive violence was to postulate two distinct ages where in fact (Nietzsche says) there was only one. What Hesiod called the Age of Gold was that of the heroes and demigods of Troy and Thebes – hence the magnificence. Then came the grimmer, unfeeling Age of Bronze. But the two, Nietzsche argues, are merely different sorts of recollection of one and the same age. The magnificence is recalled in the traditions of the aristocratic families, who had their roots in the 'great' Homeric world; the horrors are recalled by the descendants of those who were killed, robbed and dragged away into slavery. In other words, cultural magnificence and a world of violence are compatible and can coexist in time.

Nietzsche then turns away to polemicize against the taming of the blond beast, anticipating the discussion we have seen from *Twilight of the Idols*. He has not yet established anything more than the temporal compatibility of culture and terror, certainly no causal relationship. But he has given a clue to where to find a causal account, for he introduces the digression on Hesiod by the words 'I once drew attention to Hesiod's embarrassment . . .' The reference is to section 189 of the Third Book of *The Dawn of Day* (I, 1137). There we find only the same point made briefly, if a little more clearly. But if we follow the trail back to Nietzsche's very first treatment of Hesiod (not published in his lifetime, and therefore not referable back the *Genealogy*) we find something of much greater substance and value.

This is the essay 'Homer's Contest', one of the 'five prefaces to five unwritten books' which Nietzsche presented to Cosima Wagner at Christmas 1872. At one stroke we find the first full statement of Nietzsche's monistic philosophy of culture, the first use of his most famous animal metaphor, and the first (and one of the best) of his accounts of exactly how natural impulse is canalized and transmuted into cultural forms. The essay opens thus:

> When people talk of *humanity*, they have a basic idea of something which *separates* and distinguishes Man from nature. But there is no such separation in reality: the 'natural' qualities and the ones called really 'human' are inseparably intertwined. Man in his highest and noblest powers is wholly nature and bears her uncanny dual character. Those of his capacities which are terrible and considered inhuman may even be the fruitful soil from which alone all humanity in impulses, deeds and works can grow forth (III, 291).

Nietzsche's example is the Greeks. Did not they, the 'most humane people of ancient times', have 'a streak of cruelty, of tiger-like pleasure in destruction'? He lists examples – from deeds of Alexander the Great, caricatures in turn of deeds described in the *Iliad*, and from political events recorded in Thucydides like the bloody conflicts of parties in the Corcyra revolution, or the common practices of slaughtering the male population of a captured city. In these things we see into 'the abysses of hatred', and in their general acceptance by the Greeks we see (here Nietzsche is surely naïve about the degree of reflection on which such practices were based) that they 'regarded such a full release of hatred as a necessity'. However that may be, they did serve as moments of release for confined feeling: 'the tiger darted forth, a voluptuous cruelty looked out from his terrible eye'.[6]

This much is already a clue to the unitary understanding of the Homeric world: violence was something that went without saying for the Homeric audience. But what if we go back beyond the Homeric poems, which already have some warmth and mellowness through their sheer artistry? With that veil removed, we see a world of 'night and horror', ruled by Strife, Desire, Deception, Age and Death. Imagine the Greek world before it was lightened and purified by Delphi. It would be almost unbearable, and could be rendered bearable only by the creation of myths of conflict and by an acceptance of conflict (with the cruelty of victory entailed) as a basic reality of existence. Conflict, strife – 'eris' – therefore colour the ethical world of the Greeks in a way post-Christian Europeans cannot readily appreciate.

But the crucial thing is what the Greeks made of 'eris', and of its psychological counterpart, envy. These things, which the Christian moral system would consider *prima facie* evil, became the mainspring of cultural and civic achievement and the basis of stable social forms. Conflict and envy became competition: 'a new greatness takes fire from every great virtue', 'every talent has to maintain itself by struggle'. Every Greek aspires to be an instrument of his city's struggle against other city-states: 'this inflamed his egotism, and this bridled and confined it'. Only when a talent became absolute and beyond competition, or when a state became unquestionably supreme, did downfall threaten both.

The quality of this as Greek cultural history is not at issue. What is important is the principle of the transformation of potentially destructive impulses into creative action. Remove the impulses, tame them, shame them, or otherwise pervert them, and you have removed the basis for creativity. In the ultimate refinement of 'eris', the great tragedians Aeschylus and Euripides are thought of as competing with their own projected ideal of perfection in dramatic poetry, and only gradually inculcating these standards into other Greeks as their judges: what begins as a low impulse ends by creating an absolute ideal (I, 559). This account comes later, in *Human, All-Too-Human*; and it is there too, in the very first paragraph, that Nietzsche provides a general theory of sublimation which can cope with apparent antithetical concepts and show how the one may grow from the other: rationality from irrationality, aesthetic contemplation from acquisitive desire, altruism from egoism, truth from error. He calls this a 'chemistry of concepts and feelings', and he warns that its results may be to show that 'the most splendid colours are the product of lowly, indeed scorned materials' (I, 447).

Nietzsche is not, then, after all merely an aesthete delighting in amoral primitive power for its own sake. He values instinctual life as a basis, or raw material, for 'higher' activities. We can illustrate how he thought this transformation or sublimation occurred from various spheres of culture.

Social morality. Nietzsche reads hospitality as originally an attempt to lame the hostile impulses of an alien creature. 'Where people no longer feel strangers to be in the first instance enemies, hospitality declines; it blossoms as long as its "evil" precondition blossoms' (I, 1194). This analysis is very like the interpretations ethologists now place on the forms of animal behaviour which avoid open conflict – ritualizations in which a destructive instinct is diverted for the benefit of the species. Again, more cryptically (but comprehensibly if we remember the argument of 'Homer's Contest') Nietzsche links envy and friendship in the Greeks, contrasting Christians in whom there is a similarly causal but qualitatively very different link between self-contempt and pride (I, 1058).

Intellectual processes. Against Spinoza, who defined *intelligere* as 'non ridere, non lugere, neque detestari', Nietzsche argues that acts of understanding are not an exclusion of these impulses, but an intricate combination of them all, a resolution of their conflict not in the sense that they are all cancelled out, but in the sense (we might say) in which a parallelogram of forces is a resolution in mechanics:

> Before a cognitive act is possible, each of these impulses must have put forward its one-sided view of the thing or event; afterwards there occurred the struggle between these one-sidednesses and from it, occasionally, a midway point, a calming, an admission of right on all sides, a kind of justice and treaty: for by means of justice and a treaty all these impulses can assert themselves and jointly be right. We, who only become conscious of the final reconciliation scenes and last reckoning of this long process, consequently believe that *intelligere* is something conciliatory, just, good, something opposed to our impulses; whereas it is only a *certain relation between the impulses* (II, 192f).

And Nietzsche concludes that 'thinking', which has always been taken to be a conscious activity, is only a small part of our total mental life; and that deliberate conscious thinking as practised by philosophers is the weakest and mildest form (which is why philosophers have been so easily misled about the nature of cognition).

Artistic creation. Here Nietzsche is again concerned with rich and conflicting impulses which man – in contrast, precisely, to the other animals – has bred up in himself. He postulates that the maximum of conflicting impulses, compatible in a given individual with overall control, is the basis of genius:

> The highest Man would have the greatest quantity of impulses, and also in the relatively greatest intensity that can be borne. In fact: where the plant species Man appears in a strong specimen, one finds the powerful *opposed* instincts (e.g. Shakespeare), only mastered (III, 422).

This last is not worked out into a full explanation of Shakespeare's genius – one could hardly expect that – but it suffices to complete a picture of a consistent approach. Nietzsche is for all-inclusion, not exclusion. Meaningful and valuable activities are a matter of integrating and controlling the totality of psychic and physical factors, not of escaping from them or anxiously banning them. Where Schopenhauer saw art as a first release from the yoke of the Will, a step on the way to saintly abnegation, Nietzsche speaks of aesthetics as 'applied physiology' (II, 1041). Where Kant saw aesthetic experience as 'pleasure without interest', a pure contemplation which was all that remained when purpose and appetite were switched off, Nietzsche prefers Stendhal's *aperçu* that beauty was 'une promesse de bonheur' (II, 845). In his first major work, *The Birth of Tragedy*, he had shaped his own positive conception into the theory of an ideal art where Dionysian forces were controlled by an Apolline principle, the riches of chaos by the clarity of form.

In all these cases, there is a spontaneous internal transformation – perhaps therefore better termed a transition – of instinctual into cultural phenomena. Nietzsche also envisages more deliberate applications of an instinct to the task of creation. Cruelty, for example, is a necessity: 'The man who has greatness is cruel towards his own second-rate virtues and reflections' (II, 159). Since cruelty towards anything old and weak is elsewhere Nietzsche's definition of 'Life' itself,[7] greatness in virtue and thought is thus directly linked with the basic impulses of life. And the man who can be thus cruel towards himself can also have a stimulating, renewing function within his society, preventing it from going to sleep: it has always been the 'strongest and wickedest' spirits who have brought innovation in religion and morality and custom (II, 38f). Cruelty and wickedness are here so sublimated that one may well ask whether they are themselves not already metaphors.

Lastly, Nietzsche provides accounts of the transformation of whole cultures through the onslaught of racial groups with strong instincts – an analogous process to the exercise of cruelty, but in a 'historical' context. (The historicity has to be viewed sceptically – Nietzsche is working a similar vein of conjectural anthropology to the one favoured in the eighteenth century, when Kant, Schiller and Herder were its main German exponents.) The 'hard truth', Nietzsche says, about the beginnings of every higher culture on earth is that

> men with a still natural nature, barbarians in every terrible sense of the word, men of prey ['Raubmenschen'], with their force of will and desire for power still intact, flung themselves on weaker, more civilized, more peaceable, perhaps mercantile or stock-breeding races, or on old crumbling cultures, in which the last vital force was flickering out in brilliant fireworks of spirit and decay. The aristo-cratic caste was originally always the barbarian caste: their superi-ority lay not primarily in their physical but in their spiritual strength – they were the more *complete* men (which at every stage is as much as to say 'the more complete animals' ['die ganzeren Bestien'] (II, 727).

And he similarly explains the formation of the State not by any form of 'contract', but by the sudden arrival of

> some pack of blond beasts of prey ['blonder Raubtiere'], a conquer-ing and master-race which, organized for war and with the capacity to organize, unhesitatingly lays its terrible claws on a perhaps numerically superior but still shapeless, still wandering population (II, 827).

In these passages Nietzsche's favourite ideas and images come to-gether – power and wholeness, instinct and aristocracy, animal and barbarian, nature and creativity – challenging us to distinguish literal assertion from metaphor and perhaps even raising the suspicion that hectic imagination may have preceded and produced intellectual theory.[8]

The complexity of these transformation processes, whether spon-taneous or deliberate, whether on the 'historical' or the personal psychological plane; and the complexity of the cultural end-products which Nietzsche envisages – all this makes it impossible that he should ultimately value animal nature itself as an ideal for its own sake. This is implicit as early as *The Birth of Tragedy*, in familiar imagery. Speaking of the barbarians' (as distinct from the Greeks') Dionysian orgies, Nietzsche says that 'precisely the wildest beasts of nature were here unleashed', which resulted in a 'regression of Man to the tiger and the ape' (I, 27). The point is later made explicit in what Nietzsche says of the goals men should set themselves. Immediately after his announcement 'I teach ye the superman', Zarathustra asks his hearers whether they will be content with less: 'All beings before ye created something beyond themselves: and ye desire to be the ebb of this great tide and would rather return to the animal than overcome Man?' (II, 279). In the next section he calls man 'a rope stretched between animal and superman – a rope across an abyss' (II, 281). The animal is not enough, only a beginning – albeit a necessary beginning, not to be scorned. In another of Zarathustra's speeches, animal nature is the pack of wild dogs in the cellar, which had to be transformed into birds and sweet singers: the passions, directed at a chosen goal, become the creative man's virtues (II, 302). And where higher man fails in an attempt at some high goal, he is characteristically said to be 'like the leaping tiger who has missed his prey' (II, 528). Nietzsche sums up his position perfectly in *Beyond Good and Evil*, where he imagines a criticism that his ideas are merely regressive ('Bad! Bad! What? is he not going – back?') and answers: 'Yes! But you do not rightly understand him if you complain at that. He goes back as everyone must who is trying to take a great leap forward' (II, 747).

Even when Nietzsche polemicizes against the false paths man has taken in the past, against conventional morality and the sense of superiority it induced, there is still an implied rejection of the mere animal state clearly to be heard: 'Without the mistakes that lie in the assumptions of morality, Man would have remained an animal. But as it is, he took himself for something higher, and imposed stricter laws on himself' (I, 481).

This last is symptomatic of an ambivalence in Nietzsche which there is no space to explore fully here, but which is directly connected with the question of how culture can be created starting from animal nature. The possibility of such creation is what makes man an 'interesting animal' at all; and it is an inescapable fact that, however much past efforts at cultural creation may seem to Nietzsche to have entailed perversions of man, they did at least lift him off the level of mere animality. The asceticism of the priest, for all the negativity of its distorting ethic, was the first 'dangerous' and 'interesting' form of human life (ii, 778); before it, 'the animal species "Man" had no meaning. Its existence on earth contained no goal; "Why Man at all?" – was a question with no answer' (ii, 899).

At times, in fact, Nietzsche's recognition of the cultural achievement of Christianity loses its grudging note and becomes almost an open celebration – for example, in a passage from *The Dawn of Day* entitled 'All spirit finally becomes visible', which evokes the highest Catholic clerisy as 'perhaps the most refined figures of human society that have yet been'. In those (no doubt Renaissance) aristocrats on whom the subtleties of theology and the enjoyment of status had worked, 'the human countenance reaches that spiritualization which is produced by the ebb and flow of two sorts of happiness (the feeling of power and the feeling of devotion) after a calculated mode of life has mastered the animal in Man [. . .]'

The celebration runs on thus, with a side glance at the 'brutalization of the clerisy' by Luther (who was thus a throw-back to the 'bucolic crudeness' of the apostle Peter); and the passage ends with an implied elegy for lost greatness and a wistful ambition to achieve this and more by other means:

> And *this* product of human beauty and refinement in the harmony of figure, spirit and task is to have been borne to its grave along with the end of religions? And higher things are not to be attained, not even imagined? (i, 1051f).

Nor does this – usually suppressed – sympathy with Christianity stop short at the very general affinity between his and its creative intentions. For it is not always clear what separates the techniques of 'self-overcoming' Nietzsche himself proposes from the techniques of 'animal-taming' which enrage him in Christianity. If Christian morality is an inward-turning of impulses frustrated in their outward effect – a 'bestiality of the idea' resulting from the ban on being a 'beast in deed' (ii, 834) – this is surely not all that far removed from the creative use of cruelty by which man is to 'overcome' and perfect himself? There remains, of course, the fundamental difference of direction which Nietzsche asserts between a dualistic life-denying system and a monistic life-enhancing system. Yet even this distinction is maintained at the cost of considerable historical over-simplification.[9] One is left with the feeling that what mattered most of all to Nietzsche was that the act of creation should be left to the individual's free initiative, never imposed. That alone would have been enough to set him at odds with an established religion, even if its values and techniques had been in all respects identical with the ones he had developed from his own resources. Nietzsche is above all else not an 'immoralist', but an individualist, exhorting others to be individualists much as Zarathustra does:

> Then speak and stammer: 'That is *my* Good, that I love, thus it pleases me wholly, thus alone will *I* have the Good to be.
> I will have it not as a God's law, not as an ordinance of men and a low necessity of men: it shall be no signpost for me to Over-Earths and Paradises.
> An earthly virtue is it that I love: little cleverness is in it, and least of all the Reason of all men (II, 302).[10]

But to return to the main subject: if Nietzsche was so clear about the need to transform man's animal nature, why does the 'animal' thesis seem to loom so much larger in his writing than the theory of transformation? The answer lies in his imagery and its relation to the argument he was presenting. We saw how the interconnectedness of primitive impulse and cultural splendour was less forcefully, indeed almost obscurely, expressed through a scholarly excursus which could hardly compete in impact with the 'magnificent blond beast lustfully prowling after booty and victory'; and we saw how the 'blond beast' image was itself crudened, from meaning a psychological factor in man to meaning primitive man in general.

This imbalance and crudening is in part no doubt accidental, but in part surely – at some level of the literary consciousness – design. For a thinker presenting unconventional, dramatically *anti*-conventional views, there is a natural tendency to put their most challenging aspect in the strongest terms. Asking people to accept the idea that man's nature was animal, and that it had been perverted by false 'spiritualization' processes, was the prime provocation. That is surely why we hear so much of the beast of prey, and of how his presence in man is less to be feared as a danger to mankind than are sickness and degeneracy – or at least no *more* to be feared: for, if mankind is to go out, why not with a bang instead of a whimper? (e.g. II, 653; II, 863). That is why civilization is repeatedly spoken of as a technique of domestication, animal-taming, animal-caging, with – inevitably – the emotive image of the splendid captive animal preoccupying the reader's attention. So much so that he may not notice that animal vitality is also used at times to convey intellectual or cultural vitality, as when Nietzsche writes that 'civilization' means 'epochs of the deliberate and enforced *taming* ['Tierzähmung'] of Man' and 'times of intolerance towards the *most spiritual* and boldest natures' (III, 837, italics in the second instance mine).[11]

Similarly, in one of his earliest onslaughts on the desiccating effect of a misconceived spiritual or intellectual life, the essay *On the Benefits and Dangers of History for Life*, what most sticks in the mind is that opening image of the serenely unselfconscious animal:

> Consider the flock that grazes before you: it knows not what yesterday, what today is, it gambols about, eats, rests, digests, gambols again, and so from morn till night and from one day to the next, tethered close with its pleasure and unpleasure, namely to the tethering-post of the moment, and hence neither melancholy nor bored (I, 211).

Or that later splendid play on words by means of which Nietzsche undercuts the Cartesian *cogito ergo sum*, objecting that it leaves man a mere 'cogital' and not an 'animal', whereas the 'animal' is the necessary precondition of any cogitation whatsoever. This sticks in the mind, with its cleverness as a debating-point and its key word 'animal', more than the immediately following cry: 'Give me only life, and I will make you a culture from it!'; more also than does the conception of an integrative and formative power ['plastische Kraft'] which can organize the chaos of modern experience as the Greeks organized the chaos of their intellectual world, and put the historical consciousness once again in a right relation with life and culture. In the *History* essay, of course, it is Hegel and his brood, not Christianity, that Nietzsche polemicizes against. But the difference is immaterial. The point remains that he *is* polemicizing against an established cultural trend, and that his animal imagery is once again in the forefront of the attack. For the spectator of the battle, Nietzsche's constructive doctrines are very much in the second rank.

There are also, it is true, images which put these forward. No Nietzschean concept-image is better known than the superman. Yet to suggest *spiritual* qualities in visual terms is tricky.[12] The associations of the word are obstinately physical, even for the person who has actually read *Zarathustra*, if only because so much of the subsidiary imagery of that obscure book is itself physical – struggle, ascent, war. And where it is not in this way physical, it can be ambiguous in other ways. For example, Zarathustra's very first speech, 'Of the three transformations', uses the camel – a beast of burden unquestioningly bearing its load of accepted but still onerous morality; then the lion – a rebel, a destroyer of the morality of 'thou shalt' in favour of a morality of 'I will'; and finally the child – symbol of new-born innocence, a fresh start, a chance to create values *ab initio*: 'Innocence is the child and forgetfulness, a new beginning, a game, a wheel which rolls of itself, a primal movement, a sacred affirmation' (II, 293f). Here again it is likely that the 'forgetfulness' of the child will suggest the same animal-like lack of self-awareness which was the dominant impression left by the images of the *History* essay, and will thus confirm that Nietzsche is arguing against consciousness and intellect generally and in favour of a merely animal spontaneity. That there is something special about a sequence of three transformations, and that the child's innocence is not a return to but a higher analogue of the original unselfconsciousness of animals may well not strike readers who are unfamiliar with the tradition of triadic progressions and restorations in German cultural thinking, in Lessing, Schiller, Kleist, Hegel.[13]

There can be little doubt that it was his images that made Nietzsche, in his own word, 'dynamite' (II, 1152). In themselves his ideas were often not new. 'When we deny ourselves something, it should be a negative act: to make it a privation, and then to give this the positive status of a major virtue – where shall we end up?' The idea of positive morality, and specifically the content of Zarathustra's speech 'Of chastity', is here foreshadowed by Herder.[14] 'A man who is weak, but has a powerful conscience, a conjunction we mostly find' – add this, from Goethe,[15] to the foregoing, and you have *The Genealogy of Morals* in embryo. 'Man can acquire capacities and he can become an animal if he wishes. God makes animals, Man makes himself': the alternative of mere animality and self-creating humanity is succinctly put by Lichtenberg.[16] And one further eighteenth-century writer, that gentlest of Enlightened spirits, Wieland, provides an account of Christianity as a historical and intellectual phenomenon which has many points in common with Nietzsche's: Christianity tames the barbarians, stands the natural order on its head (an image Nietzsche was to use for the Christian perversion of man's instincts), becomes impure in proportion as it becomes a dominant organization, and finally yields, after causing in sum more evil than good, to a more enlightened culture. Wieland shows the same aristocratic contempt for the intellectual level of

Christianity as Nietzsche does, and also an incipient understanding of the power psychology of the priestly caste.[17] Yet none of these eighteenth-century ideas, even supposing them drawn together into a single system, would have the power to sway the imagination as Nietzsche's constant barrage of imagery does.

In sum, then, all Nietzsche's imagery points – or can very easily seem to point – in one consistent direction: towards the animal, instinctual, unintellectual, primitive, violent. The sophistication of his underlying system was no match for the simplicity of his imagery. He was thus at least in part responsible for the misunderstandings of his readers. Even though it *can* be shown that his favourite nexus – wildness, cruelty, beast, barbarian, war – was not merely the arbitrary choice of an aesthete, it was still dangerous to use these images for questions of cultural philosophy, the more dangerous because the line between metaphorical and literal statement is often blurred. In those 'historical' constructs, the barbarians are literally meant – but are they literally or figuratively meant in the plea 'where are the barbarians of the twentieth century?' (III, 690)? War is metaphorical in Zarathustra's 'Of war and warriors', but the metaphor rests on a literal declaration that war is 'indispensable' in *Human, All-Too-Human* (I, 687) – and is it metaphorical or literal in the late assertion that 'there will be wars like none yet seen on earth' (II, 1152)? It is tempting to say sceptically of all Nietzsche's writing what he said with pride of *Thus Spake Zarathustra*: 'The most remarkable thing is the involuntariness of the image, the simile; one no longer has a clear idea what is image, what simile, everything offers itself as the nearest, rightest, simplest expression' (II, 1132).

Nietzsche's inherently dangerous images and the confusion between literal and metaphorical statement now inevitably prompt the judgment 'irresponsible'. That is not a usual term in literary judgments. One would more normally speak simply of 'bad writing'. Nietzsche's fervid enthusiasm for wars and beasts and barbarians is out of touch with the reality of these things, they have become mere exhortatory and excitatory cyphers, and such a use of word and image unbacked by reality or understanding is a form of bad writing. At best it is melodramatic, at worst an embarrassment. Such passages would long ago have rung hollow and been dismissed as dated from a literary point of view, had not history rescued them in the most ghastly way: real wars, real bestiality, and culturally sterile barbarians arose and gave them a seeming prophetic substance far beyond

Nietzsche's imagining or intention. The Nietzsche case was accordingly transferred from the relatively lowly court of literary criticism to a higher one with broader jurisdiction.

III

And yet literary history and criticism remain the starting-point for an inquiry into Nietzsche's effect, because their concern is with the nature and reception of such indirect methods to convey meaning as Nietzsche often and at crucial points used. If his intention was philosophical, his means were eminently literary. We have seen a potential for misunderstanding in the way his images related to his ideas. Observing creative writers as they take over the images and their implications will show something of how that potential was realized.

This is, of course, only one part of a complex process of cultural diffusion, and it may seem artificial to isolate it. When Nietzsche sprang from obscurity into notoriety in the late 1880s and the 1890s, he affected not only writers of serious literature. His ideas were popularized by cultural journals, became thence the common coin of journalism high and low, and were assimilated with unusual speed into the climate of thought of the day. Increasingly as they gain ascendancy within it, it becomes hard to distinguish direct from indirect influence, the presence of Nietzsche's thought from the presence of a vague Nietzscheanism, personal readings of him from the widely accepted distortions that diffusion normally (and in his case markedly) brings with it. Indeed, it becomes questionable whether any such clear-cut difference exists: in some measure, the diffused influence of a popularized Nietzsche may be present even in those relatively 'pure' cases where writers responded to the ideas and images at source.

Yet these rarer cases still have a special and (paradoxically) representative significance. Writers may be more susceptible than most men to the suggestive power of imagery, but equally they might be expected to see more clearly how it is meant to function. If they prove nevertheless to be dominated by the simpler apparent implications of Nietzsche's images, then this confirms what an analysis of Nietzsche's writing suggested about the way his influence might work. And if it worked in this way and to this degree in such (so to speak) elevated cases, it becomes more readily understandable that it should have worked so powerfully on men of lesser discrimination; especially so if they received it in simplified form from the intellectual climate it had come to permeate, and more especially still if the reception was affected by political pressures or ideological manipulation.

Thus, the way Nietzsche's animal images and their implications are taken up by a number of major writers may exemplify the nature and power of his effect. There is of course another, more purely literary interest in juxtaposing texts by Gottfried Benn, Kafka, Thomas Mann, and Rilke. We see each in his own way transforming derived material into artistic texture; and we see, in this variety, the underlying unity of artistic effects and intellectual postulates which help to give the period its character.

(i)

Since our argument presupposes that all four writers knew Nietzsche's work at first hand, the evidence for thinking so must be briefly stated in each case. With Thomas Mann, it is overwhelming. To his many declarations of allegiance and the many quotations and adaptations of overtly Nietzschean ideas which his works contain, there can be added the bibliographical evidence of the Nietzsche editions and secondary literature he owned, reaching back to the 1890s when the Grossoktavausgabe of the works began to appear, and showing signs of thorough and repeated use. Mann's statements on the matter vary with the use to which on different occasions he put Nietzsche's thought, but for the present purposes the most relevant comes in the *Sketch of my Life*, where he comments that the blond beast crops up in his early work, but without the bestial element, leaving only the blondness and the mindlessness.[18]

The reference is plain. Nothing is more familiar to readers of Thomas Mann than the code of physical characteristics which 'place' the figures of the early stories either as outsiders or as normal members of society who are at home in life. The outsiders have a southern element in their parentage to subvert stolid Nordic normality and hence their hair and eyes are dark; for less obvious reasons they have other features suggesting refinement and even precarious health – tapering fingers, delicate veins that show through the skin. In contrast, the robust Nordic type has blue eyes and blond hair, which makes it mysteriously free from all problems and adolescent suffering. Certainly it writes no poetry and feels no longings – as the outsider does – for a type alien to its own.

This simple, even simplistic, notation is Thomas Mann's means of presenting visually the main problem of his early years, how to come to terms with the way his literary talents and ambitions estranged him from ordinary society. The theme is partly worked out in social situations – e.g. Tonio Kröger's failure to secure Hans Hansen as his friend, or to execute the patterns of a dance, or to interest the girl he loves. But social disharmony is only the surface. The characters' differing degree of 'fitness' for life ['Lebenstüchtigkeit'] is linked with vitality. Hans Hansen, courted with poetry, is symbolically devoted to horses. Later, when the mature artist Tonio Kröger feels cut off from Life itself, he interprets this vague term in a generally social sense, yet his doubts about the life of the mind extend to decidedly physical things: 'Is the artist a "man" at all? One ought to ask "woman" that! It strikes me that we artists all to some extent share the fate of those doctored papal singers. . . . We sing with a quite touching beauty. Yet . . .'

The writer's self-doubts are thus basic, and imply patterns of physical cause and effect. Art itself is seen as a consequence of declining vitality, a thesis spelled out in the novel *Buddenbrooks* which, as Mann said, owes its 'psychology of decadence' to Nietzsche. Conversely, Hans Hansen and his type live untroubled in society, will be happy and successful, because their vital forces are intact. They are free from 'consciousness' in any important sense. Ideal projections of Mann's brooding sense of inadequacy, they are the blond beast in social disguise.

Just occasionally the disguise slips and shows unambiguously the lurking animal and Mann's vitalist assumptions. It does so in *Tristan*, which dates from the same year as *Tonio Kröger*. Here Mann's self-doubting produces sharp satire. The writer Detlev Spinell is a grotesque figure physically and a dubious quantity artistically – he has written only one book, and spends much of his time admiring it. (His unusual surname, aptly, is the word for an obscure, not-quite-precious stone.) His aesthetic sensitivities are out of proportion to his artistic achievement. They include the need for regular visits to the sanatorium Einfried, as much for its Empire furniture as for any specific health reasons, and a passion for music, especially Wagner's. This proves fatal for a young woman patient who since giving birth to a child has suffered from tuberculosis. Though forbidden the excitements of music, she is prevailed upon by Spinell to play from the piano-score of *Tristan and Isolde* for him. The performance culminates in the *Liebestod*. From then on her condition worsens irreversibly: if organic decline can lead to art, art can further organic decline.

What prevents our taking Gabriele Eckhof's death tragically is the comic light Mann turns on the two men who are in such different ways attached to her. He satirizes her husband Herr Klöterjahn, a massive, self-satisfied, blustering, heavy-eating bourgeois, all husbandly solicitude and surreptitious maid-chasing in the corridors. But he also satirizes Spinell, the caricatural *fin-de siècle* aesthete, with his attitudes and beliefs (in substance they are Mann's own), his mannerisms ('How beautiful! My God, just look how beautiful!'), and his inability to face reality unstylized (he constructs an illusory *art nouveau* scene of Gabriele in a circle of singing damsels from which she was torn away to espouse her gross bourgeois). The confrontation between the two men when Gabriele is sinking fast and Spinell has addressed to Klöterjahn (in the same building) a highly literary letter of accusation and hatred, is one of the great comic scenes in world, not just German, literature.

It is sometimes assumed that in that scene Klöterjahn wins hands down, as is suggested in Alfred Kubin's famous cover-design for the first edition where a mountainous bourgeois stands with one foot on a tiny vanquished foe. Certainly he scores heavily. But Spinell's pen has also inflicted some wounds and to this extent he has achieved his aim (again, one that Mann himself voiced on occasion) of bringing some element of consciousness to the 'unconscious type' the world is full of. Moreover, on one view of the rules, Klöterjahn repeatedly drops points by misquoting Spinell's letter. Anyhow, even if the match is not a draw, crisis stops play: Klöterjahn is called to his dying wife's bedside. And only then does the decisive confrontation take place.

Not with Klöterjahn – but on this visit to the sanatorium he is not alone. Here is the scene that concludes the story. Spinell, after taking a stiff brandy and unsuccessfully trying to rest, goes into the garden:

The path bent; it led towards the setting sun. With two narrow, golden-edged strips of cloud across it, the sun stood large and low in the sky, touching the tops of the trees with fire and pouring a yellow-red radiance over the garden. And in the midst of this golden transfiguration, the mighty halo of the sun behind her head, a buxom person stood erect in the path, dressed all in red, gold and tartan. Her right hand rested on her curving hip, and with her left she was moving a graceful little perambulator to and fro. But in this perambulator there sat the child, sat Anton Klöterjahn junior, sat Gabriele Eckhof's podgy son!

He sat among the cushions, fat-cheeked, splendid and full of health, wearing a white woolly jacket and a large white hat, and his eye met Herr Spinell's merrily and without flinching. The novelist was about to take a grip on himself, he was a man, he would have had the strength to stride past this unexpected, magnificently illuminated phenomenon and continue his walk. But then the ghastly thing happened – Anton Klöterjahn began to laugh and shout with glee, he shrieked with inexplicable amusement, it was positively uncanny.

Heaven knows what got into him, whether the dark figure before him sent him into this wild hilarity or what sort of an attack of animal well-being seized him. In one hand he had a bone teething-ring and in the other a tin rattle. Whooping with triumph, he held these two objects up into the sunshine, shook them and banged them together as if he were out to scare someone away with his mockery. His eyes were screwed almost shut with pleasure, and his mouth was thrown open so wide that the whole of his pink palate was visible. He even tossed his head about as he whooped.

Then Herr Spinell turned on his heel and went from thence. He went down the gravel path followed by the jubilation of the small Klöterjahn, walking with the awkward concern to hold his arms gracefully and the forcibly restrained step of one who wishes to conceal the fact that he is inwardly fleeing.

Until this meeting in the dazzling sunlight (itself a 'strong' experience Spinell dislikes – 'One can be more spiritual without sun') he has avoided contact with the young Klöterjahn, this child of truly 'excessive health' which 'consumed vast quantities of milk and chopped meat and gave itself up in every respect to its instincts'. Now the child appears positively in glory. But this, and the perhaps sexual undertones in the description of the nurse, are only the beginnings of the challenge to Spinell's manly adequacy. In the third paragraph, what was merely a child 'full of health' ['wohlgeraten', itself a keyword in Nietzsche's vitalist vocabulary] is transformed ever more plainly into an animal, into *the* animal; for it is a mesmerizing approximation to the lion that Spinell is faced with. From the generalized 'animal well-being', we progress to those screwed-up eyes and then stare horrified down the beast's pink throat as it opens wide its jaws. The 'even' in the closing sentence ('he even tossed his head about . . .') has a fine ambiguity: on the surface it is one final sign of hilarity to discomfit

Spinell, yet it is surely also one more detail, the final and conclusive parallel, which suggests the king of beasts.

Spinell was not routed by Klöterjahn senior, because they were juxtaposed as social beings. Even beside a person so inadequate in some respects as Spinell, Klöterjahn's behaviour also left something to be desired, his limitations were clear. He was the stronger, but there was plenty of room for Spinell, from the standpoint of his very different world, to feel – and appear – superior. But the infant Klöterjahn is pre-social, instinctive, elemental. In his letter, Spinell predicts that the child, which has drained the life-force from so artistic a being as Gabriele, will be a pillar of society, but the worst he can say is that it will be an 'inartistic, normally functioning creature, unscrupulous and confident, strong and stupid'. This phrasing already echoes Nietzsche's evocation of primitive races; and in the final scene, Nietzsche's favourite image for those races is unmistakable. By the nature of the situation, there can this time be no exchange of words, Spinell's only weapon. The conflict is between animals, a healthy and an unhealthy one, with the weaker recognizing (as animals do) his place in the natural order and taking to flight. It is a conflict of fundamentals which tells us – however comic the literary intention – what the fundamentals of Mann's position were.

Taken together, *Tristan* and *Tonio Kröger* show it to be an ambivalent but ultimately defeatist position. It is ambivalent in that the qualities and worth of literature are to some extent maintained even in discomfiture – and Mann, after all, himself continues to write. It is ultimately defeatist in that literature is shown as an aberration from what is right and natural, and dependent for its value on recognizing that fact: for Tonio Kröger, in the end, the quality of what he writes will be guaranteed only by his wistful attachment to a 'seductively banal' alien world which neither recognizes nor lives by literature's standards of humane perceptiveness.[19] *Tristan*, more directly and drastically, shows the writer – a caricatural writer, it is true, but still one who can stand for his author in essentials – being finally weighed in the scales of nature and found wanting.

What is striking is precisely the way nature is taken as a sufficient objection to literary culture, which shamefacedly abdicates its claims. Nietzsche's cultural criticism also appealed to nature and glorified instinct – but only as a first step; for Nietzsche, as we have seen, envisaged an alternative, healthier culture, and gave some detailed indications of what its character would be. Of this there is no sign in

Thomas Mann. Hans Hansen and Ingeborg Holm will not produce a culture, nor will Klöterjahn junior. They are representatives of a pre-cultural stage which the man of the spirit, wearied by 'consciousness' and the strain of being constantly in opposition, looks yearningly back to as something stronger and purer. It seems that in so far as Nietzsche was a determining influence in Mann's early work – and of this there is every sign – this part of his message has been understood, or at least applied, too simply. Nietzsche's account of nature and instinct has monopolized attention; and for this, both Mann's later comment and the early texts themselves suggest, the image of the blond beast and its implications were largely responsible.

(ii)

Writers on Rilke habitually take Nietzsche's influence for granted – 'in the Nietzschean manner', 'like his great predecessor', 'tallies fairly well with Nietzsche' are typical phrases. The authors of two lively essays comparing the poet and the thinker tell us, while declining to spend time establishing the fact of influence, that certain verses 'spring from the very centre of Zarathustra's message'[20] and that 'Nietzsche's attitude is not found in German literature before him, but it is the central mood of Rilke's Elegies and Sonnets'.[21] Of course Nietzsche was a ubiquitous influence in this period, and there is suggestive internal evidence in some of the texts these essays juxtapose. But precisely the known ubiquity of Nietzsche should make us cautious, especially if we are dealing with anything so intangible as a mood, even though Rilke's 'radical affirmation of this world with all its agony' may recall in general terms what Nietzsche also preached.

What seems needful is to document the presence of any strand of Nietzsche's thought which we believe went into a poet's work. True, with Rilke there is the problem that he was not much given to acknowledging his intellectual debts, no doubt because he thought that 'their assimilation and transformation in . . . his art was the only thing that mattered'.[22] But we cannot leave it at that, for unless we trace the indebtedness, we shall have no good grounds for talking about 'transformation' at all.

The first-hand material, though not rich, is not quite as unrewarding as has sometimes been pleaded. Like Thomas Mann, Rilke was born in 1875 and was thus just coming to maturity when Nietzsche's thought began to take effect. There are a few scattered references to Nietzsche between 1895 and 1904. Some of them merely suggest a general respect for him, as when in 1902 Rilke unquestioningly sets him beside Plato, Spinoza and Kant.[23] More specifically, he tells his wife in a letter of July 1904 that a Scandinavian philosopher, about whose work he was already enthusiastic, 'has taken Nietzsche as medicine, and has become even healthier for it'.

Chapter and verse for what Rilke meant by 'health' is provided by the story 'The Apostle' of 1896. Here a dark prophetic figure shocks an elegant hotel dining-room with some of Nietzsche's central doctrines, delivered almost verbatim. Pity and mercy are poison to the soul. Christianity has deprived us of our instincts:

> We have been brought up like those beasts of prey which have had their inmost impulse taken from them by calculating cleverness, so that when they are tame they can be attacked with impunity with whips. They have filed down our teeth and claws and preached to us: love! They have taken the iron armour of our strength from our shoulders and preached to us: love! They have wrested the adamant spear of our proud will from our hands and preached to us: love! and thus we have been exposed naked and bare to the storm of life where the blows of fate's club come whistling down – and they preach to us: love!

The messiah 'has made the whole world an infirmary', which could mean the end of further human development; for if a messiah had preached love to 'our primal ancestors the apes, wild animals with great natural instincts', evolution would never have passed that stage. Similarly,

> our generation is not the pinnacle of the endless pyramid of growth ['Werden']. We ourselves are not perfected. We too are immature, not over-ripe as ye in your pride like to believe. Therefore onwards! Are we not to climb higher in knowledge, will and power? Shall the strong man not succeed in rising to the light from out of the constricting atmosphere of envy?

The weaker must be left to perish: 'Be hard, be terrible, be implacable!'[24]

Excessive though this seems (just because someone proposed a collection for victims of a local fire) and mediocre though the imitation of Zarathustra's rhetoric may be, it shows us how much Rilke had imbibed of Nietzsche and how uncritical his allegiance to these doctrines was – he called the story 'my half profoundly serious, half satirical confession of faith'.[25] The 'blond beast' is not invoked by name, but the slightly less graphic 'beast of prey' and the 'teeth and claws' are there. So too, less obtrusively, is an echo of Nietzsche's first full-scale essay in the criticism of excessive consciousness, *On the Benefits and Dangers of History for Life*. The proud belief in the full maturity of the present generation, which Rilke's apostle attacks and wishes to replace with new creative efforts, is the nineteenth-century assumption Nietzsche polemicized against, the post-Hegelian view that the pinnacle of world history had been attained from which all past ages derived their meaning and should be judged. (Nietzsche, more aptly than Rilke, uses the pyramid image for the view he is *attacking* – 1, 267; for pyramids do have pinnacles, they are not 'endless'.)

The echo would not be sufficient by itself to persuade us that Rilke had taken that essay to heart; nor would the passing remark in his *Bohemian Wanderings* of 1895 that he is one of the group of people Nietzsche calls 'the "historical" '.[26] More substantial evidence comes from following the one firm denial I know of that Rilke had any time for Nietzsche. One of Rilke's multifarious female attachments, the painter Lou Albert-Lasard, records in her memoir of their relationship that Rilke 'refused to approach Nietzsche. I remember the vehemence with which he rejected my suggestion that he should read him'.[27] This recollection is meant to back up the view that Rilke was essentially independent of other great figures, was only spurred by them to self-fulfilment. As further confirmation, she quotes a passage Rilke gave her at this time (*c.* 1915) from his Worpswede diary. What he had then written (*c.* 1900 – actually in his Schmargendorf diary)[28] is an eloquent rejection of mere historical values in favour of an essential inspiration by past greatness, an inner inheritance of what others have done. It is, in fact, a fine paraphrase of Nietzsche's argument for 'monumental' history in *On the Benefits and Dangers of History*, § 2 (1, 219ff), and the connection is confirmed when Rilke uses Nietzsche's word 'Historie' in stating 'what we have to fear from history and its effect', and when he uses phrases very close to Nietzsche's argument – 'those in whom a great man from the past is resurrected', or 'his fathers and forebears . . . are the contemporaries of his soul'.

One more text adds something to the picture. In 1900 Rilke studied Nietzsche's first book, *The Birth of Tragedy*, and wrote notes and one poem

on it. He was struck by Nietzsche's idea of music as a virtually autonomous force underlying all art; he paraphrases it as 'the great rhythm
of the background' and 'a free, flowing *unapplied force*', adding later that
'one must hold ready all receptacles to receive in beauty that wandering force'. He was also struck by the concept of the Dionysian as 'an
unlimited living-in-all-things, to which everyday life stands as a ludicrous little disguise'. He was interested in much of what Nietzsche
says about drama (he was still at this time attempting to write dramas
himself) and reflects particularly on the way myth, by being familiar
to the audience, avoids distracting attention from 'the sole thing of
importance, the background' – i.e. the 'great rhythm' present in art
behind its mere forms or subject-matter. It is at this point in the notes
that the poem stands; it speaks of 'sometimes hearing behind occur-
rence a breath moving which is greater than my own'.[29] It seems possible that the mature Rilke's doctrine of passivity, his belief that poetic
gifts came from a force outside him (as with the Elegies and Sonnets)
may have its roots here.

But that is another matter. What the 'Marginalia on Nietzsche' add
to our subject is some evidence of Rilke's interest in the problem of
consciousness, specifically in relation to a philosopher. For Nietzsche
in *The Birth of Tragedy*, Socrates was the original type of 'theoretical
Man', an enemy of instinct which he dissolved by logic, a 'specific
non-mystic . . . in whom logical nature by a superfetation is developed as
excessively as instinctive wisdom is in the mystic' (I, 84; 77f). Socrates
was therefore, like his artistic counterpart Euripides, a solvent of
true, Dionysian tragedy, and thus ultimately an enemy of all true art.
Only in his last days, in prison, did a voice come to him in dreams
saying 'Socrates, make music!' suggesting that he had repressed in
himself an essential element of human nature (I, 82). It is this passage
that Rilke glosses, reflecting that, in Socrates, intellectual processes
moved so fast that even impulses from his unconscious (i.e. the instinctual level) were overtaken, so that 'impoverished instinct with
its empty hands could only defend, warn, hold off' (presumably a
reference to Socrates' famous 'daemon'); and only when the logical
power had nothing to do, in prison, did instinct catch up: 'instinct
timorously put in an appearance and rang like yearning in the silence
before death. His soul longed for music. And presentiently it put its
lips, dried up by the wind of words, to the cup of sounds.'

Thus Rilke accepted Nietzsche's assessment of Socrates and of the
relation of the theoretical, logical mind to art; and in his own formu-

lations, especially those 'lips dried up by the wind of words', we hear the same kind of lament at the aridity of words, the bearers of unvital mental processes, as the self-critical Tonio Kröger was given to. Fruitfulness lies with instinct; logic, intellect, conscious thought, theory, are all its enemies.

The sum total of these indications in a formative decade of Rilke's life is to suggest an influence as real, if not as general or as much advertised, as Nietzsche's influence on the young Thomas Mann. In the area that specially interests us, the question of animal nature and instinct against consciousness, the same ideas and images are seen at work. They were in due course to help determine the ideas and images of the work Rilke regarded as his crowning achievement, the *Duino Elegies*. And lest it seem doubtful whether such early indications can properly be related to mature works – that is, whether the early influence was indeed formative – it should be said that Rilke is an outstanding example of something found in many major writers: the early laying down of an intellectual and artistic design which remains recognizable through successive layers of creative work, each of which is an attempt to realize it more fully and more precisely. A simple instance would be the proposition 'Art is the obscure wish of all things',[30] found in a sketch of 1900 and clearly anticipating the doctrine and practice of 'transformation' ['Verwandlung'] found in the Elegies of 1922.

By that time, animal nature has clearly come to play a role analogous to the one we saw in Mann's stories: it is a standard the human being falls hopelessly short of; animals enjoy pure perceptions and are attuned to the rhythms of the natural order. Gone is the idea from 'The Apostle' that a new creative phase of evolution might spring from man's remaining or restored animal instincts. That may have been a fuller, truer account of Nietzsche – 'The Apostle' is a very directly derivative work. But partly for this reason it could hardly stand up, as a personal programme, to Rilke's actual experience. His own deep disharmonies and 'strangeness' in life – the price of his extreme sensitivity and his poetic mission – were undeniable. In the autobiographical novel *The Notebooks of Malte Laurids Brigge*, the down-and-outs intuitively know Malte to be one of themselves, and he feels in his heart that this is right. 'Life' for him is far from a matter of magnificent instinct, let alone its transformation; it is compounded of miseries and terrors which it is his task to accept and transmute. That his harrowing experiences take place in Paris, the cliché-city of gay, splendid 'Life', is an irony he remarks on from the first page. All that was left was for animals to appear eventually in an elegiac light, as a distant lost ideal.

Notably, when Rilke does treat an animal in these years, it is with complete sobriety. 'The Panther', one of his most celebrated poems, is about a real observed animal, as the subtitle indicates ('In the Jardin des Plantes, Paris'). It describes with an exactitude a zoologist can admire.[31] Rilke no longer preaches animal instinct, nor does he yet use the animal to reproach man for losing his harmony with the natural order. The poem stands at a halfway point between vitalist optimism and existential pessimism. Arguably it is a necessary stage in the development from one to the other: that is to say, before animals could be used to show up man's lamentable case, as they are in the *Duino Elegies*, the poet had to penetrate their objective nature and thus lose his former illusions. With that subtle empathy and supple expression which is typical of the *New Poems*, Rilke enters into the situation of the caged panther, discovering with every nuance of observation how unbridgeable the divide between animal and man really is:

> Sein Blick ist vom Vorübergehn der Stäbe
> so müd geworden, dass er nichts mehr hält.
> Ihm ist, als ob es tausend Stäbe gäbe
> und hinter tausend Stäben keine Welt.
>
> Der weiche Gang geschmeidig starker Schritte,
> der sich im allerkleinsten Kreise dreht,
> ist wie ein Tanz von Kraft um eine Mitte,
> in der betäubt ein grosser Wille steht.
>
> Nur manchmal schiebt der Vorhang der Pupille
> sich lautlos auf –. Dann geht ein Bild hinein,
> geht durch der Glieder angespannte Stille –
> und hört im Herzen auf zu sein.

*

> His gaze, from seeing bars forever passing,
> Is now so tired that nothing is retained.
> It seems as if a thousand bars were massing,
> And then beyond the bars no world remained.
>
> The soft paws, in their strong and supple padding,
> Move in a circle, small and smaller still:

A dance of forces round a centre circling
Within which, dazed, there stands a mighty will.

Just now and then, to let an image enter,
The pupil's curtain soundlessly will part,
The image passes through the limbs' quiet tension –
And ends its being in the heart.

Everything here stresses the alien nature of the animal. There is no trace of the pathetic fallacy and no suggestion of a link between the animal's situation and man's. (It is difficult to see any ground for the assumption some critics make that Rilke is really intending a comment on the human condition.) There is indeed minimal suggestion of an animal consciousness at all. Each stanza is built up from a pure physical or physiological function – the panther's gaze, its gait, its perception – and this function is in each case the basis of the syntax. No mental subject, no thinking or feeling agency, is anywhere posited; the panther is never even the grammatical subject of a sentence. Only once is it represented by a personal pronoun in order to have some sort of impression ascribed to it (line 3); and even there, the German construction is as impersonal and neutral as the language can manage ('ihm ist' stays close to pure sensation, where the only possible translation – 'it seems' – unavoidably suggests mental processes and epistemological complexity). The three functions add up to the animal Rilke observes, yet lack a centre of coherence, anything that we should normally understand as an identity.

It would seem that Nietzsche is now no longer needed for our argument. For if the Rilke of *New Poems* has abandoned the Nietzschean idea of human regeneration from animal instinct which 'The Apostle' expressed, and if he is clearing the ground by means of his own precise observations, then that original influence can have little bearing on the animal images of his later poetry. These can surely be called his own work.

That would be so if Nietzsche were not so plainly present even in the observations of 'The Panther'. It is a truism that our observations are themselves predetermined by concepts. As the poet watches the panther, he is seeing its movements in established categories and interpreting them along particular lines. Most evident is the idea of a powerful will frustrated in its free action, yet manifested for all that in a grace which suggests the dance. If will was at the centre of Nietzsche's thought as the primal phenomenon of animal nature, dance was his recurrent emblem for a freedom from inhibiting conscious-ness. When two ideas so closely associated in their origins occur so closely associated again, it is hard to believe that the poetic imagination has not been to some extent guided.

And perhaps it is guided as fundamentally in the way it sees and presents such consciousness as the animal has. For the panther, in the first stanza, it is the bars that move – they are relative to him, his consciousness is in this sense absolute. Yet it is also limited, in that he does not reflect on his own movement, there is no relativizing self-consciousness. Similarly, he cannot reflect on the continuing exist-ence of the world beyond the ever more obtrusive bars of the cage; and since there is no reflection, there is no world.

Equally, there is no memory. This is conveyed in the last stanza, which concentrates on a single act of perception and the way it passes without trace. That inner void in the animal, the mental dis-continuity which the whole poem so impressively realizes, is put with finality in the closing line, with its two syllables' space of silence at the end. This is animal forgetfulness, the death of the moment, the free-dom from the shadow of the past as Nietzsche evoked it so powerfully in the opening section of his *Benefits and Dangers of History*:

> . . . the moment, there in a trice, gone in a trice, before it a void, after it a void, still [for Man] comes back as a ghost and disturbs the peace of a later moment. [. . .] Then Man says 'I remember' and envies the animal, which forgets at once and watches every moment really die, sink back into mist and night and become extinguished for ever. Thus the animal lives *unhistorically*: it expends itself fully in the present, like a sum that leaves no awkward remainder [. . .] (I, 211).

Will, grace of movement, unreflectiveness, forgetting: Rilke's panther is a very Nietzschean animal. As yet Rilke does not actually celebrate the lack of reflective consciousness, but it clearly fascinates him. The same fleetingness of animals' perception occurs again in the *Requiem* for Paula Modersohn-Becker which speaks of the poet having

> a brief existence in their eyes,
> which hold and slowly leave me, tranquilly,
> passing no judgment.[32]

And elsewhere in the *New Poems*, the animal's ease of forgetting be-comes something more active and sinister, almost a power to anni-hilate the human being it looks at by drawing his image down into that inner oblivion where the red blood dwells;[33] or the impenetrable eye reflects the human being in its amber as if he were an extinct insect.[34]

These are imaginative conceits typical enough of the *New Poems* but the direction is consistent: a positive mystique is built up around the thing observed, objectivity drifts towards myth.[35] It is only a step to the idealizing of animal perception and animal being which we find in the *Duino Elegies*. There animals join with other, more bizarre ideal figures (dead children, unrequited lovers, an untheological angel) as measures of man's inadequacy. The first elegy goes so far as to allege that animals actually 'notice . . . /that we are not very reliably at home/in the interpreted world'. The fourth opens with a picture of man as the leaves on a tree, pathetically ignorant of when to fall, dropping unseasonally late on to an indifferent pond; while the migratory birds, attuned to the rhythms of the natural order, have long since departed. This passage of lament over man's lost instincts ends with a familiar image, alien to what precedes it yet standing out the more powerfully for that as one whose intrinsic aptness could be taken for granted:

> And somewhere lions still walk and do not know,
> while yet their splendour lasts, of any weakness.

Then, most systematically, the eighth elegy elaborates on animal epistemology and its advantages. The animal creation, we are told, sees 'Openness' ('das Offene' – a kind of Rilkean 'Ding an sich' which our conceptual corruption and our awareness of death jointly prevent us from seeing) and the most we can manage is to catch its reflection, turned round the wrong way as we are, in the face of an animal.[36] For the rest, we can only bewail the wretched fate of always being 'opposite'.

> And we: spectators, always, everywhere,
> facing all that, never to see beyond!

where the animal, its 'mind' uncluttered by time, space, causality and other inconveniences, 'sees' absolutely:

> Where we see Future, it sees Everything,
> itself in Everything and healed for ever.

Rilke's position is thus more radical even than the young Thomas Mann's. For Mann, animal nature was a sufficient objection to culture. For Rilke, it is a sufficient objection to the most basic mechanisms and functions of human intelligence. It is true that the *Elegies* as a whole are supposed to be read as turning from lament to a triumphant affirmation of the poet's mission. But the conception of this mission neither removes nor resolves what has been said in depreciation of human nature. All of that still stands, as a document (however elevated its level and whatever its trappings of poetic eloquence) of anti-intellectual snobbery. The poet who started out from Nietz-sche's vision of man creatively transforming animal instinct ends by idealizing and mysticizing animal nature in totally regressive fashion.[37]

(iii)

Attempts to demonstrate philosophical influence can rarely be con-clusive. In European culture, centuries of often interrelated reflec-tions on a limited range of traditional problems have produced a body of potential literary material within which there are enough simi-larities to confuse most attributions. For instance, one might set be-side the opening of Rilke's Fourth Elegy, with its image of migratory birds and their sure instincts, the passage where Stephen Daedalus watches birds:

> and there flew hither and thither shapeless thoughts from Sweden-borg on the correspondence of birds to things of the intellect and of how the creatures of the air have their knowledge and know their times and seasons because they, unlike man, are in the order of their life and have not perverted that order by reason.[38]

The German tradition of anti-intellectualism itself does not begin with Nietzsche but reaches back, at least in the form of uneasy doubts about the cultural value of intellect, to the late eighteenth century, to Herder, Schiller and the Romantics; and it occasionally makes use of animal contrast figures – e.g. the bear in Kleist's essay on the puppet theatre.

Nevertheless, Nietzsche retains in this and much else a special status. Just as he once called Wagner a 'resumé of modernity' (II, 904) he himself was a resumé of intellectual traditions and problems. With his wide knowledge and acute understanding of preceding philoso-phies, and with his very accessible and stimulating mode of presenta-tion which from the first bypassed the obscure channels of technical, professional philosophy, he set before writers born in the 1870s and 1880s many ideas which they could conceivably have got elsewhere but did in fact get (along with his decisive slant on the question) from him.

As a small but exact pointer to this, we find Gottfried Benn asking the author of a book which touched on the theme of 'recurrence' what the origin of the idea and its earlier literature were – further back, that is, than Nietzsche.[39] And it is Benn who wrote the most emphatic statement on Nietzsche's intellectual domination of a literary age:

> Everything that my generation discussed, the problems it inwardly struggled with, one might say suffered from, one might equally well say flogged to death – all this had really been already expressed and exhausted, had received definitive formulation, in Nietzsche; what remained was merely exegesis.[40]

For his generation, Benn goes on, Nietzsche was 'the earthquake of the epoch'.

Such a testimonial, together with the frequent quotations from and discussions of Nietzsche (including three poems directly about him), leaves no doubt of Benn's preoccupation with the Nietzschean legacy. But once again, the attitudes change in the process of being taken over. They become more extreme and unsubtle; and the idea of progression yields – initially at least – to the idea of regression. We saw in Rilke's case how the tonic contempt for human limitations with which Nietzsche sought to stimulate a new creativity yielded to an unconstructive lament over modern man's inadequacies; and we saw that the animal images duly pointed back to the pre-human. Much the same happens with Benn. There may seem to be little similarity between Benn and Rilke on the surface, but that is merely a matter of tone and materials. Benn adds a show of science which makes his propositions sound tougher, more objective, less idiosyncratically 'poetic' than Rilke's; he uses the language of biology which his medical training placed to hand and this later leads on to a play with palaeontological terms and grand evolutionary perspectives. Yet the decisive attitudes and valuations are no more scientific than Rilke's. Quite apart from the highly dubious credentials of some of the 'science',[41] the seemingly objective materials merely lend a modern prestige to the familiar cultural pessimism which disposes them.

The distinctness of these two things is already clear in the very early piece 'Conversation' (1910).[42] Two young men are discussing possible literary styles for the present age. Benn's spokesman, Thom, argues that the sole 'refuge from ridicule', at a time when 'writing' is looked down on, lies in 'reducing things and events to their purely factual elements, placing them on a scientific basis'. He quotes the example of the Danish writer, Jens Peter Jacobsen, who was then much in vogue in Germany. Jacobsen, he says, was a great scientist, wrote a classic work on the desmidiaceae (microscopic unicellular algae) of Denmark, and hoped to make a complete survey of Danish flora. He was thus penetrating to the reality at the base of language, giving his literary language substance, 'living in the home of all these words'. As a good Darwinist, he was seeking an understanding of human life in life's most primitive forms. For the essence of Darwinism (Thom says) consists in two ideas: development, and the unity of all life. He pictures Jacobsen at his microscope:

> life, culminating in one of its subtlest exemplars, in which the spiritual, the cerebral element has frayed out into its finest and extremest vibrations, bending over another life: torpid, instinctual, damp, compact; and yet the two belong together and one single wave runs through them and both are corporeally related right down to the chemical composition of their juices.

We might almost be approaching the kind of scientific humanism Thomas Mann was later to evolve in *The Magic Mountain*, if not indeed the optimistic belief in evolutionary progress which Nietzsche mocked in his *History* essay, when he wrote that the universal historian in his pride at human development finds traces of himself in the living slime of the seas (I, 266). But suddenly Thom shifts to quoting from Jacobsen's novel *Niels Lyhne*, a passage where the hero sits looking out over the fields in 'vegetative rapture'. This one phrase sets going the following reflection:

> There he sits, Niels, who had set forth to become a great artist, who had exposed his soul to the violent sensations of modern culture and science, there he sits and feels with pleasure the tiredness in his joints and muscles that comes from physical labour, and stares as if with extinguished brain functions at the rhythmically waving cornfields. It is like a circle that closes: the results of millions of years of development, the brain-animal, the cerebral creature, now it is drawn back into the vegetative, the plant, into everything that is delivered up to day and night and heat and frost; now it sits there as if it had never been stirred out of the bliss of its brainless forebears, as if returned home, tired of the long road, at rest in the sun – an object filling space.

Gert objects that these are thoughts which Jacobsen may never have had and which he would perhaps have protested against. To which Thom only replies, evasively, that Gert must read Jacobsen again – his style really *is* scientific. That was not in question, but rather why the 'unity of life' a scientist observes should make us rejoice at the return of a higher form to the torpid peace of lower forms; or, more abstractly, why the Darwinian idea of development, which is linear and open-ended, should lead to the highly value-loaded conception of a 'closing circle'.

It evidently cannot do so without some imported criterion. What this criterion is appears in phrases like 'extinguished brain-functions' and 'bliss of its brainless forebears' – first shots in Benn's long campaign against the brain as a pointless aberration of the evolutionary process. Behind the talk of science and factuality lies the familiar modern all-too-modern unease over consciousness, complexity and metaphysical homelessness to which radically simplified states seem to offer an answer. What Rilke put in terms of vision and epistemology, Benn puts in the language of organic evolution; but the point remains identical.

How similar the associated emotions are, we can see in Benn's poem 'Gesänge' (Cantos) of 1913, with its open commitment to what the earlier dialogue only implied:

I

O dass wir unsere Ururahnen wären.
Ein Klümpchen Schleim in einem warmen Moor.
Leben und Tod, Befruchten und Gebären
glitte aus unsren stummen Säften vor.

Ein Algenblatt oder ein Dünenhügel,
vom Wind Geformtes und nach unten schwer.
Schon ein Libellenkopf, ein Möwenflügel
wäre zu weit und litte schon zu sehr.

II

Verächtlich sind die Liebenden, die Spötter,
alles Verzweifeln, Sehnsucht, und wer hofft.
Wir sind so schmerzliche durchseuchte Götter
und dennoch denken wir des Gottes oft.

Die weiche Bucht. Die dunklen Wälderträume.
Die Sterne, schneeballblütengross und schwer.
Die Panther springen lautlos durch die Bäume.
Alles ist Ufer. Ewig ruft das Meer –

I

O that we were our forebears in lost ages.
A speck of slime warm in the moor earth.
Life and death, fertilization, birth,
sliding onward in the lymph's dumb stages.

A wisp of seaweed or a sand-dune – thing
heavy below, shaped by the wind's touch.
A dragonfly head or a seagull's wing –
this even would be too far, suffer too much.

II

Lovers and scoffers, men by yearning driven,
by hope, despair – contemptible are these kinds.
We are such painful gods, by sickness riven.
And yet the God is often in our minds.

The gentle curve of bay, dark forests dreaming.
Stars big as snowball blooms hang heavily.
Noiseless among the trees the panthers springing.
Shoreline is all. Endlessly calls the sea –

This starts with the most extreme regression of all, back beyond the
animal to those primitive algae with their totally unconscious processes, and even to the bottom-heavy sand dune lying passive in the
wind. *Non cogito, ergo sum.* The extreme has a certain logic: if consciousness is the culprit, then even animals have it in some form. The
eighth of Rilke's Elegies begins, as we saw, with animals generally; but
it is then forced farther down the evolutionary scale to the insects in
order to find a more complete contrast with hyperconscious man.
Benn has gone straight to this logical conclusion: even the slightest
evolutionary advance spells unacceptable suffering.

Yet in defiance of his own logic, he also evokes another ideal to set
beside the pre-conscious algae. Yearning may be contemptible – 'und
dennoch', 'and yet'. Man the sick animal, or in Benn's more sardonic
phrase the diseased god, cannot help pondering on divinity. The final
stanza duly conjures up images of perfection: a southern coastal
landscape, itself reminiscent of Nietzsche's obsessions; and in it, with
the same unprepared yet seemingly unquestionable rightness as the
lions in Rilke's Fourth Elegy, the agile, noiseless panthers. At one
moment the poet is rejecting all higher forms of life, the next he is
making obeisance to these emblematic animals. Their appearance
hints that Benn's regressive nihilism does nevertheless go back to

Nietzsche; and it also hints at a residue of positive vitalist feeling, a remote hope habitually repressed and overlaid by a consciously hard-bitten pessimism.[43]

It is admittedly wisdom after the event to see in this poetic contradiction a potentially decisive instability, and it is a paradox to suggest that Benn's naïve optimism about the Nazis in 1933 was only the other side of his sophisticated pessimism in the years preceding, and that both attitudes have something to do with Nietzsche. But the way Benn described the event does suggest such a real connection. To begin with, he spoke of his notorious broadcasts in favour of the new regime as 'the result of my intellectual development over the last fifteen years'.[44] More specifically, at each stage of his flirtation with politics – the initial enthusiasm, then the response to outside challenge, then the final disillusion – he states his position by direct reference to Nietzsche. He is thus not merely an example of the general weakness of vitalist cultural pessimism for sudden rescuing intoxications (Mann and Rilke in August 1914, carried away respectively by the 'rebirth of the nation' and the epiphany of a 'new god' offer parallels here); he also provides a case of something rare in the history of ideas, the ascription to an intellectual influence of decisive effect in a practical matter.

What fired Benn's enthusiasm in 1933 was an alleged turning-point in modern history, which for him meant a fundamental change in the nature of man: 'a historical transformation will always be an anthropological transformation' he declared in his essay on eugenic policy (*Züchtung I*) 'Until a short time ago, Man was a being of reason and his brain was the father of all things, today he is a metaphysical being, dependent, and framed about by nature and origins.' This new (German) man had been prepared by 'a quarter-century of fundamental crisis' and brought on by an awareness of his endangered state 'in the last decade'.[45] As guarantor of this view of history he appealed, in his speech *The New State and the Intellectuals*, to Nietzsche: 'For the thinking man there has been since Nietzsche only *one* criterion of the historically genuine: its appearance as the new typological variant, the real constitutional innovation, in brief the new type, and this, one must say, is there.'[46]

Everything about these propositions is phoney: the ludicrous way evolution is harnessed to the decades and quarter-centuries of political life; the 'nature and origins' jargon common to Nazis and fellow-travellers in the early days of triumph; the fundamental misunderstanding of Nietzsche as concerned with biological mutations rather than with man's spiritual self-creation. But none of these criticisms reduces the practical importance of Benn's cultural pessimism and his attempt to transcend it, attitudes derived from and now explicitly linked with the name of Nietzsche.

The link is made again, in a curiously revealing manner, in Benn's *Answer to the Literary Emigrés*. In May 1933 Klaus Mann wrote his famous open letter to the poet he had long admired, suggesting more in sorrow than anger that Benn was grotesquely wrong in his choice of camp. Klaus Mann's account of the way irrationalism slides into political reaction culminates in the sentence: 'First the grand gesture against "civilization" – a gesture which, as I am aware, has an all too strong appeal for the intellectual – then suddenly it's the cult of violence, and then in no time it's Adolf Hitler.'[47] Benn's reply restates his theory of history and mutation and takes issue with Klaus Mann's assumptions about what civilization is. 'We can best approach this problem', Benn begins, 'by considering the word "barbarism" which crops up repeatedly in your letter.'[48] In fact the word does not occur at all in what Klaus Mann wrote. Yet Benn purports to quote him verbatim: 'In your letter it says "First comes the commitment to irrationalism, then to barbarism, and then it's Adolf Hitler".'[49] And further on he again refers to 'your philological query about civilization and barbarism'.[50]

The persistent inaccuracy is not random. The key to it is given at the end of Benn's text, where he groups three authorities who speak against eudemonism and liberalism in favour of an amoral view of history: Fichte, Burckhardt and Nietzsche. The quotation from Nietzsche is the passage which ends with the demand: 'Where are the barbarians of the twentieth century?' (III, 690). Benn's misquotations are thus not, as Loose suggests, a summary of what Klaus Mann essentially meant. Rather, the unconscious introduction of the word 'barbarism' shows the subservience of Benn's thinking to a Nietzschean pattern: he is seeing the Nazis as beneficial barbarians, i.e. imposing on the present a category established by Nietzsche's thought, and above all by Nietzsche's imagery.

Klaus Mann was right to prophesy that Benn's alliance with his mutated heroes would not last. They did not take long to reject him – by 1936 he was in the wilderness – and his disillusion with them was complete even sooner, by summer 1934. The Röhm killings of that June may have brought home to him what 'barbarism' really meant. So, having briefly sought to ride a new, 'evolutionary' wave and float his art on its politics; having believed, unlike Mann and Rilke and in ghastly parody of Nietzsche, that he could see a new culture growing up from 'vital' forces; having thought that the 'mysterious connection between the state and genius of which *The Birth of Tragedy* speaks'[51] was again discernible, he now withdrew again to the opposite extreme. That same autumn he wrote:

> Intellect and art does not come from victorious but from broken natures, of that I am convinced, and also of the fact that there is no such thing as *realization*. There is only form and thought. That is an insight you will not find in Nietzsche, or he concealed it. His blond beast, his chapters on eugenics, are still dreams of the uniting of Mind and Power. That is past. They are two realms.[52]

There is both irony and aptness in this rueful comment. It is ironic that the failed opportunist should now be so firm in his convictions, and ironic that the disciple should appear to be virtually blaming the master for his own errors – not the least of which were errors in understanding what the master wrote. But it is apt too that this grim episode should end with a last appearance of that crucial and most misunderstandable of images, the blond beast.

(iv)

By now the reader may be wearying of that animal. Certainly there is something dispiriting in the responses he elicited from the writers discussed so far: the defeatism which so readily deplored higher differentiation in favour of the primitive, and the gullibility which expected cultural wonders from the nastiest of primitive phenomena. Kafka offers a welcome change and an illuminating contrast.

There is common ground enough to make the comparison valid, both in Kafka's experience of Nietzsche and in his spiritual situation. Kafka read Nietzsche while still at school,[53] and as a student at Prague University he argued for him against Max Brod's advocacy of Schopenhauer.[54] Nietzsche remained relevant to Kafka's private concerns in later years: we find him quoting Nietzsche in a notebook of 1917[55] and at some time in 1920 or 1921 it appears that he gave Gustav Janouch *The Birth of Tragedy* as a present, always a sign (Janouch says) that Kafka had a particular regard for a work.[56] There are further possible points of contact with Nietzsche;[57] but in addition to all this, and most persuasive, the similarity between Kafka's and Nietzsche's imagery on

occasion reaches that rare degree of exactness which may, exception-
ally, convince us of a derivation on internal evidence alone. Most
strikingly, Kafka's story In the Penal Colony applies with horrifying literal-
ness the metaphors which Nietzsche had used in The Genealogy of
Morals to evoke the cruel procedures originally needed for the incul-
cation of moral awareness in the 'human animal' (II, 802).[58]

The passages in question occur in the second constituent essay of
the Genealogy, which is headed 'Guilt, Bad Conscience, and Related
Matters'. It seems an obvious assumption that Kafka, given any ac-
quaintance with Nietzsche at all, should have turned to this work: a
sense of guilt was one of his fundamental experiences, and the fictional fantasies in which it found expression show an obsession with
that 'Related Matter' Nietzsche also analysed at length, punishment.[59]

Yet a reading of the Genealogy would have a significance even beyond
these immediate affinities. Of all Nietzsche's works, it is the most
systematic and, partly for that reason, the most penetrating attack on
dualistic spirituality. If it is most obviously a critique of Christian
beliefs and principles, it in fact calls in question all forms of the
spiritual life, including (characteristically) Nietzsche's own: the
artist and the philosopher are only less evident – disguised, diluted –
forms of the life-denying ascetic, because all of them share that inver-
sion of the will from which reactive values and practices are born.

Nothing could be more calculated to undermine further the already
self-doubting Kafka. He was deeply conscious of the fact that his devotion to writing was created by his distance from normality, and in
turn increased that distance and his yearnings for a normal life, for
family harmony, marriage, community. At least as much as the young
Thomas Mann or Rilke, he was a candidate for conversion to the view
that literature and the world of the spirit were totally parasitic, without independent value, 'vitally' inferior. Nietzsche's analysis might
have led Kafka, too, to see his literary impulse as an aberration, and
normality as lying in the natural exercise of the will – an ultimately
animal will, since the Genealogy centres on man's animal nature (it
contains, it will be remembered, the first 'blond beast' passage) and on
the techniques that have been used to tame it.

But something less obvious seems to have happened. The evidence
is Kafka's late story A Hunger Artist, written in spring 1922. It was already true of In the Penal Colony that, in borrowing Nietzsche's images,
Kafka asked questions and implied answers which are independent of
Nietzsche. In A Hunger Artist it seems clear that he has attended to

Nietzsche's critique of asceticism, to the extent of once more taking over the philosopher's imagery, but without for that taking over his attitudes and convictions. This already sets Kafka apart from the young Mann, Rilke and Benn. On them Nietzsche's work *did* impose an attitude, albeit simpler than his own through a mistaking of his emphasis; but where Kafka diverges from Nietzsche, it is through a simple refusal to accept the substance of what the source says. In this respect, Nietzsche's influence on Kafka was analogous to Schopenhauer's. Both focused Kafka's essential problems and provided means for their metaphorical exploration; both cases show that Kafka combined an unusual receptivity for other men's modes of thought with a singular independence of mind.[60]

Rather than undergoing an influence then, with all the passivity that implies, Kafka was responding to a challenge, which lay in Nietzsche's trenchant analysis of the ascetic life and in his drastic metaphors: 'ascetic ideals', like the Christian values 'good' and 'evil' and the religious moral conscience, were an intricate confidence-trick played on the will; 'guilt' and 'sin' were the priestly rationalizations of a psycho-physiological perversion; poor man was confused and denatured like an animal in a cage (II, 825, 881),[61] forced to redirect his will towards a new chimerical goal – liberation from 'sin' through ascetic practices, 'the scourge, the hair-shirt, the starving body' (II, 881).

Kafka takes up the challenge in the most sporting way. By creating from Nietzsche's metaphors the figure and fate of a 'hunger artist', he is accepting to settle the issue on ground of Nietzsche's choosing. He is entering into the situation Nietzsche sketched, and offering us the view from the cage.

It is not an impassioned subjective view – typically of Kafka's late work, *A Hunger Artist* is detached and subtly humorous. The hero is an unprepossessing, at best a pathetic, figure; his art left behind by the tide of fashion, he has declined from being a major sensation by himself to fasting in an obscure corner of a circus-ground, his cage little more than a hindrance on the public's route to the beasts of prey. There he dies, forgotten and not understood. The cage is cleared of his remains and houses one of the animals instead. The closing page reads:

Many days passed, and even that [his final fast] came to an end. An overseer chanced to notice the cage and asked the attendants why this perfectly usable cage with the rotting straw in it was being left unutilized; nobody knew, until one of them was reminded of the

hunger artist by the board which used to record the number of days
he had fasted. They turned over the straw with poles and found the
hunger artist in it. 'Are you still fasting?' asked the overseer, 'when
are you going to stop it?' 'Forgive me, all of you', the hunger artist
whispered; only the overseer, who had his ear to the bars, heard
him. 'Of course', said the overseer and put his finger to his forehead,
indicating to the men the hunger artist's condition, 'we forgive
you.' 'I kept on wanting you to admire my fasting', said the hunger
artist. 'Oh we do admire it', said the overseer obligingly. 'But you
ought not to admire it', said the hunger artist. 'All right then, we
won't admire it', said the overseer, 'why mustn't we admire it then?'
'Because I have to fast, I can do no other', said the hunger artist.
'Now just fancy that', said the overseer, 'why would that be then?'
'Because I', said the hunger artist, raised his small head a little and
spoke straight into the overseer's ear, with lips pursed as if to kiss,
so that nothing would be lost, 'because I couldn't find the food I
liked. If I had found it, believe me, I would have made no fuss and
eaten my fill like you and everyone.' Those were the last words, but
still in his dying eyes was the firm, albeit no longer proud, conviction that he was fasting on.

'All right, get it cleared up!' said the overseer, and they buried
the hunger artist together with the straw. But into the cage they put
a young panther. It was a perceptible relief, even for the most in-
sensitive mind, to see that wild animal flinging himself about in the
cage which had so long been desolate. There was nothing the
matter with *him*. The food he liked was brought by the keepers
without needing another thought; he didn't even seem to miss his
freedom; the noble body, endowed almost to bursting-point with
everything it needed, seemed to carry freedom around with it too;
somewhere in its teeth, it seemed to be; and the joy of life came out
of his jaws with such powerful heat that it was not easy for the on-
lookers to stand up to it. But they controlled their feelings, thronged
round the cage and simply wouldn't move away.

The hunger artist's defeat could hardly be more ignominious. Not
only is he mocked in his dying hour by the uncomprehending and
then supplanted by a creature immeasurably superior; he has also
seemingly undone his claims to achievement and to the admiration
he always longed for by telling the secret of his fasting. Not that he
ever concealed, even in his heyday, that fasting was for him 'the

easiest thing in the world'; but then people thought he was either modest, or else boasting as a form of advertisement, or even that he meant it was all a swindle – i.e. he somehow managed to eat unseen by the guards. Now, however, he has made the crucial admission: there was no alternative to fasting, because he could never find the food he wanted. This is not crucial of course to the overseer and his men, who would be unlikely to care even if they understood; their reaction is not mentioned. But it is crucial for Kafka's readers, who have often thought that these dying words discredit the asceticism for which the hunger artist evidently stands.[62] Which in turn may lead them to see the panther in the by now familiar role of an ideal contrast-figure, and even to defend this noble representative of life against subversion by those who sympathize with the expired hunger artist.[63]

Such a view must at least seem dubious to anyone acquainted with irony, and in particular with Kafka's irony. Can we blithely take at face value the overseer's crude incomprehension? or his brutal 'get it cleared up!' and the consequences? Or the classically terse phrase ('There was nothing wrong with *him*' – in German the three words 'Ihm fehlte nichts') which hits off the panther's normality yet is also so eloquent of his limitation? Or the final picture of the crowd which nearly loses its nerve in face of the panther but recovers and is the more enthusiastic for its fright, an again classic vignette of the working of fashion, which is one of the story's sub-themes?

But stylistic disquiet will not by itself refute a thematic interpretation; nor will the knowledge, lurking in the background as we read the text, that Kafka also considered as counterpart to his hunger artist a cannibal – a less readily idealizable figure than the ubiquitous *Raubtier*. For it might be argued against the first that, if Kafka ironizes the panther, that is only part of the detached manner of the whole story; while the cannibal fragment left among Kafka's manuscripts[64] might be taken to show how extremes meet: how both predator and ascetic, in their seemingly very different ways, are exercising what is ultimately the same Nietzschean will. So we must look for the exact nuance and implications of what Kafka says; and in the process beware especially of putting together *his* meaning from what *Nietzsche* said, the relevance of which is so much in the minds of critics commenting on this text that the distinction between the two writers can become blurred.

Two themes dominate Kafka's story: the hunger artist's ambition to be recognized as the greatest of his kind, which we are told he in fact is; and the ease and naturalness, for him, of fasting. This at once yields a contradiction. People usually admire achievement that needs effort, in the case of fasting the effort of overcoming natural appetite. To seek admiration for something that comes easily is to live by one nature but seek to be judged by the standards of another. To that extent the hunger artist lives a lie. Even the fanatical devotion that makes him want to fast on beyond the limit of forty days, which his impresario knows is the longest public interest can be sustained, springs from the vain hope of somehow convincing sceptics, and is to that extent a further pursuit of admiration. His showmanly ambitions stand condemned.

But in so far as ambition is an impurity in his art, he has cast it and all showmanship off when he dies. He has fasted for an immense period unrecorded; he has confessed the full truth, albeit not understood; and he dies in the '*no longer proud* conviction that he was fasting on'. All this surely settles the only score on which Kafka's story 'disvalues' asceticism.

It will only be thought to do so in any other sense if we allow ourselves to confuse what Kafka wrote with what Nietzsche said – to say, as does another critic with Nietzsche very much in mind, that the hunger artist 'fasts . . . because he lacks the right food, i.e. because he is deficient in vitality'.[65] That is a wholly mistaken equation; it does however point up the issue. To 'lack the right food' is nothing to do with being 'deficient in vitality', but rather means aspiring to something which vitality knows nothing of. It is quite different from Nietzsche's thesis about asceticism and all its works, which is that the strong secure the objects of their appetites, whereupon the weak compensate by calling the strong 'evil', by denying that they themselves ever wanted those objects, and by exercising their (unsuccessful) wills on their own inner systems instead. 'Deficient vitality' leads to simple failure in the competition for things which are known, desired and available. They become unavailable for the purely practical reason that someone stronger has got them. Asceticism for Nietzsche results from the frustration of normal appetite.

The hunger artist is not at all in this case. Food has always been readily available but repellent to him: indeed the meal at the end of each fasting-period was his real martyrdom. He was even hurt by the sight of the 'lumps of raw meat' being carried past his cage to the beasts of prey and by the sound of their cries at feeding time. His dying words admit to an appetite as great as anyone's, but quite removed from the normal – which is a different thing from a perversion of the normal. The existence of his strange appetite leaves open the question whether a commensurate nourishment for it anywhere exists.

Here again Kafka is saying something that relates to problems Nietzsche discussed, but saying something very different. In a paragraph of *Human, All-Too-Human* headed 'Religious after-pains', Nietzsche says that, after the demise of religion, vestiges of religious feeling may lead men to believe certain scientific and philosophical ideas as a form of wishful thinking. Centuries of religion have developed an appetite which cannot be abolished at a stroke but goes on operating in this other guise: 'The hunger does not prove that a food *exists* to satisfy it, but it wishes for the food' (1, 531). Nietzsche is here concerned with the practical consequences, the intellectual self-deception which may result from wishing to believe something. He clearly implies that no such 'food' exists: the appetite is left over from a conditioning which redirected normal appetites, and these take a long time to recover. For Kafka, on the other hand, the possibility that the food does not exist in no way invalidates the appetite, since the hunger artist experiences his special appetite as quite real and quite different from the normal one, albeit only satisfiable in some far reach of the imagination. However dubious his showmanship may appear, his fasting itself is not explained – much less explained away – by Nietzsche's theory of the will to power. The spiritual world is a distinct one. Kafka remains obstinately dualist where Nietzsche was a monist. He appears to have taken full cognizance of Nietzsche's arguments and to have tested them out by realizing in a fiction the metaphors that illustrate them. But in the end he presents, gently yet firmly, a dissenting conclusion.

To say this is of course to take the hunger artist's dying words at face value and to assume that Kafka is not suggesting they rest on an illusion. Once more, there are stylistic reasons for this assumption: the story shows a scrupulous detachment from the hunger artist's melancholy lot, but hardly ironizes him in the way the overseer, panther, and crowd are ironized. But there are also grounds in Kafka's other writings. In 1912, he wrote the following in his diary:

> In me it is quite possible to recognize a concentration on the writing function. When it became clear in my organism that writing was the most fruitful direction of my being, everything pressed that way and left all the capacities standing empty which were directed towards

the pleasures of sex, eating, drinking, philosophical reflection, music above all. I grew emaciated in all these directions. This was necessary because my strength in its totality was so slight that it could only – meagrely – serve the purpose of writing if concentrated. Naturally I didn't find this purpose independently and consciously, it found itself and is now only hindered, but here very thoroughly, by my office work. At any rate, I needn't weep over the fact that I can't bear any girl-friend, that I understand almost exactly as much about love as about music and have to be content with the most superficial random effects, that on New Year's Eve I ate spinach and salsify for supper and drank half a pint of Ceres [a patent drink made from skimmed milk] with it, and that on Sunday at Max's reading of his philosophical work I couldn't take any part; the compensation for all this is evident. So I only have to throw out my office work from this collective in order – since my development is now completed and I have nothing more to sacrifice – to begin my real life, in which my face will finally be able to age with the progress of my works.[66]

This unsentimentally poignant review of Kafka's own situation relates, like *A Hunger Artist*, to normal appetite and its denial. The slightness of Kafka's 'strength in its totality' might be seen as 'deficient vitality', and he speaks of his writing life as a 'compensation' ['Ausgleich']. The proximity to Nietzsche's jaundiced view is clear. Yet Kafka's emphasis is quite different. He is, within the limits of his misery, content with the exchange. He readily accepts the need to abandon other activities in favour of this one potentially 'fruitful direction', the purpose which 'found itself' and which will become his 'real life'. All his emphasis is on the independent, given reality of this alternative life. In place of the Nietzschean ideas of perverted appetite and reactive values, we have practical consideration of the economy of a human organism: what resources it has and how these can best be used.

This idea of 'concentration' is different in kind from Nietzsche's theory of the frustration and resentful redirection of natural appetites and energies. Kafka seems to have held it consistently; it occurs again in 1916 when he considers the pros and cons of marriage for his writing. Conceivably marriage could bring it new strength – but the risk of being diverted from his purposes is greater; the single state may be more limited, but its advantages are certain, among them the fact that 'I keep all my forces together . . . Concentration on my work'.[67] One might say that he is opting for the literary bird-in-the-hand, if it were not that the proverb overstates the strength of his position. Indeed, in 1919 he himself adapts it, characteristically and illuminatingly, to his marriage dilemma. He says that it fits his situation 'only very remotely. In my hand I have nothing, in the bush is everything and yet I am compelled – so the circumstances of the struggle and the necessity of my life determine – to choose Nothing.'[68] Once more the choice seems his: what he desires is available to be seized; yet he chooses freely – albeit with some sense of a higher necessity – to renounce it and devote himself to an alternative. The reality of this alternative, even though he describes it in terms of the most radical doubt, is unquestioned. Misery here abuts on mysticism.

It is of course possible to think that Nietzsche was right and Kafka wrong about asceticism, and even that Kafka's case can be subsumed, whatever his own views, under Nietzsche's principles. But that is not part of the interpretation of Kafka, only a matter of each reader's response to the themes which Nietzsche and Kafka both treated, from very different angles. The most important thing for the present inquiry is this difference itself and what it shows, namely the spiritual resilience of Kafka, whose amply documented uncertainties made him seemingly the least likely person to resist a powerful intellectual onslaught. Yet at the centre of those uncertainties there was evidently a core of certainty – if not about answers, then about the reality of their pursuit.

This certainty was not easily to be disturbed by modish images of animal vitality. Kafka's panther is not an ideal; the closing paragraph of the story is not a celebration, but a cool account of mindless magnificence. Of course this can easily outshine the pathetic bag of bones which has just expired. But it is the hunger artist who has snatched a kind of victory from the jaws of defeat. For what is vitality? Undeniably Kafka was aware that he lacked it, that he was physically a weakling beside his father, the aptly named Hermann Kafka, or beside his cousin Robert, a 'splendid man' of forty whom Kafka just before his death recalled watching as he dived and who swam 'with the strength of a beautiful wild animal'.[69] But to assume that this awareness determined Kafka's thinking and artistic dispositions is to beg the question. Vitality in itself may be an insufficient ideal. Even for Nietzsche it was only a beginning. Perceiving this, Kafka was closer to Nietzsche in one respect, even while at odds with him in others, than those numerous contemporaries were who believed in the age's and their own decadence and were consequently so ready to be shamed by the animal splendour with which Nietzsche's cultural criticism appears to have mesmerized them.

IV

We have been looking at literary texts, and it is notoriously rash to read these as straight declaration. Literature is an indirect mode, of infinite subtlety. Thomas Mann's *Tristan* has irony and counter-irony, and perhaps a final irony escapes the self-abasement which Spinell's defeat suggests. Was there not similarly a good deal of bluff in those attitudes of Gottfried Benn's which are epitomized in his cynical jibe that the brain was 'a bluff for the middle classes'? And Rilke: can one really penetrate that esoteric world and bring back statements on which anything outside the confines of poetic feeling can be based? These are obvious objections with which to temper a moralistic response.

And yet: for all the ironies and ambiguities on which a sophisticated critic would rightly insist, literature is also the medium in which men's deepest impulses find (the word is apt for the limited intentionality of the process) expression. If it were not so, we should not value it so highly. It is thus not naïve to assume that what men say through images and the way they shape them tells us something about human affairs; it would be naïve to assume it did not.

We have watched four writers responding to the most powerful intellectual influence of their time. Having examined Nietzsche's meanings, and his potentially misleading way of conveying them, we have seen how in three cases out of four he did in fact mislead; and how in one of the three, Benn's, the effect already went beyond the bounds of art into politics. Four is too small a sample to satisfy a statistician – it was only meant to be qualitatively suggestive – but any statistician who knew German literature of the turn of the century would admit that many other choices would have been equally possible, and with similar results. In general, both at the level of literary understanding and adaptation and below it at the level of popularization and diffusion, the governing factor would remain what it has been in much of the foregoing: simplification. An example at the first level would be Georg Heym's Nietzsche-inspired longings for a literal war in the years before 1914;[70] and at the second, the pre-war mood which led naturally to the heroics of autumn 1914, some part of which can be put down to diffused Nietzsche. As Hermann Broch wrote in *The Sleepwalkers*: 'People wanted to see something unambiguous and heroic, in other words something aesthetic . . . They were caught up in a misunderstood Nietzscheanism, even though most of them might never have heard the name Nietzsche.'[71]

Simplification was indeed in some measure Nietzsche's aim: 'my ambition is to say in ten propositions what everyone else says in a book – what everyone else *doesn't* say in a book' (II, 1026). That was written in the already growing arrogance of the late *Twilight of the Idols*, but it has much truth, in a sense Nietzsche might not have welcomed. His writing, a repetitive because impassioned wrestling with certain fundamental problems, *can* be reduced – more readily than that of most philosophers – to a schema. The passion and the discrimination are lost with the total argument; what is left is a handful of fairly crude-sounding results.

This, as literary historians have observed, is very much the way Nietzsche's influence worked (it may indeed be doubted whether an influence of so sweeping a kind could operate in any other way). 'It is not really the philosophical substance of his writings that is taken up. That remains largely undiscovered. What takes effect is the basic positions, recognizable in thirty or forty sentences.'[72] That number may seem too high, and the 'sentences' might prove to be reducible to images, among them the master-images we have been concerned with; but the inference that these operated divorced from their context – that Nietzsche, in other words, was often simply not read – is surely right. It is borne out by an observation of Thomas Mann's written around 1909. Comparing what Nietzsche gave Mann's own generation with the effect he has had on the next, he says: 'For them he is a prophet they don't know in detail, whom they hardly need to have read, and whose purified results they nevertheless have instinctively within them' – results which he sums up as 'the antispiritual conception of nobility which embraces health and serenity and beauty'.[73] And in another note for the same project, he castigates some contemporaries for taking German art, once renowned for its spiritual qualities, 'with German thoroughness straight to the extremes of animalism'.[74]

That project, the never-completed essay 'Art and Intellect', shows Mann for the first time critically surveying the cultural values of his time and recognizing both their perils and his own share in them. His brother Heinrich was already seeing these perils in political, and again Nietzschean, terms. In 1910 he rebuked his contemporaries with the words: 'A modern nation . . . has no right . . . to persuade itself of its superman qualities ['Übermenschentum'] when it is still in arrears with its basic human ones ['Menschentum'].'[75] What was later to develop from these strands of Nietzsche's thought and influence there is no space, but perhaps no need, to go into here.

It was such developments – Nietzscheanism in its most debased forms, and a nation's fall into the irrationalism of which he saw Nietzsche as the fountainhead – that made Thomas Mann shape his fictional reckoning with German history into a transposed biography of Nietzsche. That work, the novel *Doktor Faustus*, is not a simple moralistic indictment, but an exposition of the tragic affinity between high forms of art and thought and lower, even evil, phenomena in which nevertheless a common impulse can be discerned. It raises the most general questions about the mutual causality of culture and society, and hence about the responsibility of artists and thinkers for what goes on in the world outside their personal concerns.

The nature and degree of Nietzsche's responsibility for what came after him, and for what by chance or intention was made of his ideas, is a subject already long debated and unlikely to be soon concluded. It can be urged that others perverted his thought, and also that the thought was too readily pervertible. The two points of view can perhaps be joined in a realistic conception of responsibility: the thinker's sense of responsibility for his thought must be sharpened by the knowledge that, in making his thought public, he lets further responsibility pass from his hands. As the batty humanist Moses Herzog writes to Nietzsche in Saul Bellow's novel: 'Humankind lives mainly upon perverted ideas . . . Any philosopher who wants to keep his contact with humanity should pervert his own system in advance to see how it will really look a few decades after adoption.'[76]

That is a perspective Nietzsche rarely adopted, and never with any sense of ultimate responsibility for the idea which has escaped from its author. It is striking how nonchalantly he speaks on one occasion in just these terms. Once more he is arguing for the 'wild beast' as the necessary basis for human culture, and he reflects that humane ages are loath to accept this truth because to do so may help the beast itself to life again. 'Perhaps I am risking something if I allow such a truth to get out: let others capture it again and give it so much "milk of human kindness" to drink until it lies quiet and forgotten in its old corner' (II, 693). Nietzsche's idea of man's animal nature is here itself become the beast, slipped loose at any hazard. It is not the least apt and thought-provoking of his many animals.

NOTES

1 References are to Friedrich Nietzsche, *Werke in drei Bänden*, 2nd rev. edn (Munich, 1960). All translations of Nietzsche, and of the other writers discussed later, are my own.

2 H. Heine, *Nordsee III. Sämtliche Werke*, ed. Walzel (Leipzig, 1910ff), vol. IV, p. 93.

3 Thus the text of *Zarathustra*, Book IV. The later variant reading in the *Dithyrambs of Dionysus* is slightly more explicit, containing the words

> Implacable to anything that looks
> Virtuous, sheep-like, fleecy,
> Stupid, with lamb's-milk-goodwill (II, 1241).

4 It seems well established that 'blond' ('fulvus') was a fixed epithet for the lion in Latin poetry, and would thus come readily to mind for an ex-professor of classics. See References (p. 218) under Brennecke.

5 Brennecke, p. 469.

6 For a clumsier variant of the tiger image from about the same time (1873), see *Über Wahrheit und Lüge im aussermoralischen Sinne* (III, 311), where conscious man is pictured as borne along by his fierce instincts as if he were riding on a tiger's back.

7 '[. . .] Life – that means: being cruel and implacable towards anything that is getting old and weak within us, and not only within us. Life – that means, then: being without piety towards the dying, the miserable and the old? Being constantly a murderer? – And yet old Moses said: "Thou shalt not kill!"'' (II, 59).

8 In an early autobiographical text on his Leipzig years, we find apropos the formative experiences of youth: 'Two years! At that age! The things that suck at the young being, the things that press their claws into the soft clay!' (III, 128). The metaphors are mixed, but they foreshadow a doctrine not yet formulated.

9 It can be objected that Nietzsche compares the worst examples of Christianity with the best examples, or potential, of paganism. Copleston, p. 127, points to the outgoing energy of figures like St Teresa and asks (p. 71) 'whether the Christian conquest of the Moors [in Spain] was not in reality the victory of a vigorous young and growing culture over an over-ripe and decaying culture?' This neatly uses Nietzsche's favourite situation of 'barbarians' conquering and reinvigorating what was in decline, but with reversed roles. It introduces a note of political reality (not to say *Realpolitik*) into an issue which Nietzsche saw as determined by a 'vitality' always incompatible with Christianity. El Cid, in other words, may have had a good deal of the 'barbarian' about him.

10 Cf. *The Dawn of Day* § 108 (I, 1080f) on the admissibility of *recommending* goals and courses of action to men, since the matter is then left in their free choice; and *The Joyful Science* § 304 (II, 179), where morality is understood as primarily positive, 'thou shalt' rather than 'thou shalt not'; or in Nietzsche's words, 'our doing shall determine what we omit to do'.

11 Cf. also on the barbarians' *spiritual* strength (II, 727) quoted above.

12 Hence Thomas Mann's remark in the *Betrachtungen eines Unpolitischen* that the superman was hard to visualize, 'unanschaulich'. Cf. *Gesammelte Werke* (Frankfurt am Main, 1960), vol. XII, p. 79.

13 This triadic pattern is present in Nietzsche as early as 1867, in the autobiographical sketch quoted above. It begins:

> My future lies very much in the dark for me, without for that causing me concern. I have a similar relation with my past: on the whole, I forget it very quickly, and only the changes and strengthenings of my character show me from time to time that I have lived through it. Living thus, one is taken by

surprise by one's own development, without understanding it; and I cannot but recognize that this has advantages, since continual contemplation and assessment tends to disturb the spontaneous [*naiv*] expressions of a character and seems slightly to hinder its growth.
Up to this point, we have the argument for 'forgetfulness' and against 'historical consciousness' exactly as in *The Benefits and Dangers of History*, but in purely personal terms (with however a hint in the wording of a possible Schillerian influence). But Nietzsche then reflects that the disturbing effect of self-consciousness *is* only an apparent one, and temporary: does not the infantryman under training fear that he may cease altogether ['verlernen'] to be able to walk because he has to pay constant attention to how it is to be done? Whereas in fact 'it is only a matter of giving him ['anbilden'] a second nature; then he can walk as freely as ever' (III, 127). This clearly envisaged final stage shows that Nietzsche from the first conceived of 'forgetfulness' and 'spontaneity' only as prefigurations of a second 'state of nature' which must be recreated.

14 *Journal meiner Reise*, in: *Sturm und Drang. Kritische Schriften* (Heidelberg, 1963), p. 295.

15 *Götz von Berlichingen*, Act II, first scene.

16 Heft F. Sudelbücher, in: *Schriften und Briefe* (Munich, 1968), vol. I, p. 519.

17 Wieland, *Agathodämon* (a novel largely made up of philosophical and religious discussions) Book 7, chapters 5 and 6, in: *Werke* (Munich, 1966), vol. II, pp. 683–99. The one clear difference – and it is crucial – between the two men is that Wieland sees in Christianity, despite everything, a *necessary* evil, since it was the only way to prepare 'future institutions' (p. 694). Like most Enlightenment thinkers, Wieland was ready to accept in secularized form the advances Christianity had brought about. Nietzsche was both more radical in his anti-Christian campaign and – his essential flaw as a thinker – wholly unconcerned about the 'institutions' which would be the framework for his ideal culture.

18 *Lebensabriss*, 1936, *Gesammelte Werke*, vol. XI, p. 110.

19 See the story's close, where Tonio Kröger reflects on what makes a mere 'Literat' into that more prestigious thing, a 'Dichter'.

20 Heller, p. 129.

21 Kaufmann, p. 231. Dehn, pp. 12f, argues a similar analogy.

22 Heller, p. 127.

23 In a note on Maeterlinck, *Sämtliche Werke* (SW), vol. V, p. 530. Cf. the story *Ewald Tragy* (1898) where a pompous man of letters is particularly satirized for recounting how he 'transcended Nietzsche', SW, vol. IV, p. 550.

24 *Der Apostel*, SW, vol. IV, pp. 452–9.

25 In a letter to Bodo Wildberg written just after the story was published, quoted in SW, vol. IV, p. 1009. 'Half satirical' refers to the opening portrayal of elegant diners.

26 *Böhmische Schlendertage*, SW, vol. V, p. 294.

27 Lou Albert-Lasard, *Wege mit Rilke* (Frankfurt am Main, 1952), p. 79.

28 R. M. Rilke, *Tagebücher aus der Frühzeit* (Frankfurt am Main, 1973), p. 125.

29 *Marginalien zu Nietzsche*, SW, vol. VI, pp. 1163–77. The manuscript, not published until 1966 in this volume, was found in the papers of Lou Andreas-Salome. This is a kind of confirmation of what had often been supposed, namely that Lou – once intimately acquainted with Nietzsche (and even sought in marriage by him) and fifteen years later Rilke's mistress – must have been one means by which the thinker's ideas reached the poet.

30 SW, vol. VI, pp. 1161f. For Rilke's own insistence on this continuity, see the letter of 13 November 1925 to his translator, Witold von Hulewicz. Incidentally, do the famous phrases it contains – 'die Bienen des Unsichtbaren', 'le miel du visible' 'la grande ruche d'or de l'Invisible' owe something to Nietzsche's 'Bienenkörbe

der Erkenntnis' ('beehives of knowledge') and 'Honigsammler des Geistes' ('honey gatherers of the mind') in the foreword to *The Genealogy of Morals* (II, 763)?

31 Cf. the letter from the zoologist Baron Jacob von Uexküll praising Rilke's 'outstanding talent for biology and especially for comparative psychology' as revealed in the 'Panther' poem. (Quoted by Mislin, p. 47.) Rilke's essays in description emulate Rodin, who in particular drew animals in the Jardin des Plantes (cf. SW, vol. V, p. 229).

32 SW, vol. I, p. 649.

33 *Ibid.*, vol. I, p. 501, 'Die Fensterrose'.

34 *Ibid.*, vol. I, p. 595, 'Schwarze Katze'.

35 It is interesting to see that Brecht picked up this element of Rilke's poem, and spoke of it in terms which are implicitly Nietzschean: 'Enter one who has been repressed and deprived of his freedom: the aristocrat! The beauty of the beast ['Bestie'], innocence in the higher sense, Nature which one is not supposed to question.' See Bertolt Brecht, *Arbeitsjournal 1938–1942* (Frankfurt am Main, 1973), p. 310 (entry of 27.X.41).

36 This passage (lines 29–32) recalls the configuration in the *New Poems*, 'Die Fensterrose' and 'Schwarze Katze', discussed above, and suggests the line of continuity linking those texts of 1907 with this of 1922. This is confirmed by the way animal images recur at all stages of the genesis of the Elegies: in 1912 (Elegy I), 1915 (Elegy IV) and 1922 (Elegy VIII), with a further instance outside the cycle in the poem 'Ausgesetzt auf den Bergen . . .' of 1914 (SW, vol. II, p. 94).

37 This point is crucial but is sometimes not perceived. E.g. Fingerhut (*Rilke*, pp. 103ff) suggests that Rilke is like Nietzsche in setting up animal ideal images as pointers to a higher development for man and not merely as pointers back to a lost simplicity. But precisely this is missing from the *Elegies*. Their one positive figure located beyond man is the angel. But he is of so much higher an order than man that his condition is unattainable. He is only ever used as a contrast figure – with man's poor emotions (Elegy II) and with man's limited achievements, which are finally presented to his judgment as valuable precisely in that they *are* limited to concrete human experience (Elegies VII, IX). There is no possibility here of triadic progression. It is a quite different situation from Nietzsche's, where the superman is a higher analogue, or actual transformation, of spontaneous animal nature – something which man can progressively move towards and, albeit with difficulty, at length become.

38 James Joyce, *A Portrait of the Artist as a Young Man* (Harmondsworth, 1964), p. 224.

39 To Ewald Wasmuth, 4 March 1929, in: Benn, *Ausgewählte Briefe* (Wiesbaden, 1957), p. 33.

40 G. Benn, *Nietzsche nach fünfzig Jahren*, in: *Gesammelte Werke*, ed. Wellershoff (Wiesbaden, 1959), vol. I, p. 482.

41 The theories Benn makes much of were already discredited at the time he used them. See Wellershoff, *Phänotyp*, pp. 74 and 125ff. – The most substantial contribution science made to Benn's work lay in provoking his disgust. First, with the endless ramifications of positivist investigation, whose orgiastic overthrow is celebrated in the sketch 'Ithaka' of 1914; and second, with the physical nature of man as (literally) dissected by a young doctor who must constantly 'live in the presence of the body', as the poem 'The Doctor' puts it.

42 Benn, *Gesammelte Werke*, vol. IV, pp. 179–87.

43 For both the idea and the image, cf. Zarathustra's 'So/Eagle-like, panther-like/ Are the poet's yearnings' (II, 535 and 1241).

44 Benn, *Gesammelte Werke*, vol. II, p. 393.

45 *Ibid.*, vol. I, pp. 215f.

46 *Ibid.*, vol. I, p. 443.

47 For the text of the whole letter, including and indicating the passages Benn omitted when he published it after the war in the autobiographical *Doppelleben*, see Loose, pp. 179ff.

48 Benn, *Gesammelte Werke*, vol. IV, p. 240.

49 *Ibid.*, vol. IV, p. 242.

50 *Ibid.*, vol. IV, p. 243.

51 *Totenrede auf Max von Schillings*, July 1933. Benn, *Gesammelte Werke*, vol. I, p. 451. It is not clear what part of *The Birth of Tragedy* actually says this.

52 To Ina Seidel, 30 September 1934. *Ausgewählte Briefe*, p. 61. The phrase 'chapters on eugenics [Züchtung]' presumably refers to the fourth and last book of *Der Wille zur Macht*, entitled 'Zucht und Züchtung'. In fact, its two hundred and thirteen paragraphs are no more concerned with literal eugenics, in the sense in which Benn was using the term in the 1930s, than are the areas of Nietzsche's writings we have glanced at. Yet when 'Zucht und Züchtung' stands as a major heading, it has the marked effect of emphasizing and literalizing what was in origin and in essence metaphorical. Book Four of the *Wille zur Macht* has various titles in Nietzsche's numerous plans, including 'The self-overcoming of Man' and 'The education of the Higher Man'. Responsibility for the final title is only very partially Nietzsche's, since it was chosen by Peter Gast and Elisabeth Förster-Nietzsche when they compiled this influential 'work' from Nietzsche's papers. We are thus touching on another problematic factor in the popularization process. Incidentally, as far as literal beliefs go, Nietzsche held that racial mixtures were culturally beneficial, especially the Jewish admixture in Europe. He was thus very far removed from the tendencies of Nazi genetic 'thinking'.

53 See the recollections of Frau Selma Robitschek quoted in Franz Kafka, *Briefe 1902–1924*, ed. Max Brod (Frankfurt, 1958), p. 495.

54 Brod, *Biographie*, p. 57.

55 In the third *Oktavheft*, *Hochzeitsvorbereitungen auf dem Lande und andere Prosa aus dem Nachlass* (Frankfurt, 1953), p. 80. Kafka meditates on the possible destructiveness of self-knowledge unless its deepest purpose is 'to make you into the man you are'. Quotation-marks indicate that this is an allusion, surely to the sub-title of Nietzsche's *Ecce Homo*: 'How one becomes the man one is' (II, 1063).

56 As communicated to Walter Sokel. See Sokel, p. 545. Much of Sokel's interpretation rests on the assumption that the concepts of this work were a basic and permanent part of Kafka's thought and artistic design.

57 See Wagenbach, pp. 126, 175 and 259 (where *Zarathustra* is noted as the only work of Nietzsche's Kafka certainly possessed).

58 This suggestion has been worked out by Pasley, *Heizer* etc., pp. 18ff and further elaborated by Bridgwater, pp. 104–11. To the passages from the *Genealogy* which they refer to may be added II, 881, on the 'cruel mechanism [Räderwerk] of conscience'.

59 *The Judgement, Metamorphosis*, and *The Trial*, as well as *In the Penal Colony*, are all in some degree punishment fantasies. All were written (or, in the case of *The Trial*, begun) in the two years from September 1912 to October 1914. The coherence of theme was clear to Kafka, who at one time planned to publish a volume containing the three short stories with the general title 'Punishments'. See Kafka's letter of 15 October 1915 to Kurt Wolff, in: *Kurt Wolff. Briefwechsel eines Verlegers 1911–1963*, ed. B. Zeller and E. Otten (Frankfurt, 1966), p. 35.

60 For the Schopenhauer case, see Reed, 'Kafka und Schopenhauer'.

61 These passages anticipate the second account of the 'blond beast' in *Twilight of the Idols*, quoted above, p. 166.

62 See Sokel, pp. 211ff; Bridgwater, pp. 111ff; Pasley, 'Asceticism', p. 108; and Spann, esp. p. 104.

63 See Spann.

64 Printed in Pasley, 'Asceticism', pp. 105f.

65 Fingerhut, *Kafka*, p. 246. Similarly, in Bridgwater's account of 'the folly of asceticism', it is notable that there are extensive quotations from Nietzsche, but scarcely anything from Kafka's text.

66 Franz Kafka, *Tagebücher 1910–1923*, ed. Max Brod (Frankfurt, 1954), p. 229. Images of hunger and a desired mysterious food are as central to Kafka as animals are to Nietzsche, but cannot be pursued here. Examples are quoted in Pasley, 'Asceticism', *passim*.

67 From the 'Fragmente aus Heften und losen Blättern', in Franz Kafka, *Hochzeitsvorbereitungen auf dem Lande und andere Prosa aus dem Nachlass* (Frankfurt, 1953), p. 238.

68 *Ibid.*, *Brief an den Vater*, p. 219.

69 This late jotting, printed by Brod, *Biographie*, p. 252, is quoted by Spann (p. 99) in his defence of the panther. Its inconclusiveness is increased by the full context, for what was uppermost in the dying Kafka's mind is mortality: six months after the remembered scene, Cousin Robert had died of a mysterious disease.

70 Cf. Heym's diary entry of 30 May 1907: 'If only there would be a war, I should be healthy', and of 15 September 1911: 'God – I'm suffocating with my enthusiasm which is forced to lie fallow by this banal age. For I have need of powerful external emotions to be happy. [. . .] I hoped that at least there would be a war now. But nothing doing.' Quoted in Martens, pp. 163f.

71 *Die Schlafwandler* (1931/2), *Gesammelte Werke* vol. II, (Zürich, 1952), p. 399. On Nietzsche's part in the war ideology of 1914, and its other ingredients, see Reed, *Thomas Mann*, pp. 214–21.

72 Rasch, p. 40.

73 *Geist und Kunst*, note 103, printed in Wysling.

74 *Ibid.*, note 29.

75 In the essay *Geist und Tat* of 1910. In Heinrich Mann, *Politische Essays* (Frankfurt, 1968), p. 12.

76 Saul Bellow, *Herzog* (Harmondsworth, 1964), pp. 326f.

References

Most books on Nietzsche necessarily have something to say on his, for a philosopher, unusual style and its proximity to literature; but there has been little concentrated work on his metaphors as such. These have been discussed at greatest length in two recent French studies: Bernard Pautrat, *Versions du soleil. Figures et système de Nietzsche* (Paris, 1971), and Sarah Kofman, *Nietzsche et la métaphore* (Paris, 1972). Indexes to Nietzsche's works – Richard Oehler's to the Kröner edition and Karl Schlechta's to the Hanser edition I have cited – almost wholly lack headings for Nietzsche's images, which is a serious deficiency considering the weight these carry. The feasibility of including such references is shown by the admirable index to Arthur Hübscher's second edition (Wiesbaden, 1948) of that other very literary philosopher, Schopenhauer.

As for Nietzsche's influence, there are innumerable references to it in studies of Thomas Mann, Rilke, Benn, Kafka, and many other writers of the period from 1890 on. A single compendious treatment is hardly conceivable. In its absence, one has to guard against working from a single compendious assumption; for although Nietzsche's name was on everyone's lips (or pen) at this time, each case needs precise individual treatment if the results are not to be assimilated into a vague *Geistesgeschichte*. In other words, a *soupçon* of positivism is a necessary ingredient in studies of Nietzsche's effects.

A good concise account of the main forms his influence took is contained in Section IV of Peter Pütz, *Nietzsche*, 2nd edn (Stuttgart, 1975). The earliest phase and some of the early simplifications have been usefully documented by Richard Frank Krummel, *Nietzsche und der deutsche Geist* (Berlin, 1974), which lists and gives a brief précis of over five hundred items published in the German-speaking area up to 1900 (a few items are later recollections relating to that period).

The following is a checklist of the secondary works which are referred to in my notes by author's name and page-number:

Brennecke, Detlef, 'Die blonde Bestie', *Germanisch-romanische Monatsschrift* 51 (1970).

Bridgwater, Patrick, *Kafka and Nietzsche* (Bonn, 1974).

Brod, Max, *Franz Kafka. Eine Biographie*, 3rd edn (Frankfurt, 1954).

Copleston, Frederick, *Friedrich Nietzsche. Philosopher of Culture* (London, 1942; reprinted 1975).

Dehn, Fritz, 'Rilke und Nietzsche. Ein Versuch', *Dichtung und Volkstum* (= *Euphorion*) 37 (1936).

Fingerhut, Karl-Heinz, *Die Funktion der Tierfiguren im Werke Franz Kafkas* (Bonn, 1969).

Fingerhut, Karl-Heinz, *Das Kreatürliche im Werke Rainer Maria Rilkes* (Bonn, 1970).

Heller, Erich, 'Rilke and Nietzsche. With a discourse on thought, belief and poetry', in: Heller, *The Disinherited Mind*, 3rd edn (London, 1971).

Kaufmann, Walter, 'Nietzsche and Rilke', in: Kaufmann, *From Shakespeare to Existentialism* (New York, 1960).

Loose, Gerhard, *Die Ästhetik Gottfried Benns* (Frankfurt, 1961).

Martens, Günter, 'Im Aufbruch das Ziel. Nietzsches Wirkung im

Expressionismus', in: Hans Steffen (ed.), *Nietzsche. Werk und Wirkungen* (Göttingen, 1974).

Mislin, Hans, 'Rilkes Partnerschaft mit der Natur', *Blätter der Rilke-Gesellschaft*, 3 (1974).

Pasley, J. M. S. (ed.), *Franz Kafka: Der Heizer. In der Strafkolonie. Der Bau* (Cambridge, 1966).

Pasley, J. M. S., 'Asceticism and Cannibalism: Notes on an Unpublished Kafka Text', *Oxford German Studies* 1 (1966).

Rasch, Wolfdietrich, *Zur deutschen Literatur seit der Jahrhundertwende* (Stuttgart, 1967).

Reed, T. J., 'Kafka und Schopenhauer: Philosophisches Denken und dichterisches Bild', *Euphorion* 59 (1965).

Reed, T. J., *Thomas Mann. The Uses of Tradition* (Oxford, 1974).

Sokel, Walter, *Franz Kafka. Tragik und Ironie* (Munich/Vienna, 1964).

Spann, Meno, 'Franz Kafka's Leopard', *Germanic Review* 34 (1959).

Wagenbach, Klaus, *Franz Kafka. Eine Biographie seiner Jugend* (Berne, 1958).

Wellershoff, Dieter, *Gottfried Benn. Phänotyp dieser Stunde* (Cologne/Berlin, 1958).

Wysling, Hans (and Scherrer, Paul), *Quellenkritische Studien zum Werke Thomas Manns* (Munich/Berne, 1967).

8

ENGLISH WRITERS AND NIETZSCHE[1]

Patrick Bridgwater

I INTRODUCTION

Nietzsche's impact on English writers in the years 1896–1914 appears to justify Wyndham Lewis's statement that he became, for a time 'the greatest popular success of any philosopher of modern times'. What sets him apart is the *kind* of impact he had. Philosophers are normally influential because in one way or another they reveal some essential truth about human nature. This is not the case with Nietzsche, although he does reveal certain truths, notably concerning the will to power, the genealogy of morals, and man's extraordinary power of self-deception. It was not this, however, that made him so influential. So far as British writers are concerned, his appeal lay in what is also, paradoxically, his greatest weakness: his capacity for generalization. This capacity ensured both that little of his work was true, and that most of it was highly stimulating.

His work reflects a fundamental dichotomy between self and anti-self, truth-seeker and myth-builder, philosopher and poet, although the generalization must not be carried too far since there is more than one kind of truth and more than one way in which it can be sought. Applying this division to his impact on English writers, we can immediately say that it was, above all, as 'poet' that Nietzsche caught the imagination of a generation. Many of the writers in question may have been drawn to him because of his search for truth, because they hoped to find in his work certain new truths to replace the discredited Victorian 'truths'; but in case after case it was the myth-builder under

whose spell they fell. Indeed, there were writers who objected to the
fact that Nietzsche was not taken seriously as a philosopher; Bernard
Shaw, for instance, wrote to Archibald Henderson on 5 December 1905
that 'Nietzsche's views, instead of being added soberly to the existing
body of philosophy, are treated as if they were a sort of music hall
performance'.[2] In fact it is the virtuoso nature of Nietzsche's performance which explains both his very considerable influence on the literary scene and his lack of influence as a philosopher in the academic
sense; but then if he took himself very seriously indeed, the fact remains that he did not take himself entirely seriously as a philosopher,
for he continually allowed the poet or myth-builder to undermine the
truth-seeker's works. As philosopher, Nietzsche was a less influential
figure than, say, William James; it was as *guru* or prophet that he made
his mark; in 1896 already he was described by W. F. Barry as 'the hero
as well as the prophet of free-thinkers'.

The very fact that on an academic level he was never influential in
this country not only points to the insularity of British philosophy in
the post-Hegelian era; it also suggests that his whole style was considered bad form, and that he was not regarded as an original thinker
at all. This last point has some justification, for however many trends
in twentieth-century thought he may have anticipated, Nietzsche was
fundamentally eclectic, a summarizer; his forte was the brilliant and
startling expression of current ideas. There is much truth in Ford
Madox Hueffer's statement (in his brilliant hostile analysis of Prussian
culture, *When Blood is Their Argument*, 1915), that 'Nietzsche in one sense
was something quite new; in another sense, he was just the opportunist expressing himself in new terms.' His impact in literary circles
was due to the fact that his ideas, for all their air of originality, were
familiar ones; this is a point to which we shall return. Certainly his
English readers did not go to him for epistemology or metaphysics or
even for an inverted moral theology; they were drawn to him because of the 'romanticism of ideas' (John Cowper Powys) generated
by his work, and because of his 'openly defiant romanticism' (Lascelles
Abercrombie), which was exactly what the late-Victorian age needed
to counter its sense of *Angst*. John Cowper Powys spoke for many
others when he said 'What we get from Nietzsche ... is the greatest of
all gifts that any writer can give us – namely, a heightening of
our dramatic interest in life.' What attracted Powys himself was
that he recognized in Nietzsche a fellow-'romanticist of ideas' who
shared his own delight in indulging in 'half-poetic, half-philosophic

generalizations about the history of human ideas'. Similarly Lascelles
Abercrombie wrote that the most notable effect of his writing was that
'it infects us with a mood . . . It pours into us a Titanic exultation
in being alive'. This feeling is important, not least for the writer.

Whatever opinion they formed of the direction and ultimate significance of his thought, Nietzsche introduced many of his readers to
what Herbert Read called 'the ferment of contemporary ideas'; to
read Nietzsche was an essential part of growing up. But it was more
than that. If H. G. Wells was right to say (in *The Research Magnificent*,
1915) that 'Life nowadays consists of adventures among generalizations', then Nietzsche was one of the leaders in this adventure. Herbert
Read wrote on Nietzsche's impact on him as 'cataclysmic', saying 'In
his company I knew the excitement of an intellectual adventure'.
There are few better or more honest descriptions of Nietzsche's impact
on a young intellectual than Read's:

> What I found in Nietzsche . . . was the complete destruction of all
> my ancestral gods, the deriding of all my cherished illusions, an
> iconoclasm verging on blasphemy. All of that I might have found
> elsewhere – there were plenty of strident atheists and persuasive
> rationalists about in those days. But I found something more in
> Nietzsche – a poetic force . . . an imagination that soared into the
> future, a mind of apparently universal comprehension. Some-
> thing still more: something which I can only call prophetic fire.

The ideas to which English writers responded were essentially
poetic ideas or myths; what mattered to them (and, I think, to Nietzsche himself) was not their 'truth' in any positivistic sense, but their
'poetic truth', in other words, their power of stimulation. Right from
the appearance of the first translations of his works in 1896, Nietzsche
was reckoned to have no 'system', and the real Nietzscheites (Ken-
nedy, Levy, Ludovici) devoted no little energy to defending him on
this score. It is not my concern here to define the limits within which
Nietzsche may legitimately be considered to have a systematic philosophy: what needs to be stressed is that English writers responded to
Nietzsche as to a poet, and were therefore happy to take his ideas in
isolation, as stimuli; they did not seek to 'coagulate [his] moods into
a philosophical system', nor did they 'demand consistency from his
ideas'.[3] After all, Nietzsche was the product of late nineteenth-
century irrationalism, and his most influential ideas (the idea of
aristocracy, the superman, eternal recurrence, etc.) are emotional

ideas in the sense both of being the product of an emotional need, and of having an essentially emotional appeal. Looked at from the point of view of his influence on English literature, Nietzsche was not so much a philosopher as the *guru* of the late-Victorian/Edwardian age. It is not for nothing that a number of writers (notably W. B. Yeats and Herbert Read, but also Arthur Symons and John Cowper Powys) approached him via Blake; the obvious parallels with Blake in turn meant that he was in some ways a familiar phenomenon, 'Brer Nietzsche', as Bernard Shaw called him.

The distinction between Nietzsche as philosopher and poet must be qualified at this stage, for the separation of philosopher and poet is false in that the two come together in his theory of fictions (cf. Bentham, Vaihinger); in other words, it is in a sense precisely as philosopher that Nietzsche is poet or fiction-writer, for he believed reality itself to be a 'fiction' or 'mythology' (cf. W. B. Yeats's 'phantas-magoria'), which helps to explain his appeal to a generation depressed by Victorian materialism. The Scottish poet John Davidson, for instance, was attracted to Nietzsche because his own fundamental belief that 'There is no such thing as naked reality' is the foundation on which Nietzsche's whole mythical artefact is built. On the whole, however, this aspect of Nietzsche's thought had little impact on English literature, although it may well have helped the American Wallace Stevens to form his view of poetry. There is another sense too in which it is wrong to separate Nietzsche the philosopher from Nietzsche the poet; as T. S. Eliot declared in 1916: 'Nietzsche is one of those writers whose philosophy evaporates when detached from its literary qualities, and whose literature owes its charm . . . to a claim to scientific truth.' Nietzsche's ideas, most of which were commonplace at the time, would have attracted little attention if they had not been so forcefully and strikingly expressed, while *Thus Spake Zarathustra* (for instance) would not have been so widely read if it had not claimed to reveal truth. More original thinkers and more considerable poets than Nietzsche are now forgotten, but at times of radical uncertainty the poetic *guru* has an irresistible appeal, particularly if he appears to encourage his readers in their self-esteem; Hermann Hesse is another case in point.

The story of English writers and Nietzsche is essentially one of sub-jective reactions and creative misunderstandings. Once his work had begun to appear in English, Nietzsche was reduced to a string of dangerous-sounding, half-understood slogans: the 'superman' (or

'overman' in his pre-Shavian guise), 'eternal recurrence', 'Dionysus',
the 'Antichrist', the 'will to power', 'beyond good and evil', 'hardness', etc. How these ideas related to one another, and what they
amounted to, did not matter. To adopt these slogans was to give the
illusion of 'living dangerously' (yet another slogan), and Edwin Muir's
nervous breakdown of 1919 showed that Nietzsche really could be the
'dynamite' which he fancied himself to be. It is not that many writers
learnt anything very specific from Nietzsche, or even that he had all
that much to teach them apart from his basic critique of morality,
and so far as England is concerned, that was anticipated by Shaw's
The Quintessence of Ibsenism of 1891; it is rather that Zarathustra's only
moral law – 'Do always what you will – but first be such a man as *can
will*' (II, 421) – gave a kind of Dutch courage to many who had lacked
the courage of their own proto-Nietzschean convictions. In his diary
for 27 August 1900, Charles Ricketts, for instance, wrote that when he
first read Nietzsche he was 'half-frightened to find in print so many
things which [he] felt personally', which is a typical, if unusually
frank reaction. Nietzsche brought out the heroic instinct, often in the
most unheroic of men; after reading *Thus Spake Zarathustra* nothing
came more naturally than to fancy oneself as 'A Hero of Our Time' –
though of course without the Lermontovian connotation of superfluity.

Reaction to Nietzsche and his ideas has always tended to be hysterical, or at least grossly subjective. This is why he was used just as
shamelessly as he himself had used some previous thinkers; given the
fundamental elitism of his thought – which is, as I have implied, what
appealed to the majority of his sympathizers, who fancied themselves
part of the elite in question – the most ironical and grotesque turn of
events was when he was harnessed up to help pull Bernard Shaw's
socialist pantechnicon, although the way in which John Davidson
used him to prop up dying Imperial Man was scarcely less remarkable.
The reaction to Nietzsche has always tended to be the sort of reaction
given to the larger-than-life-sized figure. The attempt by Holbrook
Jackson and A. R. Orage to 'reduce Leeds to Nietzscheism' was as
heroic as it was foredoomed to failure; but it is the fact of the attempt
that speaks so eloquently for the power which the German philosopher exercised over that generation. One simply cannot imagine anyone trying to win Leeds to the cause of, say, Goethe. This would be a
different matter – which is precisely the point.

In view of what has been said, it is hardly surprising that it was

Nietzsche's poetic power over which a number of British writers enthused; in particular they noted the 'ecstatic quality' (Arthur Symons) of the thought of this 'strong enchanter' (W. B. Yeats) with his 'unexampled divulsive power' (John Davidson); Edwin Muir was 'intoxicated' and D. H. Lawrence 'engrossed' by Nietzsche, whose effect on Herbert Read was 'cataclysmic'. John Cowper Powys spoke of the 'fatal intoxication' of his work, which Edward Thomas and Lascelles Abercrombie both found 'magnificent'. If Bernard Shaw said that *Thus Spake Zarathustra* outdid the Psalms, Rupert Brooke simply said 'Nietzsche is our Bible'. These comments are in themselves sufficient to confirm that it was Nietzsche's poetic ideas that left their mark on English writers. There is, certainly, no doubt that many of them took him very seriously indeed; they learnt his works by heart, three volumes at a time (John Davidson), and still had passages by heart thirty-five years later (Herbert Read); they carried his works around in both jacket pockets, and dreamt about him (Edwin Muir); they dragged his name into conversations quite irrelevantly (W. B. Yeats); they set out to 'reduce Leeds to Nietzscheism' (Holbrook Jackson and A. R. Orage); they even looked like him (George Gissing). At the same time there were naturally, since Nietzsche is nothing if not a controversial figure, those to whom he was anathema, a 'pronounced maniac' (Max Nordau), a 'useless anarchist' (G. K. Chesterton), 'frightfully vulgar' (T. E. Hulme), 'incoherent' (Thomas Hardy), 'conceited' (Arnold Bennett) – a thinker whose 'upsidedown ideas . . . might have some value for aged men' (George Meredith); evidently sharing G. K. Chesterton's view that Nietzsche as a thinker was 'quite the reverse of strong', James Stephens called him 'a female voice squealing for strength and calling its squeal philosophy'; perhaps the most outspoken comment of all was that of Aldous Huxley who remarked, after reading Mügge's biography, that '*Zarathustra* was written by a dyspeptic professor who could never refrain from over-eating when his mother sent him a hamper of sweet things, and was always sick in consequence.' What is immediately noticeable about all these comments, whether sympathetic or hostile, is the tendency to over-react, to over-state the case. Whatever else, Nietzsche is seen as a challenge to which some kind of response is necessary.

As we shall shortly see in more detail, by 1896, when his work began to appear in English, the main battles in the anti-Victorian movement had already been fought and won, and the inevitable opprobrium had been incurred by those who led the first wave of the attack on the citadel (Pater, Swinburne, Wilde, Symons, Shaw, etc.). Nietzsche therefore had a comparatively clear run. What he offered was an apparent synthesis of contemporary trends. It is this fact that accounts for the breadth of his appeal. What no one could have foreseen was the extent of his influence. In guises ranging from 'Brer Nietzsche' (Bernard Shaw) to 'the execrable "Neech" ' (Wyndham Lewis),[4] he dominated the literary world for a generation; writers as different as Bernard Shaw, T. E. Lawrence, and John Cowper Powys all sought to emulate him, while the young Edwin Muir went further and produced (in *We Moderns*, 1918) a straight pastiche of Nietzsche. To Siegfried Trebitsch Shaw wrote on 26 December 1902: 'I want the Germans to know me as a philosopher, as an English (or Irish) Nietzsche (only ten times cleverer)';[5] despite this, Shaw was not particularly amused when William Archer called *Man and Superman* a 'mere rechauffée of stale Shavianized Nietzsche'.[6] Rather later T. E. Lawrence wrote to Edward Garnett (himself a keen 'Nietzscheite') on 24 August 1922:

> Do you remember my telling you once that I collected a shelf of 'Titanic' books (those distinguished by greatness of spirit, 'sublimity' as Longinus would call it): and that they were *The Karamazovs*, *Zarathustra*, and *Moby Dick*. Well, my ambition was to make an English fourth.[7]

John Cowper Powys, for his part, read *Ecce Homo* and pretended that he too would be a 'proclaimer of planetary secrets', that 'it would be [his] destiny one day to give to the world a philosophy as startling and new as that of the author of *Ecce Homo*'. Even Louis MacNeice, most gentle of souls, adopted 'Up Dionysus!' as his slogan until his father (an archdeacon) said that Nietzsche was 'only fit to light candles with'.

Nietzscheism – to use the contemporary term – dates from Georg Brandes' famous series of lectures on Nietzsche in Copenhagen in 1888 and lasts until what was once called the Euro-Nietzschean war of 1914–18. The earliest echo of Nietzsche's thought in English literature appears in George Gissing's *The Unclassed* in 1884; the earliest direct references occur in George Egerton's *Keynotes* and John Davidson's *Sentences and Paragraphs*, both of which appeared in 1893. But to all intents and purposes Nietzsche's influence only began to be felt when the language barrier began to come down in 1896. The fact that the first English translation of *Die Welt als Wille und Vorstellung* only appeared in 1883–6, means that Schopenhauer was only discovered by English writers a short decade before Nietzsche, that being the decade of

English Wagnerism, which began with Swinburne's Wagner-poems of 1883. In Paris, too, Nietzsche had ridden in on the Schopenhauer and Wagner waves (the two are more or less indistinguishable; after all, Wagner's *Ring* was itself dedicated to Schopenhauer). Several British writers came to Nietzsche via Schopenhauer, including George Moore ('Schopenhauer, oh, my Schopenhauer') and W. B. Yeats ('Schopenhauer can do no wrong in my eyes – I no more quarrel with him than I do with a mountain cataract'); Schopenhauer was, of course, a major influence on writers of the 1880s/1890s (Thomas Hardy, George Gissing, *et al.*).

Once those much-maligned, but so influential, early translations of his work began to appear, Nietzsche's impact was immediate. In 1896 we already find Bernard Shaw writing that 'before long you must be prepared to talk about Nietzsche or else retire from society, especially from aristocratically minded society'; the truth of this remark is confirmed by incidental references to Nietzsche in novels such as Somerset Maugham's *The Explorer* (1907) and John Galsworthy's *The Patrician* (1911); in *The Explorer* there is a reference to 'the *Fröhliche Wissenschaft* of Nietzsche, who was then beginning to be read in England by the fashionable world and was on the eve of being discovered by men of letters', which is more witty than accurate. In a letter to Gertrude Stein, F. Scott Fitzgerald later remarked that 'the man of 1901, say, would let Nietche [sic] think for him intellectually'; the implications of this we shall consider presently. John Davidson's view that Nietzsche was 'the most potent influence in European thought in our time' was evidently shared by Arthur Symons who wrote in the introduction to his *William Blake* (1907) that

> Thought today, wherever it is most individual, owes either force or direction to Nietzsche, and thus we see, on our topmost towers, the Philistine armed and winged, and without the love or fear of God or man in his heart, doing battle in Nietzsche's name against the ideas of Nietzsche. No one can think, and escape Nietzsche.

A year later we find Lascelles Abercrombie saying that 'the notion of the Overman' is 'so sublime and yet so natural . . . that nowadays nobody's thought can help acknowledging its dominance'. Two years later Rupert Brooke spoke for many of the bright young things of 1910 when he declared at the Cambridge Union that 'Nietzsche is our Bible'. This unparalleled influence continued until August 1914, which, on the whole, marked a decisive turning-point – so decisive that John

Galsworthy was arguably right to say in a letter dated 28 December 1914 that 'Germanic influence on our spirit was never at a lower ebb'.

II   THE BREAKING OF THE TABLETS

Nietzsche's arrival on the British intellectual and literary scene could hardly have been more timely. Into the 'spiritual autumn' (G. K. Chesterton) of the late-Victorian age with its feverish restlessness resulting from the collapse of the hitherto accepted idealisms, his pointedly anti-altruistic philosophy came like a ray of lurid sunlight. The very fact that his philosophy, for all its brilliance and bravado, was in large measure a summation of what had gone before, of all the intellectual inclinations of the age, made his appeal inevitable. It was no doubt because of his built-in appeal to most sections of the smart intellectual world – although he impressed the vitalists and ideas-men more than the decadents and aesthetes – that Nietzsche so soon came to dominate discussion. What really needs to be stressed is how *little* of Nietzsche was really new to English readers. This applies even to the superman, the idea that had most impact on English writers; this particular idea would hardly have attracted such notice if the whole subject of evolution and 'eugenics' had not been so much in the air already; from Lamarck onwards the whole nineteenth century was dominated by the idea of evolution in one form or another.

The question of Nietzsche's attitude to Darwin is a thorny one. His comments on Darwin and Darwinism (which he recognized as 'the last great scientific movement' of contemporary Europe) were mainly hostile, although it would, I think, be unwise to take this hostility at face value. Nietzsche certainly absorbed the most general implication of 'Darwinism': man's development as part of the whole development of living things. In this sense the theory of evolution was one of his major starting-points, something which had to be overcome at all costs. Nietzsche was quite capable of writing of natural selection as the 'law of evolution', although he also objected to the idea that organisms and their kinds evolved by finding the best way of responding to, of reacting to a hostile and niggardly environment. He came to believe that it was, ultimately, an exploitative drive for self-aggrandizement, rather than the mere 'struggle for existence', which directed the evolutionary process, that is, the will to power rather than the 'mere' will to life. But having said this, the fact remains that most of his early critics and readers did not make this distinction between different kinds of self-assertion. Nietzsche may have been anxious not to have his 'superman' associated with either evolution or eugenics, but what concerns us here is the fact – and it is a fact – that it was precisely with evolution and eugenics that the 'superman' was connected by early writers on his work. In retrospect, of course, we can see that Nietzsche was not indebted to Darwin in any detailed way, for the 'superman' was essentially an emotional surrogate for 'God', and not a biological concept; it is, however, in the context of evolution that this concept can best be considered.

The ground could hardly have been more thoroughly prepared for Nietzsche: George Eliot's man-centred morality, Walter Pater's religion of art, the New Paganism of the 1880s and the 'Dionysian' vitalism of Swinburne, when combined with the impact of the Utilitarians, Darwin, Schopenhauer and Wagner, made it a foregone conclusion that Nietzsche would strike home, while the fact that he was seen as complementary to Blake means that he was regarded, from the beginning, as an essentially familiar phenomenon. And so he was, for atheism and the idea that man is his own god were imported into England by George Eliot with her translations of David Friedrich Strauss's *Das Leben Jesu* (1835, rev. edn 1840; *Life of Jesus*, 1840) and Ludwig Feuerbach's *Das Wesen des Christentums* (1841; *The Essence of Religion*, 1853). So far as the positivistic side of Nietzsche's thought is concerned, English readers had long since known G. H. Lewes's *Comte's Philosophy of the Sciences* (1853). Through their translations of Strauss, Feuerbach and Comte, George Eliot and G. H. Lewes did much to unleash the flood of scepticism which was to sweep all before it; George Eliot also had a hand (as assistant editor of the *Westminster Review*) in publishing John Oxenford's article which established Schopenhauer as a major influence in both England and Germany; we therefore have the paradox that while her novels with their underlying altruism seem quintessentially 'Victorian', no one did more than George Eliot to undermine Victorianism as such. English readers were already familiar with Darwin's 'natural selection', which involved the survival of the strong at the expense of the weak; it was this which led George Eliot, in her essay 'Shadows of the Coming Race' (in her *Impressions of Theophrastus Such*, 1879), prompted, no doubt, by Bulwer-Lytton's *The Coming Race* (1870), to consider the possibility that 'the process of natural selection must drive men altogether out of the field'; but what she foresaw was the possibility of man being supplanted by the machine, rather than by the superman. English readers were familiar, too, with Locke's and

Spencer's ethical relativism and the idea that things are good or evil only in relation to the pleasure or pain they induce, and with Spencer's philosophy of Becoming – to say nothing of Heraclitus, widely admired at the time (partly thanks to Pater's *Marius the Epicurean*, 1885), no doubt because Heracliteanism, like the Hegelianism of the time, held solace for the late Victorian because it explained the 'perpetual flux' of change in his world; besides, his contemporaries had T. H. Huxley's word for it that no better expression of the modern doctrine of evolution was to be found than in the philosophy of Heraclitus.

The *idea* of the superman had been in the air at least since 1844, the year of Nietzsche's birth, when Robert Chamber's *Vestiges of the Natural History of Creation* appeared anonymously. Nietzsche's concept of *Züchtung* seemed to provide a possible answer to the Malthusian problem raised by T. H. Huxley in his *Evolution and Ethics* (1873); after all, the idea of the selective breeding of the ideal citizen was a basic feature of late nineteenth-century utopianism (the word 'eugenics' dates from 1869). More generally, the romantic creed of individualism was long familiar from Carlyle's *On Heroes, Hero-Worship, and the Heroic in History* (1841), *Latter-Day Pamphlets* (1850), and *Frederick the Great* (1858–65); Nietzsche's own belief in heroes, hero-worship and the heroic in history is anticipated by and to some extent derives from Carlyle, as does his hatred of democracy, his advocacy of a new aristocracy, his distinction between master and slave morality, his adulation of strength, and so on; there are interesting parallels between Carlyle's Teufelsdröckh and Nietzsche's Zarathustra, although these must not blind us to the fact that Carlyle was an enthusiastic advocate of the German culture which Nietzsche never ceased to denigrate.

The basic attitudes of *Thus Spake Zarathustra* (1883–4) had been expressed in English by Richard Jefferies and Edward Carpenter long before Nietzsche was known in this country; in *The Story of My Heart* (1883) Richard Jefferies wrote that 'We must do for ourselves what superstition has hitherto supposed an intelligence to do for us', which makes it clear that by 1883 he had reached much the same position as Nietzsche; the Zarathustran idea that man should 'remain true to the earth' was expressed too in Edward Carpenter's *Civilization: its Cause and Cure* (1889). Bernard Shaw's *The Quintessence of Ibsenism* (1891) anticipated Nietzsche in replacing Victorian ethics by a Dionysian or 'Diabolonian' morality of self-realization. The idea of cyclic recurrence had been present in the poetry of W. B. Yeats from 1889 onwards. The 'Apollonian-Dionysiac duality' of *The Birth of Tragedy* recalls similar antinomies in Blake (Prolific and Devourer; Los and Enitharmon) whose *The Marriage of Heaven and Hell* (1793) anticipates Nietzsche's 'beyond good and evil'; the parallels between Nietzsche and Blake were discussed at some length by Arthur Symons in his *William Blake* (1907): 'The Marriage of Heaven and Hell anticipates Nietzsche in his most significant paradoxes, and before his time, exalts energy above reason, and Evil, "the active springing from energy," above Good, "the passive that obeys reason" . . .'. Several English writers were drawn to Nietzsche by their love of Blake. The 'Apollonian-Dionysiac duality' is also, of course, a more vigorous version of the struggle between 'Hellenism' and 'Hebraism' (Matthew Arnold) and between 'centrifugal' and 'centripetal' art-forms (Walter Pater) familiar to late-nineteenth-century readers; Pater's *Greek Studies* (consisting of essays published between 1876 and 1889), and particularly the essay 'A Study of Dionysus' (1876), helped to prepare the ground for *The Birth of Tragedy*.

However little of Nietzsche's work was actually new to English readers, his ideas unquestionably generated a great deal of sheer intellectual excitement. More specifically, it was his sovereign disdain for sacred cows that commended Nietzsche to so many. His impact on English literature can best be considered under two main headings: the iconoclastic revolt against Victorianism and all its works, and the erection of a new, aesthetic ideal to replace the discredited ethical ideal. It was the anti-Victorianism which came first and which was most fun, for, as Bernard Shaw remarked in a review of the first two volumes of *The Works of Friedrich Nietzsche* in 1899, iconoclasm is 'perhaps the one pursuit that is as useful as it is amusing'. It was because Victorianism had taken itself so very seriously that breaking the tablets gave such a heady joy and sense of daring, to say nothing of its appeal to the natural iconoclasm of youth; once this natural urge was satisfied, Nietzsche's 'openly defiant romanticism' carried an appeal that proved even more irresistible.

In his essay 'Wilde and Nietzsche', Thomas Mann compared Nietzsche and Wilde, saying that 'they belong together as rebels, rebels in the name of beauty [against the whole morality of the Victorian age].'[8] This is a most important point: that Nietzsche – even if he was himself unable to escape wholly from the Victorianism which he loathed and detested – was basically anti-Victorian and therefore appealed to the advanced intellectual of the time. What made him anti-Victorian was his rejection of morality in favour of art; he arrived on the English scene just as 'Ruskinism' – the emphasis on moral values in art with its 'high seriousness' – was being thrown out of the window. No doubt it was this that made Aubrey Beardsley feel 'quite gay' in October 1896 when a friend had sent him Nietzsche's works at his own request. Nietzsche's 'Art and nothing but art!' was a slogan that was bound to appeal to the 'advanced' intellectual who objected to mahogany furniture as symbolizing Victorianism, and was sick of morality-mongering and *Schmalz*, particularly if he had already read Pater's *The Renaissance* (1873) and Wilde's *Intentions* (1891), for Wilde and Nietzsche carry Pater's campaign successively further. The choice between Victorian and anti-Victorian aesthetics was put most succinctly by Arthur Symons in the preface to the second edition of his *Silhouettes* (1896): 'a work of art can be judged from only two standpoints: the standpoint from which its art is measured entirely by its morality and the standpoint from which its morality is measured entirely by its art.'

When Walter Pater wrote in *The Renaissance* that 'Art comes to you proposing frankly to give nothing but the highest quality to your moments as they pass, and simply for those moments' sake', he was, in his Apollonian way, expressing what was at the time a highly subversive idea: that art exists not for the sake of truth or morality, but for its own sake. When, in the essay on the School of Giorgione of 1877, he lays down the maxim that all art constantly aspires towards the condition of music, he was making much the same point: that art seeks to free itself from subject-matter or morality. This was the beginning of the end of the classicistic, ameliorist Victorian aesthetic, and the beginning of the modern religion of art. Pater and Nietzsche are united in proclaiming the pre-eminent value of art. But if members of what Yeats called the 'tragic generation' of the late 1880s and early 1890s looked to Pater for their philosophy, it is clear that some of them (perhaps including even Pater's disciple George Moore, if one goes by his dubious testimony) went beyond Pater to Nietzsche's more positively stimulating ideas. Pater may have started an aesthetic revolution, but when Nietzsche proceeded to say that life is significant only as material for art, the revolution could no longer be ignored. The Victorians liked the idea of the 'high seriousness' of art, which enabled them to indulge their love of 'art' (by which they tended to mean artiness or ornament) under the guise of puritanism; Nietzsche, who had a strong element of Victorian puritanism in his make-up, took art even more seriously, but in quite a different way. By the end of the century ethical complacency had given way to various kinds of despair as the dissolution of the nineteenth century set in, so that *fin-de-siècle* man found his solace in Nietzsche's idea that art could protect him from life.

It was in the once-notorious dialogue 'The Critic as Artist' in his *Intentions* (1891) that Oscar Wilde pronounced that 'all art is immoral' because 'the sphere of Art and the sphere of Ethics are absolutely distinct and separate'; he went on to argue that 'Life is terribly deficient in form.... It is through Art and through Art only, that we can realize our perfection; through Art and through Art only, that we can shield ourselves from the sordid perils of actual existence'. Now although the particular form of wit here is not Nietzsche's, the pointed overstatement is entirely Nietzschean, as is the idea that art exists not to convey moral truths, but to shield us from truth and indeed from life. Underlying this rejection of the Victorian morality of art is the view that 'Art is not simple truth but complex beauty', and that 'Truth is entirely and absolutely a matter of style'; when Wilde writes 'What is Truth? In matters of religion, it is simply the opinion that has survived. In matters of science, it is the ultimate sensation. In matters of art it is one's last mood', he is expressing a view which Nietzsche simply couched in a less shocking form. This is why Wilde and Nietzsche both see poetry and lying as sister arts; Wilde's 'The Decay of Lying' repeats Nietzsche's view (in *The Genealogy of Morals*, which Wilde presumably did not know) that modern man is not even capable of telling an honest lie.

To those already familiar with Pater's and Wilde's hedonistic aesthetic, Nietzsche's 'campaign against morality' will not have seemed particularly shocking; nor will Wilde have seemed so shocking to those who had already read Nietzsche, one of the most fundamental of whose pronouncements entered English literature unnoticed in 1884, when George Gissing wrote in *The Unclassed*: 'only as artistic material has human life any significance.... The artist is the only sane man. Life for its own sake? – No. ... But life as the source of splendid pictures, inexhaustible material for effects, – *that* can reconcile me [Osmond Waymark] to existence, and that only.' This is presumably an echo of Nietzsche's words in *The Birth of Tragedy* to the effect that life is only justified as an aesthetic phenomenon. It must be noted, however, that this is only a quotation from a novel which owes little else to Nietzsche; so far as I know Waymark's words have never been connected with Nietzsche until now; Gissing learnt a great deal more from Schopenhauer than from Nietzsche.

Nietzsche's 'Critique of the Highest Values Hitherto'[9] is an attack on the Victorianism which claimed to represent those values. The arrogance of the Victorian attitude, which carried within it the seeds of its own destruction, is obvious in retrospect. Even as the edifice of High Victorianism was rising to greater and greater heights, or sinking to greater and greater depths, according to whether one is thinking of morality or art, its foundation stones were being torn out one by one. By the 1890s this whole edifice named Morality was tottering and ready to fall to a determined attack; Nietzsche gave it the final push. This is why his arrival in England was so timely. He may have been 'the expiring voice of the old nineteenth-century romanticism in philosophy' in the words of the American critic James G. Huneker, but at the turn of the century he seemed rather to stand for liberation from the nineteenth century.

In his Fabian Society lecture of 27 May 1898 on 'Frederick Nietzsche: a Child in a China-Shop', Hubert Bland spoke of Nietzsche as a 'naughty child' who takes 'our most cherished articles of virtù' and smashes them one after another. But the real point was that Nietzsche did not simply destroy a number of the Victorians' most cherished illusions; he destroyed the very foundation stone – Morality. One reason why he attracted such widespread and enthusiastic attention at the turn of the century was that his ideas were a fine antidote to current sentimentality and the tendency to carry morality into every sphere of life; his 'campaign against morality' was welcomed because many of his English readers believed themselves 'in danger of being done to death by Ethical Societies'. These Ethical Societies were themselves a product of the Victorian ethos which substituted Christian morality for Christianity as such. This is why Nietzsche strongly disapproved of George Eliot, who seemed to him to be *the* moralist of Victorianism. What Nietzsche saw in George Eliot was not what we see, the intellectual power and honesty, but what seemed to him like *dishonesty*: to cling to Christian morality after one has ceased to believe in the Christian God. His own work was aimed at this particular inconsequentiality which he rightly saw as *the* nineteenth-century illusion; in Somerset Maugham's *Of Human Bondage* (1915), the poet Cronshaw, whose philosophy comes from Schopenhauer and Nietzsche, criticizes Philip for precisely this ('You have thrown aside a creed, but you have preserved the ethic which was based upon it'). Writing in the context of anti-altruism (in his *When Blood Is Their Argument*, 1915), Ford Madox Hueffer made a similar point:

The school of Strauss, George Eliot, and Herbert Spencer was essentially demoralizing – a school of thought as demoralizing for Christians as for non-Christians, since it was an attempt to combine the Christian standard of manners with a materialistic standard of values and to adopt even the Christian theory of Heaven whilst leaving out the principle of the God-head who designed that heaven or enjoined that code of manners. Such attempts to run with one hare or another, and to hunt with this or that pack of hounds, were exceedingly common in the Victorian era in this country and in Germany of the period between 1848 and 1880. They were due as much as anything to influences that acted and interacted between the one country and the other.

In so far as Victorianism as such owed a great deal to Germany, it was Nietzsche's task to counter the Germanism of establishment circles in this country; he therefore became the spokesman of the anti-Victorian movement in matters of religion and philosophy; with him the New Paganism of the 1880s returned with a vengeance.

D. H. Lawrence, who read his work in 1908/9, regarded Nietzsche's iconoclasm as necessary, and approved the new, Dionysian ideal. In his review 'Georgian Poetry: 1911–1912' he wrote:

The last years have been years of demolition. Because faith and belief were getting potbound . . . faith and belief and the Temple must be broken. This time art fought the battle, rather than science or any new religious faction. And art has been demolishing for us: Nietzsche, the Christian religion as it stood.

In the same review Lawrence wrote that 'The great liberation [a Nietzschean term, of course] gives us an overwhelming sense of joy'; there is no doubt that Nietzsche (and Schopenhauer) helped to liberate Lawrence. In *Twilight in Italy* (1916) he wrote: 'Now we say that the Christian Infinite is not infinite. We are tempted, like Nietzsche, to return back to the old pagan Infinite, to say that is supreme', and went on to spell out the 'pagan Infinite': 'Man knows satisfaction when he surpasses all conditions and becomes, to himself, consummate in the Infinite, when he reaches a state of infinity. In the supreme ecstasy of the flesh, the Dionysian ecstasy, he reaches this state.' This is, finally, the exact antipode of George Eliot's position; it has been reached, presumably, via Samuel Butler's *The Way of All Flesh* (1884, publ. 1903) and Nietzsche. Indeed, when Lawrence wrote, in *Aaron's Rod* (1922), that

'We've exhausted the love-urge, for the moment. . . . We've got to accept the power motive. . . . It is a great life-motive. . . . Power – the power-urge. The will-to-power', he was explicitly rejecting Victorian altruism *à la* George Eliot and Herbert Spencer in favour of the Nietzschean will-to-power; this is a passage which lies at the heart of the revolution of values inspired by Nietzsche.

Nietzsche may be defined as the champion or the opponent of modernity according to whether we are thinking of his philosophical or political ideas. What accounts for his impact in England, however, is the fact that it was precisely the 'transvaluation of values' that was, in one way and another, the central problem facing the generation of 1890–1914. He made his greatest impact in the years 1896–1914 partly because his work was not available in English before 1896, and partly because the 'transvaluation of values' chimed in with the birth-pangs of the twentieth century. It was in 1908 that Lascelles Abercrombie wrote 'his Transvaluation of Values is the word now', but the comment applies more generally to the whole of our period. The 'transvaluation of values' is quite simply what Nietzsche's influence is all about. Nietzsche might not always be approved, but he could not easily be ignored; as Gertrud Burdett wrote in the *New Century Review*, 'In judging . . . Nietzsche, it is well to bear in mind that we are living in a time of intellectual unrest, and of social discontents; that . . . we are ripe for new teachings, and longing for new ideas.' If there had not been this longing for new ideas at the turn of the century, this whole story would have been totally different. As it was, the very idea of a 'transvaluation of values' was irresistible; it was in 1912 that Edwin Muir wrote 'The idea of a transvaluation of values intoxicated me', but in effect he was also speaking for the many who had fallen under Nietzsche's spell in the two previous decades. Although Muir and many others accepted the new 'aristocratic' values, it was the idea or fact of 'transvaluation' as such, rather than the particular direction it took or the particular gloss put on it, that mattered. Everyone, after all, is his own superman.

III THE NEW IDEALS

If it had been mere iconoclasm, nothing more than a brilliant and sustained piece of debunking, Nietzsche's work could never have had the impact that it did have. This impact it owed to the fact that, having shattered the last of the old ideals, it offered a number of new ideals which for a time looked most attractive. To the 'tragic generation' of the late 1880s and early 1890s, whose only hope had been what George Gissing called 'The Hope of Pessimism', it offered a new hope, a new centre of belief (man), and a new set of aesthetic-based values. To an age becoming depressed by its own democracy, it offered a fascinating 'new aristocracy'. To an age unable to live with or without 'God' and 'eternal life', it offered the more advanced-sounding 'superman' and 'eternal recurrence'. To those profoundly depressed by Darwin, it offered the hope of man's *continued* evolution. It seemed, in fact, to contain a panacea for most ills.

The mid-nineteenth century was deeply disturbed by the discoveries that reached a climax with Darwin's *On the Origin of Species by means of Natural Selection, or the Preservation of Favoured Races in the Struggle for Life* (1859) and its less well-known but more important sequel *The Descent of Man* (1871). What mattered was not what Darwin said, but what he was popularly supposed to have said; the generation-long controversy that followed the publication of these two works revolved around man's origin and therefore, by implication, his future. Some idea of the perplexity occasioned by *The Origin of Species* is given by these lines from *Punch* dated 15 May 1861:

> Am I satyr or man?
> Pray tell me who can,
> And settle my place in the scale.
> A man in ape's shape,
> An anthropoid ape,
> Or a monkey deprived of his tail?

In terms of its effect on the contemporary world of ideas, *The Origin of Species* can only be compared with Copernicus' *De Revolutionibus Orbium Coelestium* of 1543. Both works dealt a profound blow to man's self-esteem and to his religiosity; more specifically, Darwinism dealt what was to be a fatal blow to Victorianism as such, for the discovery of man's animal origin and of the fact that nature actually depends on the predatory principle totally undermined the Victorian ethic. Since Nietzsche himself was in a general sense as deeply influenced by Darwin as any other philosopher of the time, it is hardly surprising that his Zarathustra should have been acclaimed in England as 'the Mohammed of Darwinism'.[10]

In practical terms Darwinism posed the question of morality – not so much the genealogy of morals as the future and the point of morality. In 1894 Thomas Common wrote urging the most widely respected proponent of Darwinism, T. H. Huxley, to read Nietzsche; on 23 March 1894 Huxley replied:

> I will look up Nietzsche's [works], though I must confess that the profit I obtain from German authors on speculative questions is not usually great.
>
> There are two very different questions which people fail to discriminate. One is whether evolution accounts for morality, the other whether the principle of evolution in general can be adopted as an ethical principle.
>
> The first, of course, I advocate, and have constantly insisted upon. The second I deny, and reject all so-called evolutional ethics based upon it.

It is most unlikely that Huxley will have had the time or the inclination to read Nietzsche at this stage of his life; had he done so, he might have approved some aspects of Nietzsche's analysis of man, but he would have strongly disapproved Nietzsche's 'evolutional ethics' which would have struck him as further confirmation of the 'fanatical individualism' of his time. In his *Evolution and Ethics* (1893), in which he recognized that 'for his successful progress . . . man has been largely indebted to those qualities which he shares with the ape and the tiger', and that 'the strongest, the most self-assertive, tend to tread down the weaker', Huxley distinguished the morality of self-restraint from that of self-assertion, and strongly advocated the former; in effect he was making Nietzsche's distinction between Apolline (or Judaic) and Dionysian (or Roman) morality. Huxley's conclusion was diametrically opposed to Nietzsche's; but the point I wish to make is that when *A Genealogy of Morals* (for such was the original English title) appeared in 1899, the very fact that some of Nietzsche's material was familiar from *Evolution and Ethics* will have made it more acceptable than it would otherwise have been.

Even in the 1890s the theory of evolution was still the centre of controversy. In 1897, for instance, there was a series on 'Human Evolution' in *Natural Science*, to which H. G. Wells contributed the view that: 'The tendency of a belief in natural selection as the main factor of human progress, is, in the moral field, toward the glorification of a sort of rampant egotism – of blackguardism, in fact – as the New Gospel. You get that in the Gospel of Nietzsche.'

Nietzsche's supposed views on the evolution of the Superman

can and did call forth two quite different reactions. Looked at from a moral (or 'Victorian') point of view, we get Wells's reaction – which did not prevent him from flirting with the 'Overman idee' (sic) in much of his work; this is the negative reaction, so to speak. The positive reaction is to stress the idea of *continuing* evolution, as Herbert Read was to do:

> Now for a philosophy of Evolution. This is where I think Nietzsche comes in. He had a philosophy of Evolution, and for that reason I think we must hesitate before we reject him as a mere prophet of brutality and force. . . . Some idea of the Superman I believe to be the essential idea of any evolutionary attitude towards Life.

Here again is a clear example of writers reacting in opposite ways to the same 'aspect' of Nietzsche's work; it is a matter of different premises. It is therefore not so much Nietzsche's view of human evolution that counts, as the fact that he can be seen to take account of it or to be 'relevant'. His position *vis-à-vis* late-nineteenth-century pessimism is similar. It is the fact that he concerns himself with the central issues of the time that commends him to so many other writers of quite different literary, philosophical, moral, evolutionary or political views; even those who disagreed with him evidently enjoyed the disagreement (*pace* Chesterton).

In the long run what mattered to Herbert Read was not Nietzsche's view of human evolution or democracy, but his view of the State. In *The Tenth Muse* (1957) he quoted from Zarathustra's discourse 'Of the New Idol' ('The State is the coldest of all cold monsters . . . the State lieth in all the languages of good and evil. . . . False is it wholly') and said that this discourse, which he still had by heart some thirty-five years after first reading it, contained the seeds of his 'philosophy of anarchism'. So Herbert Read's characteristic political anarchism had its origin in *Thus Spake Zarathustra*. For Read Nietzsche was the prophet not of evolution, but of revolution. This helps to explain why he retained his enthusiasm for Nietzsche in the post-1918 world when so many others were to reject Nietzsche and all his works in favour of the post-war prophet: Karl Marx.

However characteristic his political anarchism, Herbert Read was essentially artist and critic, and it was to the essential Read that the following passage from *Beyond Good and Evil* (II, 645f.) appealed so powerfully:

Everything in the nature of freedom, elegance, boldness, dance, and masterly certainty, which exists or has existed, whether it be in thought itself, or in administration, or in speaking and persuading, in art as in conduct, has only developed by means of the tyranny of arbitrary law ... Every artist knows how different from the state of letting oneself go, is his 'most natural' condition, the free arranging, locating, disposing, and constructing in the moments of 'inspiration' – and how strictly and delicately he then obeys a thousand laws, which by their very rigidness and precision, defy all formulation by means of ideas. .... The essential thing 'in heaven and in earth' is, apparently ... that there should be long *obedience* in the same direction; and thereby results, and always has resulted in the long run, something which has made life worth living; for instance, virtue, art, music, dancing, reason, spirituality – anything whatever that is transfiguring, refined, foolish or divine.

This passage, which Herbert Read marked in his copy of *Beyond Good and Evil*, impressed him so deeply that he wrote many years later: 'I would like to think that it has never, since then, been absent from my consciousness'. This, for him, was 'the essential message of Nietzsche's philosophy', that art – and everything else that matters in life – is above all else a matter of discipline and self-discipline. What made Herbert Read tick was the mixture of anarchism and formal self-discipline and the tension between the two. And both came from Nietzsche.

That Nietzsche influenced Read in his basic philosophy between 1911 and 1915 is indisputable; this influence is reflected in the early verse (*Songs of Chaos*, 1915) which Read later disavowed and then rather regretted disavowing. The immediate effect of his early reading of Nietzsche was a necessary disillusionment, that opening of the mind which, however painful for the man, is necessary for the artist within. In the long term it is true to say that Nietzsche permanently widened Herbert Read's horizons, gave him the basis of his philosophy of art and of his political philosophy, and – above all, perhaps – confirmed him in his own basic individualism. Read's extraordinary objectivity ensured that the influence was beneficial; the very fact that Nietzsche helped him to overcome his own youthful nihilism, shows that he at least understood Nietzsche.

The decade preceding Nietzsche's sudden arrival on the English literary scene was termed by G. K. Chesterton 'an epoch of real pessimism'. The truth of this is variously borne out by the poetry of

James ('B.V.') Thomson, by W. H. Mallock's *Is Life Worth Living?* (1882), and by the suicide statistics for the 1880s. The cause of this pervasive pessimism was, basically, the breakdown of Christianity and the impact of Darwinism; contributory causes included the influence of Schopenhauer and Eduard von Hartmann, and of Buddhism (introduced by Rhys Davids's Hibbert Lectures of 1881).

That Nietzsche's philosophy was accepted by some as an antidote to pessimism is shown by W. H. Mallock's *The Veil of the Temple* (1904), one of the earliest English novels with a Nietzschean hero, in which Nietzsche is lauded for his fearlessness and consistency:

> Nietzsche . . . had no fear of the cliff. He stood on the very edge, and heard the sea roar beneath. . . . Nietzsche, whatever his merits otherwise, is of all modern thinkers the one who has been foremost in seizing the new moral ideas which the world's new knowledge suggests to us . . . and in pushing them to their most startling conclusions. He alone has dared to attack Christianity not only as a system of dogmas, but as a system of democratic philanthropy – to denounce its tenderness for the weak – to deride it as the morality of slaves – to declare that the victories of the future will not be with the weak, but with the strong; and to tell us that this is the true message of science. . . . Nietzsche is the only explorer who sets his prow towards the ocean and steers his course by the light of the stars only.

Looking back in 1913, Holbrook Jackson argued, too, that the influence of Nietzsche on John Davidson was beneficial, because early association with the ideas of Nietzsche had directed Davidson's innate pessimism into channels of creative inquisitiveness and speculation. Lascelles Abercrombie, writing in 1908, had argued more generally that 'The grand importance of Nietzsche is . . . that he is the most ruthless foe that pessimism could have'. That Abercrombie came to change his mind is less important than the fact that both Herbert Read and Edwin Muir were helped by their reading of Nietzsche to overcome their own early nihilism. There is nothing surprising about this, for if Schopenhauer came to the conclusion that life was meaningless, Nietzsche saw this as a chance for the individual to create his own meaning; if Schopenhauer recognized man's predatory nature (*homo homini lupus*) as a cause for sorrow, Nietzsche sought to derive some consolation and positive significance from this by idealizing the predatory type; if Darwin and Schopenhauer stressed man's animality, Nietzsche saw evolution as a continuing process and therefore a challenge. Having said this, it is symptomatic of the opposite reactions called forth by Nietzsche that while a number of writers were attracted to him because he seemed to offer them a way out of pessimism, W. B. Yeats – after spending much of his intellectual life in Nietzsche's company – condemned the German philosopher for his pessimism. To John Davidson, Zarathustra's words 'Only from the grave can there be resurrection' offered a chance to transcend despair. Yeats, although enthralled by the German philosopher's myth-centred tragic aestheticism, ultimately withheld his assent to Nietzsche's fundamental rejection of Socratic-Christian thought: 'why does Nietzsche think that the night has no stars, nothing but bats and owls and the insane moon?'

It is a feature of the present story that Nietzsche continually crops up in surprising contexts and in different transmogrifications. Thus, in a letter dated 24 January 1900, Bernard Shaw wrote to William Archer of 'the new Socialist-Nietzsche generation'.[11] Now, if Nietzsche stood for modernism in his 'campaign against morality' and in his metaphysics and theology, he stood no less resolutely against modernism in the political context, which makes his impact on Fabians such as Bernard Shaw, H. G. Wells, Rupert Brooke and Eric Gill ostensibly surprising. After all, his repeated attacks on democracy are hardly less bitter than his attacks on Christianity. It is a fact, however, that those who were most drawn to Nietzsche were precisely the 'Socialistically inclined'; this point was made in an editorial in *The Nation* on 12 June 1913:

> Nietzsche has become quasi-popular for two reasons: first, as a mere writer, as a poet of startling phrases and occasional insight, but with no systematic doctrine; and secondly, as one of the innumerable forces of change and of rebellion against the existing order of things. It is a fact, we believe, that nowhere will you find more men who regard Nietzsche favourably or tolerantly than among those Socialistically inclined: they feel and welcome the destructive energy of the man, while caring little that his programme of construction is entirely opposed to their own.

There are, I think, two main reasons for Nietzsche's appeal to the 'Socialistically inclined'. In the first place, from the mid-1890s onwards, his thought had appealed to the free-thinking intellectual *avant-garde* as such, and this was, by and large, 'Socialistically inclined'. This is not to say that his appeal in such circles had anything to do with politics. In the second place, his very iconoclasm will have been welcome to some of those who were trying to combat Victorianism in the political sphere. Naturally he had virtually no political influence; his impact on members of the Fabian Society was much the same as on non-members, which is to say that it was partly moral-metaphysical, and partly aesthetic. The one exception here is H. G. Wells, who was clearly fascinated by the 'Overman'; much of his work is based on the 'antagonism of the democratic and the aristocratic idea', and the 'aristocratic idea' is based on Nietzsche; but Wells is an exception, and the fascination which Nietzsche's aristocratic idea had for him is to be explained in personal social-psychological terms.

At the turn of the century 'aristocracy' versus 'socialism' (or 'democracy') was the central political issue; there was a fair amount of aesthetics involved on either side. On 9 March 1907, for instance, A. R. Orage spoke on 'Nietzsche versus Socialism' at the Reform Club; Eric Gill was in the audience; in his address Orage sought to reconcile the two major influences on his thought at that time.

For most of those who fell under his spell, Nietzsche's aristocratic idea, his anti-democratic stance, was at the centre of his appeal. Thus Edward Garnett wrote in *The Outlook* on 8 July 1899 that 'It is *because* Nietzsche challenges Modernity, *because* he stands and faces the modern democratic rush . . . *because* he opposes a creative aristocratic ideal to negate the popular will . . . that he is of such special significance.' For some of his British readers at least (Arthur Symons, W. B. Yeats, Herbert Read), the opposition to democracy was a matter not so much of politics, as of aesthetics. Arthur Symons's words in 'A Censor of Critics' (in his *Studies in Prose and Verse*, 1904) – 'The world is becoming more and more democratic, and with democracy art has nothing to do' – are not only a Nietzsche-inspired expression of his own fastidiousness; they also express a representative point of view. Herbert Read put it more fully if less clearly in his diary for 6 March 1915:

> I don't think I am satisfied with the tendency of modern Democracy . . . it offers no encouragement to the development of the personality of the individual. It will ensure happiness, but scarcely nobility. It will be fatal to even a spiritual superman . . . in ethics I think I am an individualist. . . . What would be the virtue of the super-race to which I wish democracy to aspire? . . . I can't even decide what

Virtue is. We atheists must get away from the salvation-or-damnation test of Christianity. We must find a new test – a religion of human perfectibility. My own ideal is aesthetic rather than ethical.

This credo is wholly Nietzschean.

It is precisely the fact that people have invariably found in Nietzsche what they wanted to find, that makes valid generalization about his influence so difficult. There is much truth in the words of an anonymous correspondent of the *Sunday Times*, who wrote in March 1910 that 'Nietzsche's philosophy covers so wide a field that isolated texts may be picked out to support any cause, and unfortunately the Socialists are as unscrupulous in quoting Nietzsche as the devil in quoting Scripture.' Moreover, people's views and moods change, so that they may come to find in Nietzsche's or anyone else's thought the opposite of what they formerly found there. Thus, while Lascelles Abercrombie in 1908 saw Nietzsche as the ideal antidote to pessimism, by 1926 he had come to see Nietzsche's philosophy as 'the essence of romantic pessimism: the utter disvaluation of the apparent world by belief in the reality of the mere unpurposed energy of existence – the inner life in its purest abstraction'. Yet even at this time he continued to admire Nietzsche's 'openly defiant romanticism' – which is the important point, for what really influenced English writers was neither Nietzsche's optimism nor his pessimism, but rather his profoundly romantic attitude as such.

When George Moore remarked in 1904 that he saw in his *Confessions of a Young Man* 'a proud agnosticism and an exalted individualism which . . . lead . . . to the sundered rock about the cave of Zarathustra', his memory was almost certainly playing him false; but it was to this Zarathustran 'exalted individualism' that most of Nietzsche's English readers responded. Of all his ideas, it is the idea of the superman (together with the concomitant eternal recurrence, idea of aristocracy, and will to power) that has been most influential. The reasons are not far to seek: by the end of the increasingly anti-individualistic nineteenth century there was a resurgence of individualism, and the superman-idea was, or was taken to be, most flattering to the reader's ego. Besides, there was an in-built appeal to late Imperial Man. John Davidson's words 'The Englishman is the Overman; and the history of England is the history of his evolution' are, of course, absurd; and yet the popularity of W. E. Henley's 'Unconquerable':

Out of the night that covers me,
Black as the pit from pole to pole,
I thank whatever gods may be
For my unconquerable soul.

suggests that Imperial Man was bound to be particularly susceptible
to the superman-idea, which gave a timely boost to his flagging
morale; it is no chance that H. G. Wells quotes these famous lines when
linking Henley with the superhuman Samurai of his *A Modern Utopia*.

It was in Wells's *When the Sleeper Wakes* (1898) that the superman arrived
on the English literary scene, and from the continual reappearance of
this type in his novels and scientific romances, it is clear that the
superman fascinated Wells despite his own political better judgment.
In Chapter XIX of *When the Sleeper Wakes* Wells makes Ostrog say:

The day of democracy is past . . . the day of the common man is past
. . . this is the second aristocracy. The real one . . . Aristocracy, the
prevalence of the best – the suffering and extinction of the unfit, and
so to better things. . . . The crowd is a huge foolish beast. What if it
does not die out? Even if it does not die it can still be tamed and
driven. I have no sympathy with servile men. . . . The hope of mankind – what is it? That some day the Over-man may come, that some
day the inferior, the weak and the bestial may be subdued or eliminated. Subdued if not eliminated. The world is no place for the bad,
the stupid, the enervated. Their duty – it's a fine duty too! – is to die.
The death of the failure! That is the path by which the beast rose to
manhood, by which man goes on to higher things. . . . So long as
there are sheep Nature will insist on beasts of prey. . . . The coming
of the aristocrat is fatal and assured. The end will be the Over-man –
for all the mad protests of humanity.

If there were the slightest doubt that Ostrog's views reflect Nietzsche,
that doubt would be removed in the following chapter when Nietzsche
is listed as one of the 'great moral emancipators and pioneers' who
helped to form the future; but of course there was no doubt, for
'overman' is the word used by A. Tille to translate *Übermensch* ('superman' we owe to Bernard Shaw; a further variation is George Meredith's
'upperman'). So clearly Wells's 'nightmare of capitalism triumphant'
is based on Nietzsche; in other words, Wells is here taking the
superman-idea to its logical conclusion, and is therefore rejecting
Nietzsche. Yet the 'overman' continues to haunt his novels, in which

Wells is concerned with the issue of aristocracy (or individualism) versus socialism (or democracy). If he comes down in favour of socialism – he joined the Fabian Society in 1903 – this is only after 'aristocracy' has been tried and found wanting; and even then Wells continued to be fascinated by the superman and the idea of a 'new aristocracy'. All his writings make it abundantly clear that although he apparently rejected the superman-idea, it continued to haunt him and tempt him to the end. Wells was certainly one of those who allowed themselves to be flattered by the dream of supermanhood (the 'superman' was, after all, the Edwardian name for the 'super-ego'); it is Fabian and overman combined that make the real H. G. Wells.

The idea that 'We must replace the man by the superman' was also expressed by a fellow-Fabian, Bernard Shaw, in the 'Epistle Dedicatory' to his *Man and Superman* (1903), where he commented that Nietzsche was 'among the writers whose peculiar sense of the world I recognize as more or less akin to my own'. In other words, Shaw denied being 'influenced' by Nietzsche. In all his major pronouncements on the subject[12] he insisted that he was 'rather an impostor as a pundit in the philosophy of Schopenhauer and Nietzsche'; his knowledge of Nietzsche's work was limited. Naturally he recognized Nietzsche's significance, for he used to speak of the 'Ibsen-Nietzschean movement in morals' and of the 'new Socialist-Nietzsche generation'; but basically – and, I think, rightly – he saw Nietzsche as being, like himself, a brilliant summarizer of contemporary ideas rather than an original: not the kind of writer by whom Shaw would allow himself to be influenced!

Shaw's various writings about Nietzsche show that he took an interest in the philosopher's work from 1896 onwards and read Thomas Common's influential *Nietzsche as Critic, Philosopher, Poet and Prophet* (1901), the publication of which he is said to have recommended; he recognized Nietzsche as a kindred-spirit, a fellow-iconoclast whose 'sense of the world' was 'more or less akin' to his own, and approved Nietzsche's criticism of morality and idealism as being close to Ibsen's and to his own in *The Quintessence of Ibsenism* (1891); he took Nietzsche seriously as a moral philosopher and champion of individualism; in social and political terms he understandably regarded him as inept; he took over the word 'superman' from Nietzsche, only to use it in a non-Nietzschean context; otherwise, he was delighted by Nietzsche's *style*, and called *Thus Spake Zarathustra* the 'first modern book that can be set above the Psalms of David at every point on their own ground'.

Although Shaw was consistently Nietzschefied by contemporary critics, my own view is that he was not in fact deeply influenced by Nietzsche in any tangible way, although less tangibly Nietzsche's example certainly encouraged Shaw in his own ways. Paradoxically this is one of the main forms that Nietzsche's influence took.

The Scottish poet John Davidson got to know Nietzsche's work at second hand in 1891; once the English translations began to appear, he soon had the first three volumes by heart. He responded to Nietzsche so strongly because he shared his view of Christianity, of democracy, and of the rationalism and determinism of the nineteenth century; he too believed in the individual's right to self-determination, and rejected all external authority and moral sanctions. That he would find many of Nietzsche's ideas sympathetic was therefore inevitable. Nietzsche's *Freigeist*-ideal, his insistence on the relativity of all moral values, his announcement of the death of God and consequent rejection of the Christian morality, all these are reflected in Davidson's work, particularly in the period 1902–8, as are the myths of the superman and eternal recurrence. The Man-of-Power or Man-God of Davidson's egoistic creed:

> Henceforth I shall be God; for consciousness
> Is God: I suffer: I am God: this Self,
> That all the universe combines to quell,
> Is greater than the universe; and *I*
> Am that I am. To think and not be God? –
> It cannot be.

is closely related to the superman; it was Nietzsche who sharpened and deepened Davidson's conception of the hero. Yet he had reservations about Nietzsche's philosophy or, more accurately, about what he considered to be his Christianity; in *The Triumph of Mammon* (1907) he wrote:

> this Nietzsche was a Christian . . .
> His Antichrist is Christ, whose body and blood
> And doctrine of miraculous rebirth,
> Became the Overman: Back-of-beyond,
> Or – what's the phrase? – Outside good-and-evil:
> That's his millenium, and we'll have none of it.

Davidson's Mammon is a mixture of his own 'Lucretian materialism' and the Nietzschean superman (cf. H. G. Wells's 'nightmare of capitalism triumphant'); the debt to Nietzsche is so strong that Davidson must be considered to have been covering it up in the lines just quoted; his own conception of the sickness of Christianity, after all, came from Nietzsche.

With John Davidson, however, it is not so much particular ideas that matter as the whole tenor of Nietzsche's work and the strength of his personality and personal example. Davidson's whole approach to Nietzsche is itself wholly Nietzschean; his own ideas are most characteristic and most significant when they are closest to Nietzsche. The crux of the matter is that Nietzsche confirmed and strengthened Davidson in ideas which he had developed before reading Nietzsche. This 'negative' impact consisting in giving writers the courage of their own convictions was an important one; we see it repeated in the case of W. B. Yeats.

Like his friend Arthur Symons, W. B. Yeats was an instinctive 'aristocrat'; he was also more deeply influenced by Nietzsche than any other English-language writer. Yet although he was attracted to Nietzsche's elitism in general, Yeats differed from most of the other English-language writers involved in this story in that he remained critical of Nietzsche's central myth, that of the superman. It may be that he took to heart his father's criticism of 'the theory of the over-man' as 'but a doctrinaire demi-godship' and of Nietzsche as a 'malign' influence; no doubt he did take this criticism seriously, but more important will have been the fact that in the last analysis he himself had moral reservations not only about the superman, but about the whole tenor of Nietzsche's thought. Instinctively, of course, Yeats's sympathies were with the 'strong' rather than the 'weak', with the 'noble' rather than the 'ignoble'; confirmation of this is found in the fact that in Thomas Common's anthology (*Nietzsche as Critic, Philosopher, Poet and Prophet*), which he read in 1902, Yeats marked the passage 'The noble man regards *himself* as the determiner of worth'. Further notes in the same volume show that he had no hesitation in accepting Nietzsche's 'Natural System of Ranks and Castes', and that – like Nietzsche – he was overridingly concerned with *quality* of life, with perfection in the art of living, with life as an aesthetic phenomenon; but he also had an innate moral conservatism that prevented his aesthetic explorations from going too far.

The clash between Yeats's moral self and aesthetic anti-self is exemplified in his attitude towards the superman. There is, of course, a very close parallel between his heroic ideal and that of Nietzsche, between the Yeatsian hero and the Nietzschean superman. Yeats's hero is more truly akin to Nietzsche's ideal than are the more obviously and super-ficially Nietzschean superman-types of writers like Jack London. Yeats and Nietzsche both tend to reject 'the real world' and its vulgar, democratic ideals; they believe rather in a natural aristocracy of men whose ideals are 'not of this world'. Both believe in what Nietzsche calls 'the eternal second coming' and insist that the heroic personality must respond to tragic knowledge with joy. But although Yeats accepted the idea that the great individual is the protagonist in the drama of history, he remained critical of Nietzsche's superman as such; he saw man through Blake's eyes rather than Nietzsche's, as something to be restored to his former estate rather than 'surpassed'. Though he deeply admired spiritual heroism of the type represented for him by Nietzsche, and shared Nietzsche's ideal of 'nobility' (*Vornehmheit*), he rejected the arrogance of the superman. He approved Nietzsche's statement that the noble type of man regards *himself* as the determiner of worth on an abstract instinctive level, without in any way approv-ing the solipsism that lies behind Nietzsche's words. He therefore dis-approved of Nietzsche's 'master-morality': 'His [Nietzsche's] system seems to lack some reason why the self must give to the selfless or weak, or itself perish or suffer diminution.' Yeats's moral and historical reservations were strongly challenged by the deep aesthetic fascination which the superman held for him. Zarathustra's whole philosophy is extraordinarily close to that of Yeats's *aesthetic anti-self*; but it was his moral self that had the last word.

Yeats will have found his doctrine of psychological dualism – self and anti-self – confirmed by Nietzsche; after all, Nietzsche's all-important doctrine of self-overcoming really means the overcoming of anti-self by self. Nietzsche, like Yeats, is very much concerned with the relationship between the self and its mask; it is after his reading of Nietzsche that 'mask' becomes a favourite term of Yeats. Nietzsche's view of Apollo as the 'divine image' of the individual self, and his view of the superman as totally subjective man, will have confirmed Yeats in his view of the self. Yeats even – at times – shared Nietzsche's premise: that the individual creates his own world, what is known as reality being only a 'mythology' (Nietzsche) or 'phantasmagoria' (Yeats). In both cases this view goes back to Schopenhauer.

This brings us to the religious aspect of the question. Yeats was evidently disturbed by Nietzsche's rejection (in *The Birth of Tragedy*) of Platonic thought and his condemnation (in *Thus Spake Zarathustra* and elsewhere) of Christian spirituality. Beside the contrast of 'master morality' and 'slave morality', that is, of subjective and objective morality, in *Nietzsche as Critic* . . . , Yeats wrote:

Night { Socrates } one god night . . . denial of self in the soul
         { Christ }   turned towards spirit, seeking knowledge.
Day   Homer   many gods day . . . affirmation of self, the
                     soul turned from the spirit to be its mask
                     and instrument when it seeks life.

This annotation shows both that Nietzsche helped Yeats to establish the pattern of opposition between self and soul which is implicit in much of his later work, and that Yeats has substituted Christ for Nietzsche's Dionysus. Yet when he came to write *The Resurrection* in 1927, Yeats did so in the belief that Dionysus-worship was a proto-Christian religion. Though he later studied the whole Dionysus myth in more detail, Yeats's early interest in the myth, which came from Pater and Nietzsche, is shown by the poem 'The Magi' (1914), in which Dionysus-worship and Christianity are already juxtaposed:

> Now as at all times I can see in the mind's eye,
> In their stiff, painted clothes, the pale unsatisfied ones
> Appear and disappear in the blue depth of the sky
> With all their ancient faces like rain-beaten stones,
> And all their helms of silver hovering side by side,
> And all their eyes still fixed, hoping to find once more,
> Being by Calvary's turbulence unsatisfied,
> The uncontrollable mystery on the bestial floor.

The description of the Dionysian Mysteries here could well have come from *The Birth of Tragedy*; it shows the aesthetic fascination which Dionysus held for Yeats, for all his ultimate moral misgivings.

Dionysus gave Yeats not only his anti-self's secret philosophy, but his definition of tragedy. In his verse-plays the influence of Nietzsche is seen most clearly in the years 1903–10; but there are echoes of Nietzsche right through to 1935. There seems little doubt that Yeats will have had his own ideas clarified by Nietzsche's theory of the Dionysian 'mystery doctrine of tragedy'. *This* is where 'Nietzsche completes Blake' in Yeats's own words, for both Nietzsche and Blake see art as the means, or hope, of restoring the original oneness between man and nature. After referring to the rebirth of Dionysus, whose ritual passion tragedy once celebrated, Nietzsche writes of: 'the mystery doctrine of tragedy; a recognition that whatever exists is of a piece and that individuation is the root of all evil; a conception of art as the sanguine hope that the spell of individuation may yet be broken, as an augury of eventual reintegration' (1, 62).

This Dionysian definition of tragedy appears to have influenced Yeats's *Where There Is Nothing*; it is also reflected in the essay 'Poetry and Tradition' (1907), where Yeats defines tragic emotion in terms of Nietzsche's 'Dionysiac rapture': 'Shakespeare's persons, when the last darkness has gathered about them, speak out of an ecstasy that is one-half the self-surrender of sorrow, and one-half the last playing and mockery of the victorious sword before the defeated world.' This appears to reflect Nietzsche's view that it was the combination of tragic terror and the comic spirit that was the salvation of Greek art. In another essay, 'The Tragic Theatre' (1910), we find Yeats distinguishing between 'an art of the flood' or 'tragic art', and 'an art that we call real'. The latter, 'the daily mood grown cold and crystalline', evidently derives from Nietzsche's 'Apollonian sphere', 'that artificially re-strained and discreet world of illusion', the world of the (Apolline) art of dream, with which Yeats was so deeply concerned. But it is surely Nietzsche's Dionysus, god of tragic passion, who inspired Yeats's definition of tragic art in 1910: 'Tragic art, passionate art, the drowner of dykes, the confounder of understanding, moves us by setting us to reverie, by alluring us almost to the intensity of trance. The persons upon the stage . . . greaten until they are humanity itself.'

His basic view in the same essay, that 'tragic ecstasy . . . is the best that art – perhaps that life – can give', and that the audience participates in the discovery of a place 'where passion . . . becomes wisdom', also exactly parallels Nietzsche's view in *The Birth of Tragedy*; it was not for nothing that this was Yeats's favourite work by Nietzsche. In the last analysis Yeats shares Nietzsche's hatred of 'the real world' and his belief in art as the only remaining means of saving an otherwise doomed world. As Erich Heller has pointed out, the 'artifice of eternity', of which Yeats writes in 'Sailing to Byzantium' (1927), springs from the same view of art and reality as Nietzsche's when he defines art as 'the last metaphysical activity within European nihilism' and the world as an 'aesthetic phenomenon'. Nietzsche and Yeats are so closely linked because they both believe in the religion of Art and therefore tend to confuse the aesthetic and the moral spheres.

Yeats's immediate reaction to Nietzsche's work in August 1902 speaks for itself: the German philosopher's myth-centred tragic aestheticism enthralled him, and it is reasonable to suppose that it was partly the

252 Nietzsche: Imagery and Thought

ideas thrown out by Nietzsche, to say nothing of his fervid eloquence, that made the following year – 1903 – a turning point in Yeats's art. Nietzschean ideas and echoes play an important part in his work from 1903 to 1921, and from 1930 to 1939; there are comparatively few references to Nietzsche in the 1920s. In the first flush of his enthusiasm Yeats would drag in this 'strong enchanter's' name on the slightest pretext.

Yet although Nietzsche had considerable influence on Yeats, he was a minor influence compared with, say, Plotinus. Yeats never really lost his head over Nietzsche, as Edwin Muir was to do in 1912, though he certainly lost his moral judgment in his temporary aesthetic enthusiasm; and it is significant that right from the start he was critical of the superman-myth which proved to be the headiest of Nietzsche's ideas for other English-language writers. Yeats found many of his own ideas and interests rationalized, confirmed and justified by Nietzsche. He assimilated, criticized and in several respects went beyond Nietzsche. Thus his view that there are two paths to the spiritual world, the objective (Christian) way and the subjective ('Dionysiac') way, was confirmed by Nietzsche; but his cyclic theory went far beyond Nietzsche's. Nietzsche confirmed Yeats in his view of the self, of art, of myth, and encouraged him to claim for *A Vision* (in which Nietzsche appears as mythical Hero) the status of absolute truth. No doubt it was partly because his interests and sources (Plato, Heraclitus, Pythagoras, Goethe, Schopenhauer, Vico, Indian philosophy, etc.) were so extraordinarily close to Yeats's own, that Nietzsche proved to be such a 'strong enchanter' for the Irish poet. What Nietzsche gave Yeats was above all the courage of convictions which he already held, or, to put it another way, he helped Yeats to be himself. It is precisely because Nietzsche held such a strong enchantment for Yeats that it must be stressed that when all is said and done Yeats withheld his assent to Nietzsche's fundamental rejection of Socratic-Christian thought.

Of all British writers it was Edwin Muir who took not only the superman-idea, but the whole of Nietzsche's philosophy, most seriously. Muir 'took up' Nietzsche (the Edwardian phrase is peculiarly apt) in 1912 on the advice of A. R. Orage, and in a short time became a Nietzschean; he later wrote 'although I did not know it, my Nietzscheanism was ... a "compensation". I could not face my life as it was, and so I took refuge in the fantasy of the Superman.' In 1912 Muir was obsessed by 'images of the Superman', for his Nietzscheanism centred on his 'belief in personality'.

When Muir began writing, he was, in his own words, 'still under the influence of Nietzsche'. The literary product of his early Nietzschean-ism was the book of aphorisms *We Moderns* (1918). The Nietzscheanism is evident in both the style and the content of these texts which Muir later rejected as immature, written 'in excited ignorance'. In *We Moderns* the excitement, deriving straight from Nietzsche, is certainly much in evidence; the emphasis is on the will to power, the most central of all Nietzsche's themes; the superman-idea is there ('The fall from innocence – that was the fall from the Superman into Man. And how, then, is Man to be redeemed? By the return of the Superman!'), as are Nietzsche's view of ancient Greek civilization ('There is some-thing enigmatical . . . behind the Greek clearness of representation, something unexplained; in short, a problem'), his conception of Dionysian or Tragic man, his Dionysian morality including the cult of 'hardness', his view of tragedy as the supreme affirmation of life, the doctrine of eternal becoming, and the opposition of the Christian and the Dionysian, with the repudiation of Christ in favour of Dionysus. The section on Nietzsche, whose ideas are scattered throughout the book, conveniently summarizes Muir's view in 1918:

> What was Nietzsche, that subtlest of modern riddles? First, a great tragic poet: it was by a divine accident that he was at the same time a profound thinker and the deepest psychologist. But his tragic affir-mative was the core of his work, of which thought and analysis were but outgrowths. Without it, his subtlety might have made him another Pascal. The Will to Power, which makes suffering integral in Life; the Order of Rank whereby the bulk of mankind are doomed to slavery; the Superman himself, that most sublime child of Tragedy; and the last affirmation, the Eternal Recurrence: these are the conceptions of a tragic poet. It is, indeed, by virtue of his tragic view of Life that Nietzsche is for us a force of such value. For only by means of it could modern existence, sunk in scepticism, pessimism and the greatest happiness of the greatest number, be re-created.

Muir was soon to reject the arrogance of the superman-idea, which had done him more harm than good. In the following year, 1919, there began a reaction against Nietzsche which took some years to be com-plete. He now began to distrust the superman and to discard the mannered Nietzschean rhetoric of *We Moderns*.

By the time of his next prose work, *Latitudes* (1924), which includes a chapter on Nietzsche, Muir had achieved a rather more detached atti-tude to his former master. The rejection of absolute values and assertion of life as eternal becoming, which underlies the book, may be essentially Nietzschean; but the fact remains that Muir has by this time regained his objectivity. He quotes Nietzsche in support of his own ideas, rather than as a prophet to whom he has lost his judgment and to whom he therefore owes blind acceptance. In other words, he has come to terms with Nietzsche, who has fallen into place as part of his intellectual heritage. The Nietzscheanism as such has gone.

In 1924 Muir still held to that 'joyous affirmation of life even at moments when everything threatens to go to pieces, and an enormous strengthening of will-power', in which Nietzsche's influence on his followers was said to consist.[13] By 1926, however, he finally achieved a positively critical attitude towards his one-time idol; in *Transition* he wrote that Nietzsche 'rarely reached past a will-to-acceptance to acceptance itself', which strikes at the very roots of Nietzsche's philosophy. In retrospect Muir saw that his own belief in the ideas of Nietzsche had been a 'willed belief'.

Right from the beginning, Muir's social and Christian idealism had been basically incompatible with his Nietzscheanism, although at first he had deliberately refused to recognize the fact. A friend later reported that Muir 'quite literally drove himself ill trying to reconcile the intellectual appeal of Nietzsche with his latent Christian idealism'. There seems in fact to be little doubt that the emotional disturbance which he underwent in about 1919 was the direct result – like Nietzsche's insanity – of trying to reconcile irreconcilable opposites, a problem which others less honest than Muir and Nietzsche have solved by pretending that the opposites in question were not irreconcilable. As a young man, Muir suffered a conflict between self and anti-self – there was a very deep antagonism between Edwin Muir and his Nietzschean *alter ego*, 'Edward Moore' – and therefore took a long time to find his true self. Nietzsche *seemed* to help, and certainly kept him going for a time; but in the long run Nietzsche led him further and further away from his true self, hence the inevitable breakdown when his mind began to reject the intellectual foreign body.

If Bernard Shaw anglicized the *Übermensch*, it was H. G. Wells, W. B. Yeats and Edwin Muir who arguably took him most seriously. Other writers, it is true, flirted with the idea without taking it or themselves at all seriously; thus James Joyce, being rather in the doldrums in 1903/4, found it satisfying to think of himself as 'James Overman' (as he ironically signed himself). W. N. P. Barbellion, author of *The Journal of a*

Disappointed Man (1919), provided one of the most honest comments on this subject when he wrote, in 1914, 'Reading Nietzsche. What splendid physic he is to Pomeranian puppies like myself! I am a hopeless coward. . . . But Nietzsche makes me feel a perfect mastiff.' Many other British readers clearly derived the same mastiff-feeling from Nietzsche; the cult of 'hardness', or 'toughness' as we should call it nowadays, loomed large in British Nietzscheanism; indeed, this was probably 'most people's' main single reason for reading him. But despite John Davidson's remark about the Englishman being the overman, the superman-idea had no long-term impact in this country. Yeats, Wells and Muir were all fascinated by the idea, but rejected it for moral (Yeats) or political (Wells) reasons, or for a mixture of both (Muir). In short, the superman-idea filled a short-term emotional need; the events of 1914–18 destroyed not only Nietzsche's reputation in this country, but the world of which his myths had been an essential part.

What of eternal recurrence, then? Here the situation can be summarized much more briefly. John Davidson's theory of endless evolution and devolution will have been confirmed by the idea of 'eternal recurrence', that 'eternal cirque of heinous agony', as he called it. So far as W. B. Yeats is concerned it was the vision of eternal recurrence, more than anything else in Nietzsche, that caught and held his attention, for while Yeats's own cyclic theory is more elaborate than and in some important respects quite different from Nietzsche's doctrine of identical recurrence, he undoubtedly received a considerable stimulus from Nietzsche, whose ideas were largely derived from the same sources as his own; having said this, it must be stressed that the idea of eternal recurrence was familiar to Yeats many years before he read Nietzsche, so that here as elsewhere Nietzsche acted mainly as confirmation. Even after he had dropped his 'Nietzschean affectations of super-manhood', Edwin Muir continued to be haunted by the 'forbidding thought of the Eternal Recurrence'; this was a specific influence. John Cowper Powys, too, was fascinated by Nietzsche's myth, although he rejected the idea of *identical* recurrence as such. Of all aspects of Nietzsche's 'openly defiant romanticism', it was also eternal recurrence that impressed Lascelles Abercrombie most deeply in 1909:

> But what an astonishing piece of romanticism, so sublimely to ignore all logic, that Eternal Recurrence – symbol of man's absolute and helpless fate in one universal whole of unending circular destiny – is to be accepted as the condition of deliberate aspiration

towards the Overman – symbol of man's triumphantly free will to transcend himself and to create his own destiny!

Like so many of his contemporaries, Abercrombie is both fascinated and appalled by 'Nietzsche's formidable ideas of Overman and Eternal Recurrence'; his conclusion still stands:

> But Nietzsche's self-importance had grandeur in it. Belief in man's perfectibility is, after all, a very handsome delusion; and only a great spirit could enjoy the intellectual splendor of that appalling idea, Eternal Recurrence. . . . Life as a whole and life in itself – that is the only metaphysic classicism allows. – It was . . . precisely this immediate life-delighting value which gave their talismanic property to Nietzsche's formidable ideas of Overman and Eternal Recurrence. But in him romanticism claims them rather than classicism, because they led him into Dionysiac notions of value transcending appearance.

IV CONCLUSION

In his *Beiträge zu einer Kritik der Sprache*,[14] Fritz Mauthner criticized Nietzsche for allowing himself to be seduced by his own 'poetic' language; Gershon Weiler has glossed Mauthner's point: 'Nietzsche mistook poetry for theory and could not resist the temptation to give answers where discursive thinking has failed'.[15] This point is of fundamental importance. The tension in Nietzsche between truth-seeker and myth-builder can be explained in a number of different ways, but whatever explanation is preferred, the fact remains that he mistook poetry for truth, which naturally endeared him to the poets, since at a time when truth had become problematical, he gave them a belief in themselves. At the same time this confusion of poetry and truth was itself a thoroughly Victorian failing, which shows again just how deeply rooted Nietzsche was in the nineteenth century. This is an important point, because what Nietzsche's critics have mostly stressed is the way in which his ideas anticipate so many trends in twentieth-century thought, and also because what made him such an influential figure was precisely the fact that he was so quintessentially late-Victorian *and yet* pointed forwards.

To consider Nietzsche's ideas anew from the point of view of their impact on English writers at the turn of the century makes one realize more than ever just how much he was a creature of the century which he so detested. The superman was understood as the culmination of nineteenth-century evolutionary thought for, if Darwinism points anywhere, it points to the problem of man's *continuing* evolution, that is, to the 'superman'; many of Nietzsche's other ideas are consequential elaborations from *The Origin of Species*; there is in many of them a powerful element of wishful thinking, which strongly appealed to *fin-de-siècle* man who was half afraid of the future.

There were of course those to whom Nietzsche's very name was anathema because his ideas ran counter to their own preconceived philosophy. There is, if not justice, at least irony in this, for G. K. Chesterton (for instance) was repaying Nietzsche in his own coin for his low opinion of Carlyle, George Eliot, Herbert Spencer, J. S. Mill and other eminent Victorians (against which must be set his high opinion of Sterne, Byron, Emerson, Darwin and Landor). But – until August 1914 – the pro-Nietzscheites were far more numerous; it became the 'done thing' to 'go in for' Nietzsche. The reason for this is that the late-Victorian period was a time when all the old certainties had been shown to be or were fast appearing to be far from certain; in particular the generation from 1859 to 1895 had been profoundly shaken by *The Origin of Species* and all its religious, moral and metaphysical consequences. Nietzsche made such an impact because the age was so desperately in need of a prophet, and because he put a positive gloss on what appeared to be the profoundly disturbing facts of life. If the 'tragic generation' of the 1880s had lived on 'The Hope of Pessimism', the men of the 1890s needed an illusion of more substantial hope, and this is what they found in Nietzsche. His 'transvaluation of values' held a deep appeal for the self-consciously apocalyptic 1890s, and, besides, his witty, epigrammatical style – itself typically late Victorian – made him socially acceptable. But he became more than a posthumous social success; he became a myth (the circumstances of his insanity helped here). It is perhaps ironical that one of the most potently mythopoeic of modern writers should himself have become an essentially mythical figure, although certainly this is what happened. It is a truism to say that Nietzsche is all things to all men; most frequently he, or rather his Zarathustra, is their own super-ego. In his *Psychology and Religion* (1938), C. G. Jung wrote of Nietzsche's 'peculiar need to back himself up by a revivified Zarathustra as a kind of secondary personality, a sort of alter ego' (Freudian terminology would say 'super-ego'), and the present history suggests that a number of his British readers felt the same need (cf. the 'mastiff-feeling'). But one can go further and apply to him his own theory of fictions to argue that 'Nietzsche' does not exist and never did exist; what exists is each separate reader's Nietzsche (and Nietzsche's own 'Zarathustra').

It was as mythopoet that Nietzsche was so influential, and of all his myths none had greater impact than the myth of 'Brer Nietzsche' (alias 'the execrable "Neech"'). When all the other once-so-heady myths have fallen into oblivion, it will be this, the greatest and most inscrutable of all, that will remain.

NOTES

1 I am most grateful to Leicester University Press for permission to quote from my *Nietzsche in Anglosaxony* (1972), in which Nietzsche's impact on English and American literature is considered in detail; the present essay, which includes some new material, seeks to give a more synoptic view.
2 Shaw, *Collected Letters 1898–1910*, ed. Dan H. Laurence (1972), p. 554.
3 See C. Day Lewis, 'The Lyrical Poetry,' in R. A. Scott-James and C. Day Lewis, *Thomas Hardy* (repr. 1965), p. 37.
4 G. B. Shaw, letter to H. G. Wells of 11 September 1906, in his *Collected Letters 1898–1910*, p. 649; Wyndham Lewis, in *Blast* no. 2 (July 1915), p. 10.
5 Shaw, *Collected Letters 1898–1910*, p. 298.
6 *Ibid.*, p. 356.
7 *The Letters of T. E. Lawrence*, ed. David Garnett (1938), p. 360.
8 In *Oscar Wilde. A Collection of Critical Essays*, ed. R. Ellmann (1969).
9 Proposed title for book two of the projected *Wille zur Macht*.
10 *The Quarterly Review* (October 1896).
11 Shaw, *Collected Letters 1898–1910*, p. 138.
12 'Nietzsche in English', *The Saturday Review* (11 April 1896); 'Preface to *Major Barbara*', 1905; letter to Archibald Henderson of 5 December 1905.
13 *The New Age* (January 1924).
14 3rd edn (1923, repr. 1969), vol. I, pp. 367, 667.
15 *Mauthner's Critique of Language* (1970), p. 293.

CHRONOLOGICAL LIST OF
NIETZSCHE'S CHIEF PUBLICATIONS

1872 *The Birth of Tragedy out of the Spirit of Music* [*Die Geburt der Tragödie aus dem Geiste der Musik*].

1873 *Untimely Meditations I: David Strauss, the Confessor and the Writer* [*Unzeitgemässe Betrachtungen. Erstes Stück: David Strauss der Bekenner und Schriftsteller*].

1874 *Untimely Meditations II: On the Benefits and Dangers of History for Life* [*Unzeitgemässe Betrachtungen. Zweites Stück: Vom Nutzen und Nachtheil der Historie für das Leben*].

1874 *Untimely Meditations III: Schopenhauer as Educator* [*Unzeitgemässe Betrachtungen. Drittes Stück: Schopenhauer als Erzieher*].

1876 *Untimely Meditations IV: Richard Wagner in Bayreuth* [*Unzeitgemässe Betrachtungen. Viertes Stück: Richard Wagner in Bayreuth*].

1878 *Hunan, All-Too-Human. A Book for Free Spirits* [*Menschliches, Allzumenschliches. Ein Buch für freie Geister*]. This consisted of 638 sections in 9 chapters.

1879 *Human, All-Too-Human. A Book for Free Spirits. Supplement: Assorted Opinions and Maxims* [*Menschliches, Allzumenschliches. Ein Buch für freie Geister. Anhang: Vermischte Meinungen und Sprüche*].

1880 *The Wanderer and his Shadow* [*Der Wanderer und sein Schatten*].

The three publications just listed, *Human, All-Too-Human*, its supplement *Assorted Opionions and Maxims*, and *The Wanderer and his Shadow*, were combined in 1886 as a single 2-volume work under the title: *Human, All-Too-Human*.

1881 *The Dawn of Day. Thoughts on Moral Prejudices* [*Morgenröthe. Gedanken über die moralischen Vorurtheile*].

1882 *The Joyful Science* [*Die fröhliche Wissenschaft*].

1883 *Thus Spake Zarathustra. A Book for Everyone and No One* [*Also sprach Zarathustra. Ein Buch für Alle und Keinen*].

1883 *Thus Spake Zarathustra. A Book for Everyone and No One. II* [*Also sprach Zarathrusta. Ein Buch für Alle und Keinen. II*].

1884 *Thus Spake Zarathustra. A Book for Everyone and No One. III* [*Also sprach Zarathustra. Ein Buch für Alle und Keinen. III*].

1885 *Thus Spake Zarathustra. A Book for Everyone and No One. IV* [*Also sprach Zarathustra. Ein Buch für Alle und Keinen. IV*]. Privately printed.

1886 *Beyond Good and Evil. Prelude to a Philosophy of the Future* [*Jenseits von Gut und Böse. Vorspiel einer Philosophie der Zukunft*].

1887 *The Genealogy of Morals. A Polemic* [*Zur Genealogie der Moral. Eine Streitschrift*].

1888 *The Case of Wagner. A Musicianer Problem* [*Der Fall Wagner. Ein Musikanten-Problem*].

1889 *Twilight of the Idols, or: How to Philosophize with a Hammer* [*Götzen-Dämmerung, oder: Wie man mit dem Hammer philosophiert*]. Prepared for publication 1888.

1889 *Nietzsche contra Wagner. Documents of a Psychologist* [*Nietzsche contra Wagner. Aktenstücke eines Psychologen*]. Prepared for publication 1888; privately printed.

1891 *Dithyrambs of Dionysus* [*Dionysos-Dithyramben*]. Apparently prepared for publication 1888.

1895 *The Anti-Christ* [*Der Antichrist*]. Prepared for publication 1888.

1908 *Ecce Homo. How One Becomes What One Is* [*Ecce Homo. Wie man wird, was man ist*]. Apparently prepared for publication 1888.

NOTES ON THE CONTRIBUTORS

PATRICK BRIDGWATER is Professor of German in the University of Durham. His main publications include *Nietzsche in Anglosaxony: A Study of Nietzsche's impact on English and American Literature* (1972); *Kafka and Nietzsche* (1974); *Twentieth-Century German Verse* (2nd edn 1968), etc.

F. D. LUKE is Tutor in German at Christ Church Oxford, and a Lecturer at the University of Oxford. His publications include an article on Kafka's *The Metamorphosis* (1951) and a number of prose and verse translations, including the following which have introductory essays: Goethe, *Selected Verse* (German text with prose translations, 1964); Goethe, *Conversations and Encounters* (with R. Pick, 1966); Stifter, *'Limestone' and Other Stories* (1968); Thomas Mann, *'Tonio Kröger' and Other Stories* (1970); Goethe, *Roman Elegies* (in elegiac verse, with facing German text, 1977): Kleist, *'The Earthquake in Chile' and Other Stories* (with N. Reeve, 1978).

MALCOLM PASLEY teaches German at the University of Oxford where he is a Fellow of Magdalen College. He has written principally on the work of Franz Kafka (e.g. *Kafka-Symposion*, 1965), and is one of the editors of the forthcoming text-critical edition of Kafka. The first volume of his translations of Kafka into English, Kafka, *Shorter Works Vol. I*, appeared in 1973, and his other publications include *Germany: A Companion to German Studies* (1972). He contributed an essay on 'Nietzsche and Klinger' to *The Discontinuous Tradition: Studies in German Literature in Honour of Ernest Ludwig Stahl* (ed. P. F. Ganz, 1971).

PETER PÜTZ is Professor of German at the University of Bonn. His publications include *Kunst und Künstlerexistenz bei Nietzsche und Thomas Mann* (1963; 2nd edn 1975); *Die Zeit im Drama* (1970; 2nd edn 1977); and essays on literature from the eighteenth to the twentieth century.

T. J. REED is a Fellow of St John's College and Lecturer in German in the University of Oxford. His publications include *Thomas Mann: The Uses of Tradition* (1974) and essays on German literature and thought from the eighteenth to the twentieth century. He was co-founder and is editor of *Oxford German Studies*.

J. P. STERN is Professor of German at University College London and Professor-at-Large at Cornell University. He is author of *Ernst Jünger: A Writer of Our Time* (1952); *Re-interpretations: Seven Studies in Nineteenth-Century German Literature* (1964); *Thomas Mann* (1967); *Idylls and Realities: Studies in Nineteenth-Century German Literature* (1971); *On Realism* (1972); *Hitler: The Führer and the People* (1975); and two books on Nietzsche to be published in 1978 and 1979.

MARY WARNOCK is a Senior Research Fellow of St Hugh's College Oxford, having previously been a Fellow and Tutor in Philosophy. Her publications include *The Philosophy of J-P Sartre* (1963); *Existentialism* (1970); *Imagination* (1976); and *Schools of Thought*, a study in the philosophy of education.

W. D. WILLIAMS has been Professor of German at the University of Liverpool since 1954. His publications include *Nietzsche and the French* (1952); *The Stories of C. F. Meyer* (1962) and various editions and articles on nineteenth- and twentieth-century German literature: the work of Mörike, Fontane, Mann, etc.